Dawson's
Avian Kingdom

Dawson's Avian Kingdom

SELECTED WRITINGS BY WILLIAM LEON DAWSON

EDITED BY ANNA NEHER

FOREWORD BY GRAHAM CHISHOLM

SANTA CLARA UNIVERSITY, SANTA CLARA, CALIFORNIA

HEYDAY BOOKS, BERKELEY, CALIFORNIA

Library of Congress Cataloging-in-Publication Data

Dawson, William Leon, 1873-1928.
  Dawson's avian kingdom / edited by Anna Neher ; foreword by Graham Chisholm.
      p. cm.—(A California legacy book)
  ISBN 978-1-59714-062-1 (pbk. : alk. paper)
  1. Birds—California. 2. Dawson, William Leon, 1873-1928. I. Neher, Anna. II. Title.
  QL684.C2D34 2007
  598.09794—dc22
                              2007016214

Cover Illustration and Design: Lorraine Rath
Interior Design/Typesetting: Lorraine Rath
Printing and Binding: McNaughton & Gunn, Saline, MI

Orders, inquiries, and correspondence should be addressed to:
      Heyday Books
      P. O. Box 9145, Berkeley, CA 94709
      (510) 549-3564, Fax (510) 549-1889
      www.heydaybooks.com

Printed in the United States of America on 50% post consumer recycled paper.♻

10 9 8 7 6 5 4 3 2 1

Contents

COWBIRDS, ORIOLES, BLACKBIRDS, MEADOWLARKS, AND BOBOLINKS

FINCHES AND OLD WORLD SPARROWS

Foreword

Graham Chisholm

Director of Conservation, Audubon California

AS A YOUNG BIRDER IN THE MIDWEST, I was usually either exploring the Missouri River bottomlands or combing through my meager collection of bird guides, seeking to learn how to tell subtle differences between species of flycatchers or fall warblers.

Back in Omaha, I searched through antiquarian bookstores, looking through old musty tomes with titles like *Birds of America* or the Life Histories of North American Birds series by Arthur Bent, hoping to find more knowledge there. But I felt rebuffed by their flowery or idiosyncratic descriptions from the field, a language at once dense and sentimental. A disciple of the first wave of conservation biology, I found these Victorian viewpoints irrelevant and old-fashioned.

It was a heady time to be a birder, even in Omaha and even pre-Internet, as each year brought new information about the science of bird identification. More sophisticated bird books emerged that took identification to new levels that had seemed unimaginable in the early 1970s. The rise of modern birding knowledge over the next two decades led my friends and me to become fearless in our belief that there was no identification problem that we could not overcome—fall sparrows, quiet flycatchers, immature tanagers—all could be surmounted. The DNA wave arrived with a promise to reshuffle our understanding of the bird world. Species were split—Plain Titmouse became Oak Titmouse and Juniper Titmouse, and many others followed suit. Our knowledge seemed increasingly exact, and as a bonus for birders, there were more species to count.

Yet all this new knowledge also seemed narrow. Our field guides were to the point. The focus was on identification—we looked for primaries, secondaries, tertials, and variations in molts. Natural history was secondary. There were important exceptions, though, as some birders realized that intuition could help identify birds. The recognition that a bird's "jizz"—the immediate feeling that one picks up, whether it be related to size, behavior, or some other characteristic—could be essential in identifying a bird opened a new window for me. In truth, this came at a time when many of us were also growing weary of just birding. And I was itching to move West.

A move to graduate school at the University of California at Berkeley provided the opening I needed to become acquainted with birders who, like me, wanted more. We wanted a broader understanding of natural history—what *is* that shrub that the California Thrasher is sitting on? We also turned our interest to "birding with a purpose," or "citizen science." We started doing more than just participating in Audubon Christmas Bird Counts; we signed up to help on breeding bird survey routes or atlas projects. We started becoming observers—observing all birds, everyday birds, and noticing behaviors that we might have ignored in our quests to identify species. I realized that seeking birds—new birds—wasn't fulfilling. I was becoming happy with deep looks at common birds, watching them feed, following them back to their nests, and just spending time getting to know them in their landscape—in the California landscape.

This brings us full circle, back to early field ornithologists like William Leon Dawson, who was always one of the best "whole bird" observers. Now, here I have to admit that my first encounter with Dawson's *Birds of California* was short (that Victorian thing again), and after having rebuffed it more than a quarter of a century ago, I was surprised to find Dawson on my desk again.

This was because Malcolm Margolin, pied piper of California's natural and cultural heritage, told me that Heyday Books was reissuing a portion of Dawson's work. This time, I was charmed. Phrases such as "Lilliputian bedlam," "fellow mountaineer," "busy little midgets," and "tricksy bushwhacker of song" all brought smiles to my face. Taught to avoid anthropomorphizing animals, it was hard to not cringe at expressions like "What a piece of mischief is the sparrow!" Yet Dawson's descriptions of birds and their behavior are accurate and true to the observations of those who have spent days watching birds in California. While the style is more flowery and the path often less direct, it is clear that Dawson brought a tremendous knowledge of California and its birds, plants, and natural habitats to inform his seminal work.

Dawson spent hours, days, and weeks watching birds. He knew birds and he knew California. While this version of Dawson's work has been trimmed to remove passages that are less likely to be of interest to the nonscientific reader, there is still a lot of science between the lines. We learn much about our California birds, their habits, their songs, their preferred trees or perhaps their favored meals. We get "the whole bird." We also get a deep sense of Dawson's passion for the land that those birds depend upon.

In an age when "modern science" guides our decisions, Dawson reminds us that a connection to the heart remains important—and that a little whimsy never hurt anyone. I hope his words open many hearts to California's birds, inspiring us to take action on behalf of the California Condor, Black Rail, and Snowy Plover and other species that are our California heritage.

Dawson reaches out through time to show us that, more than science and policy, perhaps a charmed heart is the most potent weapon we can wield in protecting this great and rugged land.

The Egg Man: A Biography of William Leon Dawson

Terri Sheridan

GENTLY LIFTED TO HIS FATHER'S SHOULDER, four-year-old William Leon Dawson peered into a Brown Thrasher's nest and thrilled at his first sight of neatly arranged eggs still warm from their mother's breast. Though no one realized it at the time, the glimpse into that nest might well have been a gaze into a crystal ball. For it was this experience that set Dawson on a path that would eventually lead him to become one of the world's greatest egg collectors.

Born February 20, 1873, in Leon, Illinois, Dawson was the only child of William Edwy Dawson and Ada Eliza Adams Dawson. He was just five months old when the family traveled by covered wagon to settle a homestead in Rush County, Kansas. Dawson spent his first nine years exploring this prairie farm and the countryside beyond the fencerows. It was during these boyhood wanderings that he developed his gift for observation and love for the out-of-doors. In 1882 the Dawsons moved again, this time to northern Illinois so that the senior William could pursue a degree in theology. It was here, at the age of ten, that the young Will collected his very first egg, from the nest of a Prairie Hen. Remembering this event in later years, Dawson regretted having left the rest of the eggs behind. Within a month of his first egg, Dawson had eighteen more—all collected from common prairie species. Collecting eggs would become an unbeatable addiction for Dawson; twice he tried to kick it by giving his collections away, only to start collecting all over again in new locations.

Seeing their son's insatiable desire, Dawson's parents provided him with an egg drill and a subscription to *The Young Oologist*. If they couldn't discourage the hobby, they reasoned, they might as well support it.

When the Dawson family relocated to Washington State in 1885, the eggs from fifty species of birds were carefully packed and transported with them. It was while living in Seattle that young Dawson met Frances Etta Ackerman. The two were smitten, and when it came time for college, they both enrolled at Ohio's Oberlin College. In 1895 the two were married. Etta never could have predicted what their life together would become. Taking a break from their studies, they spent the following year in Okanogan County, Washington, where Dawson worked as a home missionary and Sunday school teacher. As the parish boundaries were larger than the state of New Jersey, Dawson often traveled by pony to reach outlying communities. He used his long hours on the trail as an opportunity to gather information on the local birds. He would record 145 species during this time, leading to *A Preliminary List of the Birds of Okanogan County, Washington.* *

Dawson was to be paid $600 for a year's work, and the parishioners were to come up with another $100 worth of goods and services for the family. As the parish was a poor one, there was not always much to spare for the Dawsons. The "goods" usually came in the form of beans, beans, and more beans, which Etta became quite adept at preparing any number of ways. With Will away much of the time, Etta was left to "make do." Their house was made from three shacks that had been placed together to give them a bedroom, parlor, and kitchen. They had an outhouse at the back of the lot. Water had to be drawn from Lake Chelan and carried up to the house in ten-gallon oil cans slung across the shoulders and supported by a yoke. As the two planned to return to Ohio, Etta took a teaching job in the next town to help bolster their savings. Although the hours were long for both of them, they did manage to squirrel away enough money to return to their studies at Oberlin.

While at Oberlin, Dawson alternated between zoology and theology courses. He donated his egg collection to the college museum and began a mentorship under Lynds Jones, ornithology professor and founder of the *Wilson Bulletin*. Their lifelong friendship would result in many

* Dawson, William L. 1897. "A Preliminary List of the Birds of Okanogan County, Washington." *The Auk.* 14:2, pp. 168–182.

trips into the field and more than one publishing venture, including *The Birds of Ohio*,* which was published in 1903. Eventually, Dawson decided to follow in his father's footsteps and earned his degree in theology. Preaching would take him to a "moribund country church" in Ahtanum, Washington, where the Dawsons' first son was born, and then to Columbus, Ohio.** However, this career as a minister was to be short-lived. Dawson could not ignore his itch for ornithology. Using poor health as an excuse to leave his second congregation, Dawson again turned his attention toward egg collecting and the natural history of birds.

At a crossroads, the Dawsons returned to Washington in 1904, this time with two young sons in tow. Will's next project was to be a book about Washington birds. Wounded from the criticism he had received regarding the illustrations published in his previous work, Dawson set about learning the craft of photography and cultivated a relationship with artist Allan Brooks. For a scientific assistant, Dawson chose the distinguished ornithologist John Hopper Bowles. The result was the founding of Occidental Publishing Company, the sole purpose of which was to publish *The Birds of Washington*. When the two-volume work was released in 1909 it was characterized as "scientifically trustworthy," with illustrations "noteworthy for their excellence."***

Encouraged to write *The Birds of California*, Dawson moved the family to Santa Barbara in 1910. By this time, Dawson had the support of many ornithologists worldwide and his egg collections were growing exponentially. Santa Barbara had become an important stopover for prominent field biologists, like Joseph Grinnell, on their travels between northern and southern California. Etta Dawson was called upon at all hours of the day and night to provide them with tea and a

---

*   Dawson, William L., and Lynds Jones. 1903. *The Birds of Ohio*. Columbus, Ohio: The Wheaton Publishing Co.

** Dawson, William L. N.d. Biographical Notes. Unpublished manuscript in George Grinnell correspondence files, Museum of Vertebrate Zoology, University of California, Berkeley.

*** Allen, J. A. 1909. "Dawson and Bowles's 'The Birds of Washington'." *The Auk*. 26:3, p. 328.

bite to eat, while Dawson himself held court with his latest oological theories and hair-raising tales of his exploits in the field.

The Dawsons' third child, a daughter, arrived in 1913. With his California bird book still incomplete, Dawson set out to fulfill yet another dream—that of a Museum of Comparative Oology. In 1916, this museum was born at the back of the Dawsons' Santa Barbara property in the form of a small studio office with an adjacent corrugated storage shack to house the collections. The advent of World War I made funds scarce, but Dawson's creative knack for fund-raising and his recruitment of members willing to contribute both collections and time to his endeavor kept the museum and its reputation alive.

Dawson's leadership created an institution of worldwide renown. With the museum's reputation in good stead and members of the board tending to many of the day-to-day operations, Dawson was able to take a leave of absence and, with the support of Ellen Browning Scripps, finally complete *The Birds of California* in 1923.* His celebration was to be short-lived, however, as a falling-out with the Museum of Comparative Oology's Board of Trustees led to his resignation a short time later. He was forced to leave his collections behind as he gathered face and regrouped his supporters. (The museum still exists, expanded in mission as well as physical appointments, as the Santa Barbara Museum of Natural History.)

Dawson would go on to found another institution, the International Museum of Comparative Oology. Under the auspices of this new institution he set out to write two more books, about the birds of Mexico and the birds of Florida. He traveled extensively in both areas, compiling checklists and field notes. He solicited subscriptions and sponsors for both of these projects, but was never able to raise enough money for the publication of either.

Dawson's last project was to be a revised edition of *The Birds of Ohio*. He wanted to produce a work for Ohio that had an illustrated

* Dawson, William Leon. 1923. *The Birds of California*. Los Angeles, San Diego: South Moulton Co.

magnificence equal to his California volumes. This was not to be, however: while traveling from Florida to Ohio, Dawson caught a cold, which turned to pneumonia. He died April 30, 1928, at the age of fifty-five, leaving his life's work unfinished.

Etta was left heartbroken and financially obliged to sell most of his collections, including eggs and nests, photography, artwork, and even his personal journals and field notes. Although some of his egg and photograph collections remain at the Santa Barbara Museum of Natural History and many of his journals and field notes are now part of the Ohio Historical Society archive collections, there are still missing pieces from the life of William Leon Dawson. Even so, his work continues to touch the lives of both ornithological scholars and amateurs, and his spirit lives on in the colorful prose he used to describe his beloved birds. Certainly, he had the soul of an artist. In the summer of 1929 Etta and the Dawsons' daughter Barbara climbed eleven thousand feet into the Sierra Nevada to scatter Dawson's ashes into his beloved Crystal Lake.

Terri Sheridan is Museum Librarian at the Santa Barbara Museum of Natural History.

INTRODUCTION
Anna Neher

A CONFESSION: Before encountering William Dawson's *The Birds of California*, I did not like birds.

Oh, they seemed a pleasant enough accessory to garden, forest, field, or cityscape, but no more. Certainly I was no birder. I would not be caught squatting in the brambles for hours on end logging sightings—or worse, hunched over field guides, scrutinizing the distinguishing marks between a Common Redpoll and a Pine Siskin. And doubtless many a gardener or outdoorsperson, turning a far more fervent eye toward the feathered kind, nonetheless balks at the thought of engaging in actual "bird-watching." For who would encounter nature encumbered by binoculars and an American Ornithologists' Union checklist?

When such casual or disinterested readers first open one of the original tomes of *The Birds of California*, now musty and faded with the decades, little do they know what awaits. Here there are daring exploits (both human and avian), furtive encounters, descriptive passages of fanciful excess. Intrepid birders scale Sierra cliffs and crouch waist-deep in muck in pursuit of their elusive quarry, while for page upon page the drama of birdlife unfolds. Birds woo mates, defend their nests, feed their young, steal from each other, fight each other, eat each other, all in a rich roll call of character sketches sufficiently vital and persuasive to draw nearly any reader into Dawson's avian world.

To read Dawson is to wake up. It is to distinguish, one morning, individual birdcalls from the morning cacophony, or to suddenly be struck by the cocky tilt of a Scrub Jay's tail feathers. It is to pass an afternoon tracking a mother Junco's cautious, food-laden comings and goings. As Dawson would say, it is to look with the eye of "the poet, the interpreter, the apologist—the mystic, even—the at-all-times bird-lover."

At its best, nature writing opens the reader to a world that was previously inaccessible—whether that be the fastness of the Sierran wilderness or the Spotted Towhee scratching at a patch of dirt out back. It shows the reader how to see. Dawson's text is a work of love, informed by years of patient observation and a near-encyclopedic knowledge of California birdlife. His gift to California letters resides in his ability to open our senses to the natural wealth of this state.

This collection brings together those passages of *The Birds of California* that, through wit, eloquence, and keen perception, most powerfully grant entry into California's avian kingdom. In making selections, every effort was made to represent that kingdom in all its abundance and diversity. Still, the longtime birder may note the absence of some favorite species considered indispensable to any collection on California birdlife. I can only offer that literary merit, as well as a desire to avoid repetition among similar entries, took precedence over any attempt to generate a complete, authoritative field guide.

It is also worth noting the omission of many passages of more scientific than literary merit. Dawson was as much an ornithologist as a writer—his commitment to oology is of particular note—but his technical contributions are not necessarily of interest to general readers. For meticulous observations on the sizes and shapes of eggs, and unflagging attempts at phonetic transcription of birdsong, I refer readers to the complete text.

Perhaps even more vocal than Dawson the scientist is Dawson the conservationist. Throughout *The Birds of California*, he fiercely advocates for his birds against all comers. Be his opponents sportsmen, farmers, legislators, or developers, he squares off with unbridled zeal, sometimes co-opting entire entries in the service of woeful lamentations or involved counterarguments to vilified proposals. His urgent, firsthand accounts of dwindling populations are as relevant today as when they were written. Some writers have represented Dawson as an engaged naturalist in the spirit of John Muir.

Yet environmentalism in the early twentieth century was still a nascent force in the minds of American nature lovers. Dawson occasionally betrays a restlessness within his own strictures, a nostalgia for the heady era of ornithological quest, when museum collections were half empty and the wilderness was ripe with fresh discoveries. In particular, his proclivity for nest- and egg-hunting reveals an enthusiasm far exceeding his staid defense of these practices in the service of science. He even gives voice at moments to a measured appreciation for the sportsman's particular understanding of his quarry. In this sense, Dawson represents and embodies a transition in birding, natural science, and human interaction with the natural world. I have made space for passages that evoke practices and precepts that are now lost to us.

Dawson's Avian Kingdom is a sampling of a sprawling, epic text that was a decade in the making, and whose creation sent the author across the vast array of topographies and ecosystems that form the state of California. As a tribute to this state and to its wealth of avian diversity, it is as pertinent today as it was in 1923. If you have long been a birder, you will find much to refresh and confirm your interest. If you are new to the avian kingdom, you will never look at birds the same way again.

Happy reading, and happy birding.

Dawson's Avian Kingdom

Loons and Grebes

COMMON LOON
Gavia immer

VIEWED STRICTLY AS A WATER-BIRD, as Nature intended, the Loon is a paragon of beauty. Alert, supple, vigorous, one knows himself to be in the presence of the master wild thing when he comes upon a Loon on guard in his native element. The bird seems to move about almost without effort, a single backward kick of one of those immense paddles serving to send it forward at any desired speed, while the head is turned inquiringly from side to side as if to take your measure. A shout, a false motion, the flash of a gun, and the wild thing has vanished, leaving scarcely a ripple to mark its recent resting place. It reappears, if at all, at a surprisingly great distance, and if really alarmed, only the head is thrust out of water to take breath, get bearings, and disappear again.

Under water the Loon moves with great rapidity, using its wings to assist its progress. It is able, thus, easily to overtake a fish, which it transfixes by a stroke of its dagger-like beak and brings to the surface for consumption. When the water is clear enough to admit of it, it is a delight to watch the air-bubbles which cling to the diver in the translucent depths, like a silvery coat of mail, and which he shakes off only upon emerging at the surface again.

In singular contrast to the Loon's facility and grace in the water is its behavior upon land. Since the feet are placed so far back, it must stand nearly upright, penguin-fashion; and its walk is an awkward, shuffling performance; or else, as is more likely to be the case, the bird flounders along on all fours. It is said not to be able to take wing from the ground at all. In rising from the water the bird humps over in an agony of effort, rising only by slow stages, first by threshing the surface of the water with wings and feet, then by combined running and flying, until the feet clear at last, and the aspirant attains a proper motion. Once started, the Loon's flight is swift and powerful, the wings accomplishing by rapid vibration what they lack in expanse.

Because of their infirmity of gait, the Loon usually nests quite near the water's edge, on some wood-bound lake or solitary mountain mere, so that it may glide into the water, unobserved, at the approach of danger. And because the eggs are of such a perfect mud color themselves, there is little attempt made to conceal the nest. On the contrary, a position on some promontory, or projecting log, is chosen, so that the bird may command with its watchful eye a wide stretch of territory. Treasure trove the Loon considers the stub of some submerged tree broken off at the water line. Here, if the water is quiet enough, she heaps up a miscellaneous mound of grass, moss, roots, and floating stems. The external diameter of this island citadel may be as much as three feet, and its depth one; but at another time the bird is as likely to deposit her eggs on a sandbar with little or no pretense at a nest.

WESTERN GREBE

Aechmophorus occidentalis

IT IS AS A WINTER VISITANT along the kelp-line offshore, in lagoons, and on the larger interior lakes, that the Western Grebe is commonly known to Californians. The fall arrivals are somewhat unsophisticated, and will permit us to drift up close enough to observe the cruel blood-red eye which appropriately accompanies the javelin beak. The necks of these birds are very mobile and their heads are scarcely at rest for an instant, save as the gaze is riveted by fear or momentary curiosity. If fishing is dull and the observer on his good behavior, the company will float at ease rather than excite itself to pull away; and now and then a bird will seek relief by reaching upward and outward with one of its green paddles and wagging it vigorously—apparently with no intended slight.

Fish form the principal diet of these grebes, and in the pursuit of them the birds exhibit great dexterity. Schools of herring and the like are followed until capacity is exhausted. In diving, the Western Grebe's head describes a loop with lightning rapidity, and the body springs forward as though to accept a challenge from its vanishing leader. Considerable depths are visited, and the bird is by preference a fisher of the channels, leaving the shallows to his smaller kinfolk.

Like all others of the group, the young of the Western Grebe tumble out of the shell into the water, and the saturated mass of decayed vegetation which for a time held the eggs is never known as home. When the brood is hatched, the young birds clamber upon the mother's back, or the father's, as the case may be, and have a ride quite to their liking. Nothing more convenient than this floating palace could be devised; besides being a raft and a diving bell(e), it is fitted up with feather-stuffed cushions for repose, and upon it meals are served frequently, *a la Grebe*—since it is said that the mother can twist her neck around without difficulty and bestow a selected morsel upon whom she will of the expectant flock.

Horned Grebe
Colymbus auritus

APPARENTLY NOTHING IS MORE ATTRACTIVE to a school of herring (all little fish which attend school are herring for practical purposes) than a maze of piles supporting a wharf. They crowd into the shadowy aisles and survey the retreating vistas with the dumb wonder of children at Karnak. A few nibbles at the hieroglyphics traced by barnacles on the pillars, or tweak in mischief at the wan whiskers of the serried anemones. Suddenly a silver shudder thrills the school. A flash of white sides is followed by a dash for the depths, and there emerges from the tumult a gray apparition which resolves itself into a panting bird. An instant gleam as of fins near the bird's beak tells you that another fish has gone to grebe; but just how you cannot tell, for it was all so sudden. The diver pauses a moment to consider the danger of the kindly eyes that stare down on him, recalls that art is long and fish are fleeting, and is off again hot-foot to urge the merry chase under water.

They are innocent, happy little souls, these Hornies, and one is tempted to look upon them as children, especially if he is used to the grown-up Westerns. Once I stole upon a little company at early morn, as they rested after a long migration flight. Six of the dainty creatures were dancing before me on the gently ruffled surface of the water-works pond. They saw the bird-watcher plainly enough some thirty feet away, but accepted him as a part of bountiful nature and gave themselves to slumber. In sleeping they draw the head back and settle it between the shoulders, thrusting the bill down, precisely, to the right. Now and then one lifts its head and describes a wary circle of reconnaissance, but is soon reassured and resumes its slumbers. While taking these cat-naps in my presence, they swim and whirl automatically and maintain their general position, as though gifted with double consciousness. There are five males in the company, with one female, and the white of their breasts and throats glistens purely in the morning sun, for it is autumn; and I steal away with a sense of privilege, as though I had seen fairies caught out of bounds.

Albatrosses, Shearwaters, and Petrels

SHORT-TAILED ALBATROSS

Diomedea albatrus

NO ONE WHO HAS NOT SUFFERED the pangs of solitude, or the worse pangs of ill-assorted company long endured, knows with what glad acclaim a fellow mortal may be hailed. He is for us an authentic outpost of life and a dear pledge of that wholesome, myriad-pressing, human contact for which our hearts have come to ache. So upon the trackless ocean, the sight of a bird brings to the watcher a sudden electric thrill. Our eyes devour the vagabond with quick apprehension, and there springs up within us a world-conquering, class-obliterating sense of fellowship.

Those who have studied pelagic species just off shore—and there are no more fertile fields for such study than those afforded by several of the gregarious species of these ocean wanderers—can form little conception of the average desolation of the oceanic wastes. Dr. T. W. Richards gave us the most adequate expression of it when he testified that during a voyage of twelve thousand miles, he saw not over one hundred pelagic birds all told—one bird every hundred miles! Yet in all probability ten million albatrosses and a hundred million shearwaters and a billion petrels were at that very time scouring the seven seas. It takes a good many sea-birds to go around if all seafaring men are to have a comforting glimpse of one now and then.

Wind is a prime requisite of Diomedeine happiness, and it is amid the roaring Forties of the Antarctic seas that these birds appear to best advantage. The stouter the gale the more certain the bird's advance against it, for Nature has taught the bird a subtle alchemy whereby it can resolve the forces of the wind so that the upthrust plus gravity much more than balances the resistance of the onsweep, to the end that the bird rides splendidly against the wind without other effort than that of holding the wings at a certain angle.

But while the albatross is a good sailor, he is a poor oarsman. When the wind fails, the birds are becalmed, and they sit the waters, it may be for days at a time, rather than try to endure the exertion of a labored flight. Indeed, in default of wind, the bird finds great difficulty in rising from the water at all, even though assisted by powerful strokes of the feet.

Dark-bodied Shearwater
Puffinus griseus

YOUR ONE BEST BET TO SEE A MILLION BIRDS is to post yourself on some sea-cliff, anywhere from May to October, and to watch for a dark line of hurrying Shearwaters outside of the kelp-beds, perhaps half a mile or so offshore. It is a mere chance, then, for Shearwaters hunt in great hordes, and the main host may be operating anywhere between Baja California and Alaska.

But to see them all at once! That, too, is easy if you know the magic talisman. It is *herring*. The million Shearwaters are looking for a school of ten million little fish; and when this populous kindergarten is located—lucky for you if near shore—an electric thrill runs through the circle. The original discoverers have plumped into the water; those immediately ahead have wheeled about; while those behind have speeded up with an impulse which almost immediately affects the entire line. The pace is furious, and the water is instantly black with settling birds. The first comers have snatched their prey from the surface; their immediate successors have had to dive to moderate depths, probably not over three or four feet. The fish themselves have taken alarm and gone below, but they will reappear in a minute or so at some distance, only to be set upon in fury by the augmented company of beaks.

Beal's Petrel

Oceanodroma leucorhoa beali

ON JULY 20, 1906, THREE OF US, in company with two expert Indian surfmen, set off in a canoe from La Push to visit this rock a mile offshore. The sea was fairly quiet and the sky was perfect, but the swells crashed and roared about the base of the rocks, and landing with cameras was a difficult operation. Once ashore, we were obliged to scuttle between waves to the nearest point where it was at all possible to scale the rock.

Immediately upon arrival our attention was called to tiny openings in the grass, the orifices of subterranean burrows. The tunnels are about two and a half inches wide at the mouth, and run in from two to three feet. They seldom run straight, but twist about at random, widening as they proceed, until a considerable nesting chamber is reached.

Here, according to the season, may be found two adult birds, a bird and an egg, or a bird and young. When removed from the nest, the parent bird appears dazed and blinded, and seldom seeks to escape by flight. Taken into the hand, it jams its head into the recesses of the fingers, thinking only of cover. Placed upon the ground, it pokes about the grass in a fidgety, near-sighted way, looking for a hole, and does not scruple to enter the hole of a neighbor rather than remain under surveillance. Once one flew from the hand and made off to sea with a bewildered, hesitant motion, a jerkiness somewhat similar to that of a Nighthawk at close quarters. Others I threw into the air, and they too made off to sea sheepishly, like waifs caught sleeping on a park bench and told to move on.

We had been working in the turf plot looking only for fresh eggs and taking pains to replace the chicks—tiny balls of slate-colored down with feet of a deathly pallor and bills jet black; stupid, also, as balls of mud—wherever found. But after having waded through the heavily grassed portion of the island once or twice, the thought occurred to us that there might be petrels there. Judge of our surprise, however, when we found the vegetable mold a perfect labyrinth of petrel burrows! The whole half-acre of grass proper was a *seething mass of petrels*. Yet from all that host not a sound to betray their presence! The sun shone calmly and the breeze blew benignly. Nothing disturbed the serenity of the day save the restless quaverings of the always hostile gulls. There was nothing, in short, to indicate that beneath our feet lay a buried city, not once populous and now deserted, but *now* teeming with life, a city of storm-waifs, gathered from an expanse of a thousand watery leagues, a city perhaps more populous than any other colony of the class Aves within a hundred leagues, lying silent where the eye saw only waving grass. The promise of the situation so wrought upon us that we determined to return at evening sometime later, and did so on Monday evening following, July 23rd.

We arrived a little after nine o'clock, provided with matches, bedding, and water, and prepared to spend the night. We found the island still silent, but we used the remaining moments of twilight to further determine the limits of the colony; and found that the dense salmon-berry thicket was likewise occupied by petrel burrows.

At about ten o'clock the first note was sounded—from the ground. In quality like that of a tiny cockerel, in accent like that of a glib paroquet, came the cry, *Petteretteretterell, etteretteretterell*. The second phrase is slightly fainter than the first, and is, therefore, just suggestively an echo of it. After ten minutes, or such a matter, one sounded in the air. By and by came another and another. And so the matter grew until by eleven p.m. the air was a-flutter with sable wings, and the island a-hum with *t*'s and *r*'s and *l*'s.

The air was full at all times of circling birds, at least several hundred of them, probably several thousand. They flew about excitedly, much more nimbly than in the daytime, but still erratically, incessantly clashing wings with their fellows and now and then colliding with such force that they fell down into the grass. Those which flew about uttered from time to time the characteristic cry, but those a-wing were but a small portion of the total number in evidence. The grass swarmed with birds working their way down through to the burrows, or else struggling out, all giving from time to time the rolling cackle which is the accompaniment of activity; while from the ground itself came an attendant chorus of cries. Taken altogether, there were thousands, perhaps tens of thousands, of birds in motion, and the total effect of the rustling and the cackling (or crowing) was a dainty uproar of notable proportions, a never-to-be-forgotten babel of strange sounds. And in this fairy tumult not the least element was the peeping and whining of the chicks, both tended and untended.

Cormorants and Pelicans

FARALLON CORMORANT
Phalacrocorax auritus albociliatus

LANDSMEN ARE SLOW TO REALIZE THE FERTILITY OF THE SEA. Its great expanse is so little broken at the surface by the irruption of life that we cannot easily comprehend the vast and varied resources either of its depths or of its teeming shallows. The gulls, the gooneys, and the man-o'-war-birds serve to heighten this superficial impression which we get of ocean's scanty fare, for we find them traveling a league for a bite, and a day's journey for a full meal. Not so, however, with the cormorant. Here is a bird, the very symbol of voracity, built to seize and swallow and speedily digest. When we see him and know his ways, we realize the long-suffering of the great mother, and the boundless provision she has made for her hungry children.

Cormorants of more than forty species range along the hundred thousand leagues of earth's shore-line, well distributed in all save Arctic and Antarctic waters; and they constitute the mightiest race of fishers ever known, save those born of the teeming waters themselves. The piscatorial peculations of men are as a dot beside their unceasing pillage.

The name "shag," from the old Saxon *sceacga*, hair, undoubtedly refers to the crests, which are so characteristic a feature of many species of cormorants. Speaking of crests, fashions are various; and in the case of the Farallon Cormorant, at least, very variable.

Unlike the Baird's Cormorant, which is nervous and flighty to a fault, the Farallon is a plain, home-loving body, very amiable if treated with reasonable consideration. Partly because of her more phlegmatic disposition, and partly, no doubt, because most of her eggs have hatched by vacation time (which is as early as most of us get around to pay a visit to the sea-bird isles), it is often possible to get very close to brooding birds of this species. I have sat down on the very door-step (marble or merely white-washed mattered not) of a shagine home and visited with the occupant to heart's content.

A typical cormorant rookery is, of course, foul from every conceivable source. The nests and rocks are white with excrement, and with this the callow young are more or less besmeared. Then about the nests lie fragments of uneaten fish, and to these flies swarm in myriads. Add to the general raciness of odor an occasional overdone egg, and you have a fine unsavory mess of it.

Young cormorants are perfectly helpless when hatched, and are, if possible, uglier than young magpies. Not only are they coal black and as naked as sin, but their heads are scarcely larger around than their long necks, and a nestful of them looks more like a bundle of young black-snakes than anything avian. The characteristic orange upon the gular area of the adult is reflected by a pale yellow, sharply contrasting with the posterior black, even in the very youngest specimens; while youngsters half or two-thirds grown are covered with a coarse black down. When disturbed at the nest the younglings quit their quarters and waddle off clumsily to the farthest nest of the immediate group, where they stand on the defensive a dozen or twenty strong. When brought to bay, and, of course, after they have disposed of the contents of their crops, no matter where, they thrust out the neck at the intruder and open the gullet, until it almost makes one dizzy to look down it, emitting the while a sound between a hiss and a bark, intended no doubt to be frightful, but really only dismal or ridiculous.

If the shags take a heavy toll of the finny tribes, they pay fearful tribute, in turn, to their ruthless overlord, the Western Gull. From the time the first egg is laid, one or the other of the parents must mount guard incessantly to keep the marauder at bay. The gull is a coward and cannot stand up under well-directed blows of the shag's beak; but once let the owner's attention be diverted, and the gull slips in to snatch an egg or a stripling youngster. Human intrusion is welcomed by the gull with loud acclaim, for in the great colony of shags many will flee in fear before the man. This is the gull's opportunity, and he will gobble the uncovered eggs in a trice, or return again and again until all the bantlings are appropriated. It may be the law of nature, but it always arouses in the beholder feelings of indignation to see a gull seize a helpless black baby by the neck and bolt it in midair, in spite of frantic kicking and squirming.

Your shag is no ballet dancer. Water is her native element, and she is not ungraceful in the air, but lighting on a sprangly mesquite bough is a more difficult matter. As the contact is about to be made, the performer is convulsed with an agony of apprehension. The tail-brake is set hard, the wings are back-firing, the splay feet are held tense, while the acuteness of anxiety is most convincingly shown by the rigidity of the hyoid apparatus which makes an acute angle in the throat. As often as not, the bird misses her footing and scrambles madly, while her disconcerted neighbors roar protest.

BRANDT'S CORMORANT

Phalacrocorax penicillatus

BRANDT'S CORMORANT IS BOTH MORE SOCIABLE—or, strictly speaking, gregarious—and more wary than its milder-mannered cousins, the Farallon and the White-crest (*P. a. cincinatus*). Nevertheless, Brandt's is a familiar figure on the piles of the unfrequented piers, as well as on the rocky headlands of our entire coastline. If the bird is not exactly of a mind to fly at the first alarm from a passing steamer, it stands with wings half open, that, should necessity arise, no time may be lost in making good its escape. Again, a group of them will sit on a low-lying reef, or even on a floating log, with wings half extended, "drying their clothes" in the sunshine. The wings as well as the feet are used under water, but we cannot guess why the cormorants more than other aquatic species should be averse to wet plumage.

The birds nest in large close-set colonies, which, partly no doubt for sanitary reasons, they relocate from year to year. At least a last year's nesting site visited on the Farallons was not only buried in white-wash, but contained an appalling number of sodden squab skeletons. The new site chosen for the season of 1911 was on the north slope of Maintop, and by the last week in May was in a furor of nest-building activity. The interested actions of hovering gulls suggested that community tactics had been engendered as much by fear of the gull as anything else. An isolated nest might easily be surrounded by a mob of these pious marauders, and its occupants crowded or lured away; but in a closely occupied colony it is the invader who is surrounded, and a half-dozen writhing necks surmounted by beaks of no mean power are too much for the Larine nerve. But it is also amusing to see how the Brandt's Cormorants prey upon each other in the matter of building material. They are always grabbing at each other's haypile in passing, and once an absence is noted or an easy mark discovered, the ungenerous neighbors fall upon the nest and lug it off piecemeal. One bird I saw seized a beakful which for bulk was half as large as himself—a magnificent haul.

The newly hatched young are mother naked, and of a repulsive greasy black appearance. At the age of a week or such a matter, they are covered with a thick black down, well sprinkled upon the sides with white. The gular area is of a livid blue-black color from the outset, and young Brandts may thus be clearly distinguished from young Farallons, with which they occasionally mingle when frightened. A young cormorant is no mean climber. Armed with sharp claws, and hesitating not a moment to use wings in lieu of hands, an unsettled squab can scramble back up a very steep bit of rock. The social instinct is very strong in times of danger, and a hundred bantlings will huddle together in a single seething mass of apprehension.

The details of infant nursing are fortunately obscured from the eyes of a reluctant public. The "operation" takes place in the parental throat, down which the youngster thrusts his serpent-like head. Do not, therefore, accuse the gentle shag of cannibalism when you detect in it the act of swallowing the first six or eight inches of its infant's anatomy. Baby has been invited to help himself, and he will presently emerge from those fish-lined depths in radiant if disheveled triumph.

BAIRD'S CORMORANT
Phalacrocorax pelagicus resplendens

HARD EXPERIENCE, AS WELL AS INNATE SUSPICION, has led the Baird's Cormorant, long since, to forsake the comfortable quarters of her easy-going kinsmen, the Brandt's and the Farallon, and to rear her young on the bosses and inaccessible ledges of grim sea-cliffs. The ridges and crests belong to the larger shags, but the sides are her domain. Her calculations are not always infallible—your shag is no Plato—but ungettability has been her life study, and her average attainments in this line are noteworthy. The sculptured pillars and crannied sea-walls of our smaller coastal islands are an especial delight to her, while some of the sheer walls upon our mainland promontories permit fairly gratifying opportunities for study.

Cormorants plunge into the wildest waters as fearlessly as sea-lions, and they carry on their fishing operations about the shoulders of booming reefs which humans dare not approach. Wings are used for propulsion as well as the powerful full-webbed feet. The nostrils, moreover, of all adult cormorants are permanently closed, so that we have here perhaps, at least among those *who can also fly*, the world's champion diver. After luncheons, which occur quite frequently in the cormorant day, the birds love to gather on some low-lying reef, just above the reach of the waves, and devote the intervening hours to that most solemn function of life, digestion. There is evidence that the birds discuss oceanic politics on these occasions—the benevolent assimilation of a twelve-inch buffalo cod is presumed to be sufficient occupation for union hours.

White Pelican
Pelecanus erythrorhynchos

WELL DID THE PSALMIST OF OLD choose the pelican as the symbol of the wilderness. "Dead" seas and salty, the mighty evaporating pans of the desert, have here given rise to a race as weird, as majestic, as gracefully uncouth, as any that have ever adorned the pages of time. The White Pelican is an embodiment of an elder age, a legacy of the opulent days when Nature took thought of her winged children, and recked not of the reign of man, man the ruthless, man the envious, man the destroyer. For eons the great white birds have circled and soared over the desert wastes of interior western America. For generations uncounted they have fished in the salty waters of Lake Lahontan, of Lake Bonneville, and their successors; or they have foregathered ashore in snowy windrows to meditate, to digest, and to gladden withal the retrospective eye of the rare man who, like his Creator, enjoys the simple bliss of the undisturbed wild. The pelican and the wilderness stand together in their mute appeal. When the one is fully "reclaimed," the other must perish.

It need not be supposed that these ponderous fowls, the largest of water-birds by avoirdupois, are to be set down as awkward simply because they have big bills. Viewed at a distance, as they rest on shore or near some low mud island, their stately ranks present a most impressive spectacle. In flight they are calm, almost majestic; and their white plumage, set off by black wing-tips, makes a fine showing in the morning sun. They sit the water almost as gracefully as swans, and "tip" in a dignified way, immersing the entire head and neck—again much after the fashion of swans. Being provided, also, with an extensive system of air-sacs, they ride high and get credit for all their inches.

The pelican lives upon an exclusive diet of fish, and he uses his great gular pouch as a dip-net, or scoop, rather than as a creel for transportation, as was formerly supposed. He prefers little fish to big ones; and, indeed, the big fish rarely come his way, for he does not plunge from midair, after the fashion of his brown cousin, *P. o. californicus*. After a successful haul, the fisher bird raises his head, contracts the bellying net, or pouch, ejects the water, and swallows the catch. It sometimes happens that the bird makes a greater catch than he can handle, or, at least, greater than he has time to swallow during the rush of a successful drive. In this case he retires to shore with a full basket to effect a readjustment or to discard a clearly proven surplus.

CALIFORNIA BROWN PELICAN
Pelecanus occidentalis californicus

SYMBOL ALIKE OF THE SEA'S STRANGENESS and of her prodigality, there is perhaps no other bird whose appearance would so perfectly assure the landsman that he had arrived as this uncouth Adonis of the ocean-front, the California Brown Pelican. We will concede, without argument, that the bird is impossible. It is an incarnate jest, if you will, a piece of apprentice work perpetrated by one of the lesser divinities of Nature's workshop. An adobe artist with an imagination like Doré has taken a perfectly good goose and tricked it out with a huge fish-net which it is pledged forever to wear, and the public is expected to laugh at the poor bird's plight. But somehow we do not laugh. The bird has accepted its lot with such becoming meekness; it is able to view life with such imperturable gravity; above all, it has met its situation with such transcendent skill, that we can only wonder and applaud.

For what, after all, is more adroit than the flight of a pelican? With three or four leisurely strokes the bird acquires a momentum with which he can glide with incredible accuracy just above the surface of the water. Or if he is hunting at a higher level, the bird is able to check his momentum, to put on brakes midair, in less than the distance of his own length, and to plunge with the speed of thought upon his finny prey. If the run of fish is good, this feathered hydroplane heaves to upon the water. With beak held perpendicularly, or nearly so, he surveys the depths with tiny beady eyes, or thrusts again and again with a stroke as swift and sure as that of Cousin *Ardea*, he of the strong spear.

When the pouch is full, or when a turn of the tide sends the quarry down for a season, the birds haul out on a sandbar or other lonely spot and ruminate. Here they stand in solemn companies with bills depressed, for the weight of these members is quite too great to permit of their being carried at right angles; and here they survey an approaching stranger like myopic grandfathers peering over an array of befogged spectacles. Or else, if the way is quite clear, the pelican turns his head about and lays his bill comfortably along his back for a snooze; or else, in the last stage of relaxation, he squats upon the ground and disposes of both neck and bill in a jack-knife fold which rests upon the back.

If the casual acquaintance with these fowls permitted by shore-line loiterings is seductive, a visit to their haunts at nesting time is rewarding in the extreme. Not elsewhere, save upon some separate planet, may the observer hope to obtain such an impression of the utterly different. Indeed, a pelican rookery at the height of the season is a chapter from the Mesozoic age—nothing less. Here man is the outlaw, the anomaly; and, save for the dire portent of his presence, life in a pelicanry moves off in obedience to alien standards. Its very dimensions seem grotesque and unreal. There is no point of contact with previous experience; and the visitor, whether fortified by scientific purpose, or urged only by the vulgar curiosity which afflicts our kind, knows that he is an outsider, an intruder, a companion of gulls and ravens, before whom the law-abiding citizenry of this elder world stands silently reproachful.

The author pleads no more serious a purpose than an oological quest, and the securing of some pictures, to justify a brief exploitation of a province of this elder Eden; and (with consummate hypocrisy, if you will) he urges that such visits be *not* repeated. For the truth is, pelicans pay a fearful price—to the gulls—for any invasion—however intended-peaceful—of their colonies. A man is at best a potential marauder, and so long as his intentions are under suspicion, nests are uncovered and eggs grow cold or are snapped up by the predatory gulls.

But if you insist on turning buccaneer "just for this once," man the thwarts and help us pull this gear from the launch over to the landing place. A benevolent government, under necessity of maintaining an automatic light upon this dangerous headland, has provided a crude system of ladders whereby the intrepid, albeit camera-laden, may scale this 200-foot wall of basalt. The top of the island, once gained, is suddenly level. There is nothing visible save grass and sea and birds—these and quaint groves of a palm-like vegetable under whose scanty shadows the pelicans are huddled. It is incredible! a bird squatting upon a nest which rests upon the ground, and yet looms half as high as a palm tree! The illusion is perfect; but the "tree" is *Leptosyne gigantea*, a composite, which rises to a height of six or eight feet, and which supports on naked stems, two inches in diameter, a sudden crown of leaves, finely divided, like those of a carrot, and a few coarse yellow flowers.

We unlimber our photographic gear, and dedicate a leather case to such eggs as we may require, and then prepare to rush the colony for mass effects. Splendid! The whole earth seems to be in motion, and a thousand aeroplanes launch into the air. There is no noise of propellers nor yet of sputtering exhausts. Nature has perfected her models long since, and her motors meet the test of absolute silence. Pelicano, Model A, is a weird-looking craft, but a skyful of him is as efficient as so many swallows. There is no crashing of fusilages, and never an aileron impinges upon the rights of all that skyful. It is wonderful! awe-inspiring! It is only when the excitement has died down a little and the birds decide to settle again, that the show changes from grandeur to comedy. A pelican looking for a place to land is grotesque beyond the power of exaggeration. With legs straddled out at divergent angles and heads drawn back, the birds are preparing for the inevitable, and you rather expect a series of crashes. The birds appear to also; but somehow no casualties result, and you come to suspect that it is just a pose intended to enhance the effect of a surprising deftness.

Soon the ledges are lined with grave senators, and the birds gather in open places to view with impeccable decorum the ravages of the ruthless human bipeds. But, really, you know, it is not nearly so exciting to rob a colony of unresisting Quakers. Those bills might be terrible if they were plied in righteous indignation. The challenge of those great throats, if they were fiercely vocal, might rouse us to a corresponding fury. But this placidity is disarming. "I guess we've got enough, boys."

Auklets, Guillemots, and Murrelets

CASSIN'S AUKLET

Ptychoramphus aleuticus

THE PETREL POPULATION OF THE ISLANDS lying off the coast of California is not large; and Howell is probably correct in his surmise that this species outnumbers all our other small pelagic birds combined. The case was quite otherwise on the coast of Washington, where in 1907 we had just discovered the presence of Cassin's Auklets on a rocky islet which was tenanted by some 40,000 Beal Petrels.

Determined to get a line on the night-life of this interesting colony, we returned to the mainland for blankets and other supplies and had the Indians land us by canoe at nightfall. The distant lights of the Indian village and the myriad stars entertain us, but the real performance does not begin till well on toward ten o'clock. Now for the orchestra. "*Petteretteretterell, etteretteretterell*"—it is the tap, tap of the petrel conductor calling the island to attention. Soon ghostly forms steal about in the gathering gloom. Voice answers voice as each moment flies. The flitting shadows become a throng, and the chorus a tumult. But in the grand melange there is a new note. A quaint, burring croak wells up from the ground, elfish, gruesome, portentous. The Cassin's Auklets are waking up. Heard alone, the auklet chorus reminds one of a frog-pond in full cry. As one gives attention to an individual performer, however, and seeks to locate him in his burrow, the mystery and strangeness of it grows. The vocalist is complaining bitterly of we know not what wrongs. We must be within three feet of the noise as we stoop at the burrow's mouth; the volume of it is ear-filling; yet its source seems furlongs off. Now it is like the squealing of a pig in a distant slaughter pen. We lift our heads and the stock yards are reeling with the prayers and cries of a thousand victims. And now the complaint falls into a cadence, *"Let meee out, let meee out, let me out."* A thousand dolorous voices take up the chorus. The uproar gets upon the nerves. Is this a bird lunatic asylum? Have we stumbled upon an avian mad-house here in the lone Pacific? And are these inmates appealing to the moon, their absent mistress?

Nay, rather, it is the eternal infant. It is the voice of elemental hunger we hear, and we are powerless to answer. Oh, the unwearying importunity of the hungry child! Earth nor heaven shall forget him while he draws the breath of want. Listen, ocean! and hearken, ye still spaces! "Let me eat, let me eat, let me eat!" Anxious fathers and distraught mothers hurry to and fro under the lash of the myriad hunger cry. There are some sounds of satisfaction here and there, but they are drowned in the universal shout. Hour after hour goes by and still the fury of demand increases. Fast and faster whirls the ministering host. High and higher rolls the tumult—until tired nature (human nature) asserts herself and we drop off to sleep—to awaken only when the sun is an hour high and the silence of the island is unbroken save by a few quavering gulls.

The Cassin's Auklet seems incapable of controlling the force of its flight, and the wonder is that they are not every one of them dashed in pieces in a single night in their effort to locate their proper burrows. In this respect they remind one of nothing else so much as beetles or moths which come hurtling into the region of candle light, and, without an instant's pause for presumed necessary recovery, begin an animated search for an imaginary exit. This crash-and-crawl method seemed not exceptional but characteristic. It was especially noticeable in the paved area just outside our workroom doors. (We occupied an outbuilding of the light-keepers' quarters.) Crash! announced the arrival of another food-laden wanderer from the unknown. The impact against the building invariably stunned the bird so that it fell to the ground, but immediately it began a frantic search, and as likely as not, before we could lay hands on it, it disappeared under a crack in the doorstep. *"Right here,"* from a certain spot under the floor announced the home-coming, and so enthusiastic would be the reception accorded the tipsy reveler that for a time all human conversation above had to be suspended.

PIGEON GUILLEMOT
Cepphus columba

ON THE CHANNEL ISLANDS, which are more or less protected from the prevailing winds which sweep the northern coast, the Pigeon Guillemots are occupying their nesting caves by May. With us, the birds have little need to provide artificial tunnels in the earth, as is their habit further north, but they nest instead in any available cranny from the water's edge to the summit of the cliff. On the mainland and sea walls or on the larger islands, the birds see to it that they are out of the reach of prowling foes. As one clambers over the rough sides of the rookery, these birds tumble out just ahead like sleepy children, and plunge with all speed into the nearest water, by way of getting their wits collected. After a refreshing dive, they join in turn the growing company of their fellows, who bob and hiss from beyond the kelp line.

If partially reassured, the bird realights upon an exposed surface of the rock, and opens a carmine mouth of inquiry. Others join him, and soon your motives are being discussed by a whining company of these wondering wights. Their only note is a cross between a hiss and a whine, and it has no great power; but a large company of these birds can produce a mild chorus, which takes its place among those primal sea sounds which haunt the sympathetic soul forever after. It blends curiously with the voices of "the dry, pied things which be in the hueless mosses under the sea," and which are set a-murmuring when the tide runs out.

These guillemots are not ungraceful while at rest, and it goes without saying that they exhibit the perfection of motion in the water; but on land they move about with an awkward shuffling gait, and in their shorter flights about the rocks they thrust out their great red feet cornerwise, and almost excite derision for their awkwardness.

They are, in the main, peaceable folk, and in the larger colonies are gregarious to such an extent that one can rarely distinguish paired birds. On the whole, however, I am inclined to consider them strictly monogamous—at least in the avian sense, which takes account of only one season. Sportive pursuit often takes place in the water, and the rapidity with which these birds can appear and disappear at the surface would be instructive to the aspirants of the old swimming hole.

A cock-fight between rival suitors is apt to be quite a spirited affair. As they face each other upon the surface of the water, the combatants hold their tails, inconspicuous at other times, bolt upright; and this, with their open mandibles disclosing a bright red mouth and throat, gives the birds a somewhat formidable appearance. The actual scrimmage, however, is likely to take place beneath the water rather than upon it; and the onlooker has no means of guessing the battle's progress till the weaker bird bursts from the water like a flying fish, and so by change of scene gains a momentary advantage of his pursuer, or owns defeat outright.

MARBLED MURRELET

Brachyramphus marmoratus

FOR THOSE WHO LONG FOR "SOMETHING DIFFERENT" we recommend a steamboat ride along, say, the Straits of Georgia, or across the eastern arm of Juan de Fuca on a blowy day in December. To be sure it is a bit chilly out, and there are spiteful dabs of rain between whiles, but the forward deck is clear, for the helpless ones are crowded in the cabin playing poker or scowling gloomily out of the windows. We may have the bow to ourselves—you and I—and what a glorious company of sights and sounds there are about us! Every blue-gray wave has a voice, and the gray-blue wind tries every tone with its deft fingers. The chorus smites upon the prow with its never-ending climaxes of spray, to which our staunch boat opposes only its patient methodical sighing. Now the wind laughs, and while it marshals its serried ranks for a fiercer charge, our drummer boy, the trusted flag-rope, beats furious tattoo. Crash! Poof! Poof! We win!

But there are those who enjoy the conflict of the storm even more than we. Above the whining of the waters and the crashing of the prow come shrill exultant cries, *Meer-meer, meer-meer.* The Murrelets are in their element, and they shriek to each other across the dancing waters like Tritons at play. Perhaps association will partly account for it, but somehow the note of the Marbled Murrelet seems of itself to suggest piping gales and rugged cliffs beset by pounding surf. It is the articulate cry of the sea in a royal mood. And not a thousand Murrelet voices are required to transport the hearer to Alaska forthwith.

Save in summer, the Murrelets appear chiefly in pairs, and it is interesting to note the harmony of action in the case of mated birds. They sit upon the water, usually abreast, from one to four feet apart, and in flight they maintain the same relation. In rising from the water they do not patter, after the fashion of the grebe, but burst out by a sudden effort. They do not, however, always succeed in getting quickly under way, for they sometimes bump along over the surface like a skipping stone, and are even quite baffled if they are called upon to clear an unusually high wave. Once a-wing, however, they vibrate the pinions with extreme rapidity and appear to move like winged bullets.

Because so agile, they are often quite venturesome, and the pursuit of fish is sometimes carried on before a wharf-load of beholders. About the docks of one of the navy-yards these birds are especially fearless.

They look like little men-of-war themselves, as they lie at anchor on the surface of the water; but when they get news from below by wireless, they are off like a flash, down, down into the cool green depths. They do not swim under water, but fly rather. At first one may see the wing-strokes, incisive, rapid; then only the quickly disappearing white of the bird's nether parts is visible; and lastly, a slowly rising line of bubbles which mark the first dozen feet or so of the diver's course. When surprised at close quarters by a steamship, the bird oftener escapes by diving than by flight, and so confident is he of his powers in this regard that he tarries to indulge the last possible moment of curiosity before going below.

Herons, Bitterns, and Ibises

PALLID GREAT BLUE HERON
Ardea herodias treganzai

As a picturesque feature of the landscape or, oftener, the water-scape, the Heron has no rival. Whether standing motionless upon the flats, with bills elevated, or depressed, according as men or fish are the objects of current moment, or whether flapping slowly across the scene, they lend just that touch of sedate life which the artistic eye requires.

The Great Blue Heron is, with us, the largest of its kind; and while not exactly graceful on the one hand, nor majestic on the other, it presents that peculiar combination of the two which we are pleased to call picturesque. While standing knee-deep in the water of some pond or stream, awaiting its customary prey of minnows or frogs, it may remain for an hour as motionless as a bronze statue; then with a movement like lightning the head is drawn back and suddenly shot downward, and a wriggling fish is transfixed on the spear-like beak. A deft toss of the head puts the fish up and transfers it to the inside, and the bird moves with quiet, measured step to another station, or else rises heavily, with slow flaps, into the air.

During the breeding season these large birds are gregarious. Their immense nests—as big as a washtub, Finley says—are by no means to be concealed, so the colony seeks protection in the depths of a tule swamp; or else resorts to the heights of forest trees difficult or impossible of access. In the absence of the old birds, the youngsters, awkward, scrawny, ill-favored little brutes that they are, spend most of their time squabbling and trying to push each other out of the nest. There is with most herons a considerable disparity of ages, and consequently of sizes, in the brood. The runt gets trampled or smothered in the early days, and one or more decaying carcasses of younger sons are a familiar enough component in the lining of a heron's nest. Now and then one of a contentious brood succeeds in toppling a brother off the platform and down the long abyss; but oftenest the pursued one escapes along the branch; or, if he falls, catches on a limb below, and scrambles back to safety, "tooth" and toe-nail. If he does fall to the ground, it is all day with him, for no matter what the state of his skin upon arrival, the parent birds never trouble to look him up.

American Bittern

Botaurus lentiginosus

"I WILL MAKE IT A POSSESSION FOR THE BITTERN and pools of water, saith the Lord" (Isaiah 14:11, A.V.). Nothing presents to the average mind a more vivid picture of desolation than a waste of swampy waters. It is "miasmatic," repulsive, and, above all, useless. And the bittern, who dwells there, has become the very symbol of desolation. Doubtless, the prophet had first descried the bird at rest, with his head drawn in, his plumage relaxed and drooping, like a rudely thatched roof, and he himself looking not unlike a deserted hut, fit emblem of the melancholy morass. But if the prophet's observation stopped there, he missed knowing one of the oddest, weirdest, most elusive, and most versatile of all the feathered kind.

The bittern has no desire to become famous. When suddenly flushed, the bird makes off with a low, frightened *quawk* on heavy, noiseless wings; but if he has a moment's warning and the ghost of a show at concealment, our bird stretches instead to an enormous height, holding the long bill vertically, and becomes rigid. Instead of a bulky fowl, he has become, to all intents and appearances, a slender reed-clump; and it requires the closest scrutiny to distinguish the bird with his streaky yellows and greens and browns, even after he has been pointed out.

The moonlight serenade which this ardent lover accords his mistress is one of the most outlandish performances in nature. Take an air-tight hogshead and immerse it suddenly in water with the bung-hole down; then allow the air to escape in great gurgles, say a caskful at a time, and you will get but a faint idea of the terrifying, earth-shaking power of the "Thunder-pump" at close range. *Umph-ta-googh, umph-ta-googh* groans this absurd wooer, and the swamp quakes with apprehension. The case is serious, for the bird accompanies the cry with a motion which suggests the miseries of the Scriptural whale, and each successive Jonah has a long way to go before reaching fresh air. Maria likes the noise and—well, love *is* like sea-sickness, at certain stages.

LEAST BITTERN
Ixobrychus exilis exilis

ONE IS TEMPTED TO APPLY THE WORD "AWKWARD" to this bird, as he is ordinarily noted in daylight. See him as he springs up suddenly from your feet in the cat-tail tangle—the flapping wings, the straightening neck, the legs clumsily dangled until the bird's balance is gained, the noisy plash with which he settles into the reeds again—all this seems awkward enough. Or if you persist in dashing after the stranger, having noted his exact whereabouts, see him as he stretches to an incredible length, and stiffens to the semblance of a reed-stalk—slender, immovable, the very counterpart of any of his sere and lifeless companions. In this position, if you avoid betraying your recognition by a too knowing gaze at the bird's eye, you may even get close enough to seize him in the hands. The bird apparently realizes what a sorry figure he cuts on wing, and flies only as a last resort. Even when he wants to make a reconnaissance, instead of taking a turn a-wing, he climbs carefully up some upright stalk, wren-fashion, and squints furtively over the tops of the reeds.

Amused criticism, however, turns to admiration when we note the marvelous dexterity with which the bird threads the lawless mazes of a cat-tail swamp. Now plashing softly through a shallow, now scrambling nimbly over opposing vegetation, he can soon quit dangerous territory if he will.

But the Least Bittern is a bird of the night. When evening falls, he goes to his accustomed hunting-ground with strong, sure flight. These birds do not often wait for the game to come to them, as is the habit of that patient fisherman, the Great Blue Heron, but they move about with lowered head and outstretched neck, industriously searching for slugs, frogs, tadpoles, beetles, and their kin. Even field mice are sometimes caught by a rapid run and a flashing stroke.

Wood Ibis

Mycteria americana

THE STORKS ARE RATHER STUPID BIRDS, perhaps because they are such gluttons. They are, however, shrewd enough in procuring food, if Audubon's account be correct. He says that a large company of them will enter a shallow pool of water and stir up the mud by dancing about, until the frenzied fish, frogs, and young alligators, venturing too near the surface, are rapidly knocked on the head in turn by the birds' powerful beaks, and there left to float until the drive is completed. Then the birds gorge themselves, and stand about the margin of the pond in sated rows while digestion wrestles with its task.

It was Audubon, too, who would account for the well-known habit which these birds have of mounting into the air and soaring about at great heights during the later hours of the morning, by calling it an aid to digestion—a sort of morning constitutional, necessary to well-fed burghers who would avoid gout. Whatever may induce these storks to play the buzzard for a time each day, they certainly present a pleasing and impressive spectacle, as, with plumage rendered striking by reason of its contrasting blacks and whites, they wheel aloft in majestic circles whose dizzy and distant mazes test the eyesight.

White-faced Glossy Ibis
Plegadis guarauna

THE FIRST VISION OF IBISES THE AUTHOR EVER HAD was during the spring migrations at Santa Barbara. A dip in the road, where the tongue of an estero crossed, was suddenly lighted up by a burst of black forms—a flock of land-locked Cormorants, I thought momentarily. But the "shags" were too graceful by half as they breasted the strong wind; and as they hovered questingly, in exquisite syncopation of flight, my recovering senses grasped the significance of wine-red reflections. White-faced Glossy Ibises! What splendid birds they are! A score of them, a very vision of the elder day; whereas all modernity is one gibbering sparrow! I stopped the motor instantly; and, reassured, the ibises settled back into the wet grass, and resumed immediately their search for food. Here, again, they seemed the very embodiments of grace, as they turned and twisted, or probed for insects in the soft mud, or reared their sinuous necks for a moment of inspection. And what marvels of color! reds and greens and purples, which resolve into black with distance. "More, anon, you beauties; I'll track you to your haunts! Just now my plates are gone; the wind is blowing a gale; and the motor is urging homeward. I will leave you to your wayside fare."

Ah, well, I have seen them since, hundreds of them—not thousands, as formerly—in migrations, characteristic haunts in the flooded sections of Los Baños. The birds breed annually somewhere within a radius of twenty miles of the town of Dos Palos; but as the flood conditions are never twice alike, the colony shifts from year to year, and I have not been so fortunate as to find it in three trials. The birds are said to build in loose colonial fashion, several hundred pairs in an area of forty acres, selecting for the purpose the least accessible mazes of the "tule" or giant *Scirpus*. The nests are merely platforms of broken-down tules, augmented, or not, with some interlacing of loose stems. The eggs, three or four in number, are of a rich dark bluish green, quite the handsomest in the entire heron order.

The chief interest of the nesting region attaches to the appearance and spectacular flight of the wide-ranging groups of foraging birds. Pairs or squads or small platoons are likely to be flushed anywhere within ten miles of the central rookery. At such times the self-conscious birds vault into the air with startled cries, not unlike the grunting of pigs, *moik*, or *oigh, oigh*. A flying company, coming upon observers in ambush, will flinch or corkscrew most picturesquely (not to say pathetically) each for himself. But left to themselves, they fall into line behind some trusted leader, and move off at a very businesslike pace. In my opinion few sights in the marshes equal the vision of a passing company of Bronze Ibises, timid mementoes of the elder magnificence.

Ducks, Geese, and Swans

MALLARD

Anas boschas

THIS, THE CONTEMPORARY ANCESTOR OF OUR DOMESTIC DUCK, enjoys a distriution almost world-wide, and has been from earliest times the best known of swimming birds. Although nowhere in America so abundant as formerly, it is still the standard with which we compare all other species, both in point of excellence and in numbers. Being somewhat less gregarious than the Teals and the sea-ducks, the Mallards are found in pairs or small parties, wherever a swampy pool or a widening of the brook affords a resting place, and one may easily recognize their fitness for domestication in the fact that they can content themselves with a little six-by-eight puddle when the whole world lies before them.

While on the water the birds spend much time "tipping" for food. Heads under water and tails pointing skyward, they search the bottom for mollusks and crustaceans, or feed upon various kinds of aquatic plants which choke sluggish streams or line the edges of ponds. When hunger is satisfied, they frequently disport themselves upon the water, diving, throwing water over their backs, and splashing about with great ado, much like boys in the old swimming hole. Nights, especially in thickly settled regions, are habitually spent feeding, either by dabbling, or in long forays to stubble-fields, and woods where acorns abound, so that much of the daytime is spent sleeping just on shore, with one leg drawn up and the head tucked comfortably under the wing.

There does not exist in Nature a more engaging sight than that of a mother duck tending and piloting her brood. It does not make much difference as to the species. Baby ducklings are irresistibly cunning, every one of them. They sit on the water like corks, or race after their mothers like toy steamboats, or stick their fluffy little heads under water in an obedient effort to do as mother does. The mother herself is the soul of anxiety. And who wouldn't be worried with a dozen babies at once, be they never so good! Minks think them cunning, too, and coyotes, and water-snakes; and whoever saw a farmer boy who would not dash into a pond pell mell at the sight of ducklings. All heedless the capture, but never a true-hearted lad who did not repent and let the peeping captives go.

CINNAMON TEAL
Querquedula cyanoptera cyanoptera

IF THE BIRD-LOVER CONFESSES a somewhat languid interest in the old standbys of duckdom, Mallard, Widgeon, Shoveller, and the rest, the species which have quacked and spattered their way through literature for generations, it is a far different matter with our champion of the West. For him we are not ashamed to confess a fresh interest and a kindling of desire. Whether our attitude be that of sportsman, bird-lover, or student, surely no more alluring spectacle could be afforded than that of a flock of these brilliant chestnut-colored ducks when they rise suddenly from a wayside pond at the break of day. It is as though fragments of the rich red earth, from which we are all made, had been startled by the impact of the sun's rays upon the water, and were fleeing toward heaven—earth, air, fire, and water, all in one burst of momentary splendor.

A favorite play on the part of these Teal at mating time is leap-frog. A bird will vault into the air and pass over another's head and down again with a great splash; whereupon the other, as likely as not, will return the compliment. This passage occurs oftenest between two males, and does not appear to have any unfriendly motive. When the fortunes of the ensuing season are being decided, the ducks become very much absorbed in their business. At such a time I once stole up through the reeds, where, upon a little "two-by-four" pond, I could survey six or eight Cinnamon Teal disporting themselves and indulging in courting antics. A male would follow about very closely after his intended, and bob his head by alternately extending and withdrawing his neck in a very lively fashion. Now and then the female would make some slight acknowledgment in the same kind. In at least one instance I witnessed a decisive moment; for, from pretended indifference in the presence of her suitor, a duck suddenly responded to his long bobs of invitation by bobs of approval, equally emphatic, and given face to face; and immediately thereafter she seconded the favored swain in his efforts to drive off discredited rivals.

SHOVELLER
Spatula clypeata

ONE GLANCE AT THE LONG, BROADLY SPATULATE BILL of the "Spoon-bill," or Shoveller, is quite sufficient to establish the bird's identity in the mind of anyone who has ever even heard one of its names. This huge bill not only gives its owner a top-heavy appearance, but gives the impression of a larger bird than the measurements warrant. The bird is rather less of a vegetarian than most of its kind. It eschews grain, and is not so partial to water-cresses and succulent browse as are Mallards and Widgeon. The roots of aquatic plants are eaten, but insects, tadpoles, snails, and small fish are a preferred diet. Much of the bird's food is secured in the shallow water or mud, which is scooped up liberally and sifted through the lamellae of the beak until only edible portions are retained.

Highly gregarious at all times, it is in the pursuit of food that the Shovellers have developed a communal habit, called by the sportsmen "milling." This operation may be carried on by a dozen or by a hundred birds *en masse*, and consists of paddling with increasing speed upon the surface of the water, presumably with *the outside foot*, until the whole mass of birds experiences a rapid circular or elliptical motion. The birds' bodies are in actual contact, but their heads are all below, greedily sifting the turbulent waters, whose hitherto hidden dainties their combined efforts have succeeded in stirring up.

Pintail
Dafila acuta tzitzihoa

WHETHER AS THE OBJECT OF ADMIRING GLANCES or covetous, whether as a flying target, a table bird, or, better still, as the subject of Brooks's brush, the lordly Pintail deserves, it seems to me, first place in the consideration of the connoisseur. The Mallard is the contemporary ancestor of the domestic duck, and as such is perhaps entitled to early notice; but the Pintail is the epitome of all that makes ducks interesting. He is as handsome as any (save the Wood Duck, who is a professional beauty), and to the splendor of a tasteful color-pattern he adds both a sinuous gracefulness of movement and a bearing of conscious nobility which no other duck exhibits. Mark him sitting high on the water, reflecting the morning sun from his snowy breast, swaying the mobile neck in sagacious scrutiny, and raising the slender, tapering tail aloft, like an ensign, and you know you are dealing with an avian equal, a bird of quality and resource.

Pintails are wary birds, and when mingling on the water with other species are usually the first to give the alarm. Being of a sociable nature, and also fastidious as to personal appearance, they spend a good deal of time on shore preening their feathers and gabbling amiably, or else napping. Here, by the exercise of proper precautions, they may be stalked; and owing to their habit of bunching closely when taking to wing, a second barrel may be even more destructive than the first. As single winged targets, they are among the most difficult, as their flight is extremely swift, perhaps the most rapid of any of the ducks. Or so the sportsmen tell me.

But who wants to shoot, anyhow? Come with me, and we will bag five hundred ducks of a dozen species with our double-barreled binoculars. If you must have trophies, remember that the best photographs of wild ducks have never been taken yet; nor (with humble apologies to the Major) the best pictures painted. The scene is Laguna Blanca (at its best, while thoroughgoing protection was in force); the date—shall we call it December 4, 1912? Several hundred Pintails occupy the preening beach. Some are dozing; others are making their toilets with most becoming diligence; while others still are parading up and down, like distinguished visitors at a pleasure pier. Other hundreds have hauled out upon the broken-down tules, at a point where the water is deepest and the landward maze most impenetrable. A shout, a clapping of the hands, and all is attention. A thousand birds slip silently into the water and push out watchfully from shore, a more than Spanish Armada for splendor, ready at an instant to take the air. It were a pity to frighten them, but who does not love the harmless bedlam of bird-wings, and especially the down-rush of stiff-set duck-wings, intent on shelter—when confidence has been restored!

Wood Duck

Aix sponsa

BEYOND CONTROVERSY, the Wood Duck of America is one of the most exquisitely beautiful of living creatures. Among the ducks themselves only one species, the Mandarin (*Aix galericulata*), of China, approaches it in elegance; and this is not so strange, since the Mandarin is a kinsman, or, in scientific parlance, a "congener," of our bird. Linnaeus called the Wood Duck "the bride" (Latin, *sponsa*, bride); but of course it is the bride*groom* who wears the jewels, and inherits the products of Oriental looms and dye-stuffs, for *males must strut and females must work* is the rule among ducks as among most other groups of birds. Literally *all* the colors of the rainbow belong to this bird in his nuptial plumage—with black and white thrown in for good measure. The Wood Duck is our one vision of tropical splendor, a thing too beautiful and, as the event has proved, too confiding to entrust to our vandal generation.

The Wood Duck is notable not alone for the gaudiness of its attire. In action it is graceful and agile and pleasing. Birds of this species frequent, or used to frequent, secluded swamps, lagoons, and shaded waterways. They are swift and graceful fliers, and they are able to traverse the mazes of the forest with the ease of pigeons. They perch readily upon the branches of trees, and even walk along them without hesitancy. To the aquatic fare offered by the surface and depths of woodland pools is added the flying insects of the forest home, and the tender shoots and leaves of plants in spring. Acorns are a favorite food in fall, and upon these the birds sometimes stuff themselves to repletion. They evince an interest in fallen rice also; and if the stock could be nursed back to normality, they would doubtless do their part in protecting the rice grower against the "volunteer" crop which he so much dreads.

Canvasback

Marila valisineria

Viewed under a bright sun, as on a refuge pond, a resting company of care-free Canvasbacks is an inspiring sight. Both by reason of his size and his judicial calm, the Canvasback looks more substantial and more important than his lesser kinsfolk. That high-arched bill, melting in to a sloping forehead—it looks somehow more suitable, more efficient, than the sudden angle of Cousin Redhead. The Canvasback is an opulent burgher. His head and neck are covered with conventional black and vandyke brown, and for the rest he is clad in flowing magisterial robes of canvas, save as a black velvet waistcoat points a contrast, and restrains his rotundity. Or, with head under wing, he looks like a man-of-war lying at anchor. No need to keep a lookout. This is the international fleet at rest.

When the siesta is over (and "Cans" have to sleep o'daytimes in these troubled years), the flock deploys for food. Canvasbacks are deep divers. When in search of snails or clams, they must achieve depths of twenty or twenty-five feet. More commonly, their search is directed toward aquatic plants, and these they pluck up by the roots, bringing their plunder to the surface for consumption in the case of major hauls. As likely as not, the saucy Widgeon presents himself before the astonished burgher upon his emergence, and snatches away a portion or all of his innocent swag. Well, never mind; there is plenty more at the bottom; and it is quieter down there anyway.

AMERICAN GOLDEN-EYE
Glaucionetta clangula americana

OF ALL WING-MUSIC, from the droning of the Rufous Hummer to the startling whirr of the Ruffed Grouse, I know of none so thrilling sweet as the whistling wing-note of the Golden-eye. A pair of the birds have been frightened from the water, and as they rise in rapid circles to gain a view of some distant goal, they sow the air with vibrant whistling sounds. Owing to a difference in wing-beats between male and female, the brief moment when the wings strike in unison with the effect of a single bird is followed by an ever-changing syncopation, which challenges the waiting ear to tell if it does not hear a dozen birds instead of only two. Again in the dim twilight of early morning, while the birds are moving from a remote and secure lodging place to feed in some favorite stretch of wild water, one guesses at their early industry from the sound of multitudinous wings above, contending with the cold ether.

Golden-eyes associate in small flocks, usually of not more than eight or ten individuals; and because of the prominence of their snowy plumage they find themselves obliged to maintain a wary lookout wherever found. The birds, the males at least, ride high upon the water, yet they dive with extraordinary ease and wrest most of their living from the depths. On salt water the birds venture up on shore as often as they dare, and it is to be feared that they are not fastidious in the matter of their food. Mussels, crabs, and marine worms are commonly eaten, and that bugaboo of northern beaches, the decayed salmon, is also greedily devoured, so that the birds are usually unfit for culinary consideration.

When the youngsters are hatched they are either allowed to spill out upon the ground, or into the water, if the nest is so fortunately placed; or else they are transported upon the back of the mother bird, clutching tightly at the ruffled feathers of the neck with their tiny bills.

The imagination cannot but follow the adventures of children so romantically cradled and so magically whisked about by fairy flying carpets (whatever the precise method of attachment thereto). If we had to be a duck, we would elect to have golden eyes and to chase mischievous water bugs through limpid icy pools, while nodding little fir trees looked on and applauded. I am sure, too, that *clangula*'s bright-eyed offspring do enjoy their youthful hours. A group of four which we sighted on a lake of northern Washington were no sooner made out than they paddled over in our direction, as curious as we were. When their curiosity was satisfied, the jolly quartette resumed their interrupted sport, which seemed to consist of a spirited game of tag.

Harlequin Duck
Histrionicus histrionicus

THE SCIENTISTS DERIVE GREAT SATISFACTION from their attempts to tell us why certain things are so and so, and we nod gravely from time to time in pretended comprehension; but there are matters which are better left to folk-lore. We can understand in a measure how the partridge came to look like dead leaves, and the snipe like dead grass, but who must say in terms of cold logic how the Harlequin acquired his fantastic livery? No; it must have been in this wise. The first Harlequin, before he was a Harlequin, that is, was of a nearly uniform slate color, with some relief of dull cinnamon. But, clad in this somber garb, folks mistook him for a Coot, which were a misfortune indeed for such a dainty creature. Driven to desperation he sought out Mother Nature and begged to be retouched. This the good dame, being in a whimsical mood, consented to do. She seized a brush from the nearest pot of paint, which happened to be white, and gave her discontented subject, between fits of laughter, sundry daubs and slashes with it, ten to a side, sending him forth at the last a very—Harlequin.

Surf Scoter
Melanitta perspicillata

THE PROW OF ANY ONE OF A THOUSAND coasting steamers, ferries, or river boats affords an ideal opportunity for the study of winter bird-life in Pacific waters. Wanton shooting from such stations has been practically discontinued, so that knowing birds postpone flight till the last moment at the approach of a steamboat. No birds are more frequently encountered than the Scoters, Surf and White-winged; and it is a source of never-ending enjoyment to observe their behavior on such occasions.

At first it is presumed that the boat will pass at a considerable distance. In default of this issue the birds decide to outswim it, and bend low to their task. But the monster approaches. The coots stop rowing and wag their heads inquiringly from side to side. It certainly is coming. Whatever shall we do? Finally, one bird pulls himself together and begins to pound the water with his wings and feet. The rest follow suit with much grumbling and wheezing, and soon they are really off, pattering and scooting over the water. But Flagstaff's wind gives out (and he is the handsomest of the company). He is too fat to fly, and he gives up after a few strokes, falling back panting into the water. There is always one resort left an honest sea-fowl. You quench your curiosity in his gaudy head-gear, bending low over the railing, and as the steamer is almost upon him, the bird dives, swiftly, surely, confidently, quite out of harm's way, and does not reappear short of a hundred yards.

The head of the male Surf Scoter presents one of the most bizarre appearances in nature. It has only the Tufted Puffin for a rival, and I think that "the odds are even" here. Try to conjure before your mind's eye the colorings of the Scoter's bill alone: black, white, pink, yellow, cadmium, orange, and carmine, and those displayed not only in transitions but in the most abrupt contrasts. Add a swelling which involves not only the base of the bill but the whole anterior portion of the head; then a white eye; then two patches of dazzling white on black ground for the rest, and you have this Beau Brummel of the seas.

But the ladies like him; they have to, for they are such homely bodies themselves that the perversity of attraction must be mutual. I have seen a Surf Scoter courtship in mid-April. Five males are devoting themselves to one female. They chase each other about viciously, but no harm seems to come of their threats; and they crowd around the female as though to force a decision. She, in turn, chases them off with lowered head and outstretched neck and great show of displeasure. Now and then one flees in pretended fright and with great commotion, only to settle down at a dozen yards and come sidling back. If she will deign a moment's attention, the flattered gallant dips his head and scoots lightly under the surface of the water, showering himself repeatedly with his fluttering wing.

CANADA GOOSE
Branta canadensis canadensis

HONK, HONK—HONK, HONK! What a stirring sound is that which summons us from whatever task indoors, and hurries us out hatless, breathless, into the crisp March air to behold a company of wild geese passing forward into the frosty North! *Honk, honk!* We think madly of our gun upstairs, for the geese are provokingly near, and we hear the thrilling swish of the low-sweeping wings; but we take it out in great boasts to our similarly hatless neighbor, of what we could have done if the gun had been put together and we had known that those foolish geese were coming right over town. And when the great birds become a row of trailing points on the northern sky, a fever of strange unrest burns within our veins, and we wonder through what ancestral folly our wings were clipped, and our race condemned to unceasing barnyard toil.

The Canada Goose has only two cardinal points on his compass, north and south; and unlike most migrants, he does not go by the map, nor follow favorite paths through the air, but flies straight over hill and dale, city and hamlet alike, until the goal is reached, or until the weather discourages further movement for a time. The geese move usually at a considerable height, forming open V-shaped figures, with the oldest or strongest gander in the lead at the apex; or else in single oblique lines. Each bird demands as clear a field as possible, and this is best secured by an arrangement which allows each goose to look over the wing of the one next preceding, right or left, according to the branch of the V which it occupies. The line of march shifts and changes under the eye, as the hindmost birds become dissatisfied with their positions, and change sides, or as tired leaders give place to fresher birds; and the changes are accomplished not without much lordly discussion in high-pitched *honks*.

Like most geese, this species feeds principally upon grass and tender herbage, berries, sedge-roots, and aquatic plants. Their suspicion of all mankind is deeply planted and freshly watered, but the goose psychology works under several limitations. A lone goose for instance, having none to counsel him, appears at times to be quite incapable of making a decision, and allows the fatal approach of the hunter. The situation is further compromised if the lone bird happens to alight among decoys. "It's plumb scandalous," reasons the bird, "the man is coming and these birds stand here like clods. But they ought to know; they were here first." And the real bird awaits his doom.

The sitting goose remains at her post for four weeks, and she is attended by the gander who maintains a constant vigil at her side and accompanies her during the foraging trips. The goslings, when hatched, are covered with down of a bright grass-green hue, mottled with a shade of olive. They swim from the shell; and by the second or third day they have attained such robustness that their capture by hand from a boat is a very difficult matter. Hiding is the long suit of the mother goose when in charge of a tender brood; and if surprised at such times in open water, she manages to "scotch" down and hug her feathers close until she does not appear above one-third her normal size. If the ruse is discovered she flees reluctantly and summons her mate, who joins his anxious cries with hers, *Honka-honka-honka!*

Whistling Swan

Olor columbianus

THE CASE OF THE WILD SWAN is one of the saddest in American annals. Majestic as well as graceful, of noble proportions as well as harmless conduct, world-wide symbol of purity and charm, the stately beauty of the swan was altogether such as to excite admiration and to deserve chivalrous treatment. But what do we see instead? Extravagant praises of the quality of swan's flesh! instructions for hanging or garnishing or flavoring with herbs; or worse than that, records of slaughter—slaughter gigantic, wanton, insatiable, and now alas! irremediable.

During migrations the swans move in small flocks, forming a "flying wedge," or V-shaped figure, with some trusted patriarch in the lead. Their flight is exceedingly swift, being estimated by competent observers at one hundred miles per hour—probably twice that of the geese. For all they are so powerful on the wing, they rise from the water rather reluctantly, and prefer, if there is room enough, to distance pursuit by swimming. Because the neck of the swan is so long and hung at the water-line, the bird can explore the bottom freely in shallow waters in its search for roots and mollusks, without making any ungainly motions with the body. Indeed, there is a peculiar disconnectedness between the operations of the swan proper and its far-reaching head— as though here were a white boat sent down to grapple for hidden treasure. Ashore, its gait is a rather ungainly waddle, the foot being folded and lifted "unco high" at every step.

The Whistling Swan is a noisy bird at best. A flock of them exhibit great individual variations of notes, and they can create a chorus which is mildly worse than that of a political jollification meeting. The bass horns, of tin rather than brass, are blown by the old fellows, while the varied notes which seem to come from clarionets are really due to cygnets. The birds set up a great outcry when they have done or are about to do anything important, as when preparing for the flight northward, or when welcoming a company of their fellows to the feeding grounds.

No fitter emblem of purity and grace will ever be found than this matchless daughter of the wilderness, the American Swan. If we are impelled to admire the stately beauty of the domestic bird, as it moves about upon some narrow duck pond of our own contriving, how much more shall we yield tribute of admiration to this native princess, spotless and untamed! Whether seen as a garniture of some inland mere, or descried aloft as a bank of winged snow, no vision of Nature will ever thrill us with a deeper romance than does the wild swan.

Falcons, Hawks, Eagles, Condors, and Vultures

PRAIRIE FALCON

Falco mexicanus

THE PROBLEM OF EVIL HAS ALWAYS BOTHERED the theologian, and
he is bound to wrestle with it, because inconsistency is intolerable in
religious thinking. But the bird-lover cannot be consistent. Within
his little province he cannot "love good and hate evil," for to do so
were to lose that *joy in variety* which is his endless delight. Nature herself
is inconsistent—fearfully so. Indeed, it is she who has set theology's
problem. And if there be a "higher unity" or "religious synthesis" (and
I believe there is) we as nature students have naught to do with it. If we
are to find satisfaction in things as they are, if we are to enjoy nature,
external nature, we must surrender ourselves to admiration of beak
and talon no less than of wing and song.

All of which is artful preface to a declaration of love for that arch
scamp and winged terror, the Prairie Falcon *(Falco mexicanus)*. Ruthless
he is, and cruel as death; but ah, isn't he superb! To recall his image is
to obtain release from imprisoning walls, glad exit from formal gardens
and the chirping of sparrows. To recall his scream is to set foot on the
instant upon the bastion of some fortress of the wilderness. Away with
your orange-bowered bungalows! Give me a sunburned battlement in

the hills of San Luis Obispo County. A plague on your dickey birds! Let me dare the displeasure of the noble falcon as he falls like a bolt from the avenging blue and shrieks out his awful rage. Curse for curse and blow for blow, you jolly old pirate! Hide your treasures in the remotest cranny of the uttermost wilderness, if you will, and I shall find them; and if I find them, they are mine; and if I reach them, you may wreak your vengeance on whom you will. I will not even reproach you for the rape of pullets nor the carnage of quails. Go to it, old sport! Fill the air with shrieks and call heaven to witness what a rogue you are! Aye, but you're a gay fowl, and I'm o'er fond of you!

All the traditions of chivalry, save gentleness, and all the associations of romance gather about this bird. In speed, in grace, in prowess, and in skill, he is the peer of any; and in the choice of nesting sites he is excelled by none. Picture, if you please, a granite cleft in the foothills. The road at the bottom winds deviously over intersecting talus beds, "rock slides," while the sun-kissed battlements of riven rock tower on either hand to the height of a thousand feet; and they clear their own debris in sheer walls of at least half that height. About the brink of the precipice a dozen Prairie Falcons are at play. It is courting time and the birds are showing off. The females are the larger birds, but it is their turn to sit in the boxes while the aspirants perform. The doughty males are not really contending—only renewing their vows as they come hurtling out of the heavens, screaming like all possessed and cutting parabolas whose acuteness is a marvel of the unexpected. The female screaks in wild approval, or takes a turn herself because she cannot contain her fierce emotions. The rock walls resound with boisterous music, and the observer feels as though he were witnessing the play of elemental forces—riotous, exultant, unrestrained, the very passion of freedom and conquest.

The falcon is king of birds and he knows it. Ferocity gleams in his eye and menace quivers in his talons. Mastery is his element; his very wings flash confidence; and caution is to him a thing unknown. The much-vaunted eagle is a craven beside him, and nothing affords the smaller bird greater delight than to hector his lethargic kinsman.

The flight of the Prairie Falcon is always easy and graceful, being oftenest accomplished by a succession of short wing-beats alternating with a sail. The bird mounts rapidly, and if intent on distant hunting grounds, is, because of its light coloration, soon lost to eye. It is hardly possible to exaggerate the swiftness of the falcon's flight through comparison with that of any other bird. I should say that the White-throated Swift alone excels it.

The bird makes little fuss over the capture of small game. It simply materializes out of the empty blue and picks up a gopher or a blackbird as quietly as you would pluck a flower. The approach has doubtless been nicely calculated. The thunderbolt, launched from the height of half a mile, has been checked every few hundred feet by a slight opening of the wings, that the falcon might gauge the caliber and intent of the victim; and the final plunge has, therefore, the speed and accuracy of fate. In case of larger game the quarry is knocked headlong by a crashing blow, after which the assailant turns to try conclusions as to weight. But the falcon prefers always to snatch, and when small game is abundant, the bird is less likely to disturb rabbits or poultry.

The two handsomest sets of eggs in the extensive M.C.O. series were obtained on successive days in the Shandon country, and the finding of both resulted from a combination of professional suspiciousness, *durch-heit*, and happy accident, which taken together constitute "collectors' luck." A page from the note-book gives the details as follows:

"In another canyon a male Prairie Falcon keel-hauled a passing eagle, and I marked his approximate range of interest upon his return in lordly mood. There were many possibilities, but I tried first a likely-looking Raven's nest a hundred yards away. The effect was electrical. Out shot a female Prairie Falcon as though touched by the bullet; and when she had caught her breath, she filled the air with fierce aspersions, perhaps pardonable under the circumstances.

"The ascent was tedious and the sun torrid; but the descent over a conglomerate escarpment some ninety feet in height was rewarded by a set, ¼, of the darkest eggs of this species which I have ever seen—so dark, indeed, that I first exclaimed 'Duck Hawk!' incredulously. The amiable birds did not omit to offer comments anent my skill as a rope artist; and the female made some beautiful swoops at my head—always a solace under such circumstances. Ah, me! What a rascal is the oologist who enjoys such objurgations! But I'll own to it. And as the indignant lady stood upright in her empty cell, I turned and blew her a kiss and promised to come back another year."

Peregrine Falcon
Falco peregrinus anatum

THE NAME DUCK HAWK IS REALLY A TRIBUTE to the skill and prowess of this highly endowed bird; but it is belittling, nevertheless, to institute a comparison, however remote, between the noble Peregrine and the multitudinous "Hen Hawk" of the vulgar conception. This is the PEREGRINE FALCON, if you please, the American bird being no different, save for a somewhat whiter breast (which only enhances his beauty) from the "falcon gentil" of song and story, the most courageous, the most spirited of all birds of prey. Like the Prairie Falcon, it secures an intended victim either by striking it from above and bearing it down to earth by its acquired momentum, or else by snatching it from the ground with incredible swiftness. Many stories are told of its seizing and making off with wounded game from under the very nose of the hunter; and it is especially fearless in its pursuit of wild ducks, which it is said to follow systematically for days at a time during the migrations.

It is undeniable that chickens occasionally fall victims to this dark corsair, but Bendire is of opinion that the falcon rather disdains such stupid quarry, and is sure that they sometimes engage in the pursuit of poultry from sheer mischief without intention of harm. Certainly the Peregrine need not deny himself any luxury which his appetite craves, and young meteors would be quite in his line if they were only a little more juicy.

For a nesting sight the Peregrine Falcon chooses an inaccessible cranny in some commanding cliff. In default of shelter, an exposed ledge midway of some sheer precipice will do as well. The southern Coast Ranges offer a considerable variety of rounded pickets of lens-shaped cavities, left either by the defection of a nodule, or else by the evanescence of some frail substance once resident in the sandstone. These chambers are naturally lined with clean dry sand, and they afford ideal homes for falcon or condor. The birds exhibit a deep attachment for a given locality, and although they may shift from niche to niche, they will not desert their chosen cliff for anything short of gunfire.

American Kestrel
Cerchneis sparverius sparverius

THIS HANDSOME LITTLE FALCON is unquestionably the best known, as it is the most abundant, bird of prey in the West. While it shows a preference for open situations, its breeding range extends from the Colorado Desert, at points below the level of the sea, to the forests of Humboldt and Del Norte counties, and to the limit of trees in the Sierras. It is equally at home in the sahuaro patches bordering upon the Colorado River, the oak groves of San Luis Obispo, the rocky defiles of San Diego County, or the pines of Modoc. Commanding points of rock are sure to be worn smooth by the clasp of many sharp-spurred claws, and treetops serve for sentry boxes whenever the birds pass that way. Telegraph poles are regarded as a special convenience, since they traverse the treeless stretches which afford no other watch-tower; but fence-posts will suffice in default of more elevated stations. From such points of vantage as these the birds attentively watch the happenings on the ground, and dive down whenever they consider that their presence is needed by mouse or grasshopper.

Always graceful, the Sparrow Hawk is seen to best advantage during the courting season, when the male reaffirms his fondness for his life-long mate by circling about her as she sits upon the treetop; or he measures the height of his devotion by ascending to the clouds before her, and dashing himself at her feet again with shrill cries of *Killy, killy, killy*. To hear the snarling clamor of the birds, one would think that they were not getting on nicely; but this is a mistake, for the high-pitched conversation is really very amiable in character, and neither bird would think of parting from its consort, for however brief a space of time, without a screamed farewell of unquestionable tenderness.

Sparrow Hawks nest in holes in trees when these are convenient, using either natural cavities or the deserted tenements of Flickers and other woodpeckers. The higher these rented quarters, the better the birds are satisfied, but holes not over four feet from the ground are of record. In default of such accomodations, old Magpies' nests or even open-topped Crows' nests have been utilized; but a more comon expedient is to resort to the romantic crannies and hidey holes of the rocky cliffs. In such situations this diminutive falcon appears to recall his noble ancestry; and I have fancied that he was here a shade more valiant in defense of his young. Certainly the Red-tail does not care for that particular stretch of cliff; and the Prairie Falcon seems to regard the lesser spitfire with quaint indulgence, or else to treat him with that magnanimous unconcern which a Newfoundland shows to a terrier.

Osprey

Pandion haliaetus carolinensis

WHETHER OR NOT FISH IS PROPER BRAIN FOOD depends, as someone has wittily remarked, "more upon the brain than it does upon the fish." An exclusive diet of fish has not made the Fish Hawks either brainy or valiant. We need not be troubled on the latter score, though, for in a family where prowess and tyranny are almost synonymous, it is a comfort to find birds who mind their own business and exhibit a proper humility.

The Osprey preys exclusively upon fish, and covers long stretches of water in its tireless search. It flies along at a height of fifty or a hundred feet above the water, and when its finny prey is sighted, pauses for a moment on hovering wings, then drops with a resounding splash, often quite disappearing beneath the water, but rising again quickly with a fish firmly secured in its talons. The bird upon rising immediately adjusts the catch, placing it head foremost, so that it will offer the least resistance to the air in flight. Not infrequently the hawk secures a fish which it is barely able to handle, and occasionally it strikes one so large that it is drawn under and drowned before it can disengage its claws.

Clear water is essential to the Osprey's success, for he must needs see and strike from afar. The bird has little use, therefore, for the silt-stained waters of the lowlands, and it avoids the storm-tossed waters of our western coast. The more placid seas which surround our southern islands, San Clemente, Catalina, and the rest, afford a congenial summer home; and a few linger here through the winter. In the interior, the Osprey is likely to show up almost anywhere during the spring migrations, especially along the north-and-south-trending valleys, such as the Sacramento, Owens River, and the Colorado.

A typical Osprey's nest is a huge aggregation of sticks, bark, and trash; and is placed either on the top of a broken pine or fir stub or else lodged on some convenient cliff or isolated spur of rock. If the rock or tree is surrounded by water, so much the better, for it assures immunity from predatory mammals, including, to some degree, their worst enemy, man. Persecution, however, sometimes drives the birds to the deep woods, miles from their fishing grounds. If the female is on, the male, tired of fishing, is likely to be standing at her side. Both birds will rise upon our approach, and will poise in midair above our heads, suspicious of oological intent, and uttering, therefore, feeble screams, or "whistles," of protest, *ki-ik, ki-ik, ki-ik.*

The home life of the Osprey is ideal, and the nesting Osprey deserves protection, if for no better reason, because of the conspicuous devotion of the male bird to his mate and young, and because of the touching obedience of the latter.

MARSH HAWK

Circus cyaneus hudsonius

HUMILITY IS THE LEADING CHARACTERISTIC of this "ignoble" bird of prey, whether we regard its chosen paths, its spirit, or the nature of its quarry. Preeminently a bird of the meadows and marshes, it usually avoids the woods entirely, and is to be seen coursing over the grass and weed tops with an easy gliding flight. Since it flies at such a low elevation as neither to see nor be seen, over the limits of an entire field, it oftenest moves in a huge zigzag course, quartering its territory like a hunting dog. Now and then the bird pauses and hovers to make a more careful examination of a suspect, or drops suddenly into the grass, seizing a mole or cricket and retiring to a convenient spot—a fence-post or a grassy knoll—to devour its catch.

The food of the Marsh Hawk consists almost entirely of meadow mice, young rabbits, ground squirrels, garter-snakes, frogs, lizards, grasshoppers, and the like. In hunting for ground squirrels the bird flies higher and secures its prey by a headlong dash, pinning the victim to the ground and making sure of the kill before rising. So great is its fondness for mice that one may, with sufficient cover for concealment, succeed in calling the hawk very close by imitating the squeak of a mouse in distress.

As the breeding season approaches, the male Harrier, feeling the impulse of the ennobling passion, mounts aloft and performs some astonishing aerial evolutions for the delectation of his mate. He soars about at a great height, screaming like a falcon; or he suddenly lets go and comes tumbling out of space head over heels, only to pull up at a safe distance from the ground and listen to the admiring shrieks of his spouse. "At other times," says Mr. Ernest E. Thompson, "he flies across the marsh in a course which would outline a gigantic saw, each of the descending parts done in a somersault, and accompanied by the screeching notes which form the only love song within the range of his limited vocal powers." This operation is not necessary in order to win his mate, for he is supposed to have won her "for keeps"; but, after all, it is well enough to remind her now and then that he is a very good fellow—for she is a size larger than he and a little exacting in matters of courtesy.

Sharp-shinned Hawk
Accipiter velox

Millenniums of agonized terror voice themselves afresh in the pitiful cries which break out among the lesser fowl, especially the Linnets and the Bush-tits, whenever the Sharp-shin is astir. Many birds dive instantly for cover, but members of these two species, whose sole dependence seems to be in numbers, are thrown into a helpless panic. A wave of vocal despair sweeps the woodland, and each individual is seen to be fluttering abjectly while it utters those chittering distress notes. Not the devil himself, appearing suddenly in a congregation of worshippers, could occasion such consternation as comes to the little feathered folk cringing before the expected blow. The blow must fall and someone must die. Aie! Aie! But when the grim destroyer has made selection, or passed on, how swift the recovery! The sun is still shining, buds are sweet, and grubs are juicy. What, ho! birdlings! "On with the dance. Let joy be unconfined!"

The hawks proper, of which this bird is a typical representative, may lack the spectacular wing feats and noble bearing of the falcons, but they are still very bold and rapacious birds. Indeed, it would be hard to picture a more alert and blood-thirsty creature than this sharp-taloned little hawk as it scours the brush patches or open fields in search of feathered prey. The flight of the Sharp-shin is at times as swift as an arrow and as direct, but it is skilled in doubling and twisting; and no bird, save a swift or a swallow, can escape it in the open. Coming upon a flock of blackbirds, the hawk makes instant choice of a victim, and pounces like a flash upon it, either snatching it in midair, or bearing it to the ground and transfixing it with claws which pierce the vitals and cause instant death. If unsuccessful in its open attack, the hawk will either pursue through the mazes of brush or weed, or else retire quickly to thick foliage, there to await with the patience of a statue the first stirrings of the frightened quarry. The prey, when caught, is held at "arm's length" until quite dead, and then either eaten on the spot or else carried up to some elevated perch.

Both birds assist in the duties of incubation, and they are unusually brave in the matter of sticking to the nest under fire. No amount of rapping on the base of the tree will flush the sitting bird, and it will not often leave until the nest is almost reached. When disturbed both birds will make a high-spirited defense; and the female, who is, of course, the larger, will dart at the climber so boldly as occasionally to brush him with her wings. A wrathful *yip, yip, yip, yip, yip* is likely to accompany this attack; and the notes serve again to remind one of the bird's affinity to the Cooper's Hawk.

Mexican Cooper's Hawk

Accipiter cooperi mexicanus

Next after the American Kestrel (*Cerchneis sparverius sparverius*), the Cooper's Hawk is the most abundant and the best distributed hawk in California. This does not necessarily imply that the bird is most in evidence, for it is wary and furtive to a degree, insomuch that it is able to maintain itself almost unnoticed in some sections where gunfire is unusually vigilant. Where not persecuted, however, it is possessed of a lively curiosity, and will appear unexpectedly at one's elbow, as though desiring to profit by any woodland commotion likely to set the little birds astir. It is thus, no doubt, that it has learned to dance attendance upon deer or cougar thrusting through the brush.

One never gets a clearer insight into the possibilities of cruel rapacity than when a Cooper's Hawk comes dashing up into a thicket where you have been ogling sparrows, and baffled of his victim, stands for a moment panting in his rage, and flashing malevolence from a blood-red eye. It is as though an emissary of the nether world had broken from cover; and one feels all the virtue of a just cause in putting him to death.

So quick, as well as stealthy, is the bird in action that in nine cases out of ten it is the Cooper's Hawk who gets the bird, and the unwary Buteo who gets the shot. His lurking presence contributes more than any other factor to the deadly hawk-fear which occupies the background of the bird psychology. When he has recently shown himself, the bird world gets panicky like a spirited horse. After that, every flying shape is a hawk and the signal for a scramble to shelter. I shall never forget how a company of ducks, chiefly Cinnamon Teals, on Laguna Blanca, were thrown into the wildest confusion by the sudden arrival of a Great Blue Heron. "My! What a fright you gave me," gabbled a dozen ducks, as they checked their mad effort and settled back to puddling. A moment later the Cooper's Hawk did appear, and a watchful Killdeer, who saw him first, set up a sharp *tee dee dee*, which put the ducks to rout and nearly upset the heron. The ducks, forty of them, now dashed into the nearest clump of tules, and the heron, seeing that the fishing was spoiled anyhow, took himself off grumbling.

WESTERN GOSHAWK
Astur gentilis striatulus

A MILD EXPERIENCE OF THE FEELINGS of a chicken befell my partner while we were camped near a trail in the northern Cascades. It was late in June and the ornithologist was not aware that a certain stretch of woods which the trail cleft belonged to a highly virtuous pair of Goshawks, until Whoof! Buff! the blue terror struck a blow from behind and sent the bird-man sprawling. He had, moreover, quick need to defend himself with sticks and stones, for the bird was back again in a trice, and a tough sombrero alone saved him from severe scalp wounds. Of course there was a nest hard by, and we found it, some sixty feet up, in a dense stand of fir trees.

I accepted the photographic challenge which the discovery afforded, but first improvised a coat of mail, wherein a stuffed knapsack did duty for a helmet, and a wrapping of dunnage bags was designed to protect the shoulders. Like Don Quixote, I set out to meet my foe, but the "gentil" bird had respect for knighthood even of this decadent type, and forbore to offer further indignities. As she left the lists she indulged a stentorian cackle, *ak, ak, ak, ak*, a note which reminded one again of the Cooper's Hawk, save that it had a deal more of menace in it.

The Western Goshawk is excelled by none in display of cunning or prowess. At times, indeed, the thirst for blood appears to dull its discretion, and it will return to seize a fowl even after it has been shot at; but oftener it marks the gunner from a distance and awaits the unguarded moment at the poultry-yard. After sighting game, this hawk does not soar and hover, after the manner of the Prairie Falcon; rather it approaches in a horizontal direction at a low elevation and under partial cover of vegetation, then darts down suddenly or makes a quick side turn, seizing its victim deftly, and off again to a distant station. Having once got the lie of the land, a Goshawk will make requisition on a poultry-yard two or three times a day, and may elude capture altogether, be the owner never so incensed over his losses.

Western Red-tailed Hawk

Buteo borealis calurus

THE ALABAMA HILLS, IN INYO COUNTY, are reputed to be the oldest geological formation in America. By this I suppose it is meant that this modest escarpment of granite represents the core of a continental ridge older than the towering Sierras, which now dwarf them into insignificance. The superficial details might be as recent as those of any other granitic exposure; yet to the eye it is not so. It is rather as though the authentic eld had been preserved intact. We came upon it after sunset, my son and I, and the glory of it smote us like a vision of Neptune with his bearded hosts. Surely we had stumbled upon a bit of the elder world, reserved by sorcery from the accustomed gaze of man. With bated breath we gazed, until we plucked at our flesh to see if we, too, were turned to stone. And as we gazed, a Redtail, lifting silently from an unseen ledge, winged across the chasm with such confident modernity that the spell broke in laughter.

A "Burke's Peerage" of the birds might not mention the Buteos under the head of royalty—*Falco* and *Aquila* are the autocrats *par excellence*—but Redtail's patent of nobility is very ancient, and is based upon the same claims as those which human lords have set up: viz., a predatory ancestry, unbroken possession of certain broad acres for many centuries, and a frowning castle upon some sightly hill. In this last respect the bird is not surpassed, in the Pacific states at least, by that arrogant old Hapsburg, the Prairie Falcon himself.

As to the broad acres, chiefly game preserves (to carry out the whimsy), the royal claim comes first (because, forsooth, the falcon is the swifter bird); and there is always a horde of retainers—Sparrow Hawks, Burrowing Owls, Magpies, and Ravens—to consider, before the overlord may count his yearly rental of ground squirrels, rabbits, mice, snakes, lizards, and the lesser fry. Moreover, in these evil days, the pirate Danes have swept down on the Redtail's coasts, have torn his acres with the plow and have burnt his gopher-fields with fire. Worst of all, these ruthless invaders, having no use themselves for sage-rats, yet deny them to their rightful owner, the Redtail; and they pursue him fiercely with engines of destruction when he ventures to sample an imported Danish fowl. Verily, these be troublous times for the aristocracy. Alackaday!

Once a male Prairie Falcon, whose eyrie we found later, took it into his head to persecute a Redtail. He circled about rapidly and hurled himself again and again at the hawk, but each time, at the expected moment of contact, the Buzzard [Hawk] turned deftly face up, presenting his talons to the persecutor; and each time, of course, the Falcon swerved short to avoid the parry. Both the birds were very much in earnest, to judge from the harsh cries which escaped them at the moment of "present talons"; but it was evidently an old game and an idle one, too, for no matter at what range or from what angle the Falcon struck, the Redtail was always ready, with a quick half-somersault, to receive him. Conducted thus in the open in a fierce glare of sunlight, it was surely a battle for the gods to witness—even though the issue was only a draw.

GOLDEN EAGLE

Aquila chrysaetos

BECAUSE OF THE RACIAL WEAKNESS FOR SYMBOLS and striking generalizations, we have been taught that the Golden Eagle is the embodiment of all regal qualities, including courage, magnanimity, and valor in defense of offspring. There is some foundation for all this. In his mountain home the majestic flight of the eagle truly bears the grandeur of the scene. Cradled on a beetling cliff and schooled in the clouds, it is little wonder that the eagle should have become for us the symbol of both prowess and aspiration. Even in captivity there is something awful about his piercing eye, and the unrest of the royal captive appeals to all that is chivalrous in our natures.

But the reputation of the eagle race, quite as in the case of our own, has been made by a few individuals, and their feats are a revelation of the possibilities inherent in the breed rather than chapters from common life. Never shall I forget the pained disappointment over my first eagle's nest in a northern country. The situation was romantic enough—a ledge of rock some three hundred and fifty feet up on the side of the gulch, and seventy-five feet clear of the talus below. At the time of my first visit, May 18th, the nest contained two eaglets about six weeks old. Armed with a stout birchen staff, I worked my way over to a secure footing within a dozen feet of the nest. The remaining distance was a nasty bit of climbing, and I preferred to await the first onslaught of the outraged parents where there would be some chance of defense. Fudge! The fire-eating birds appeared once or twice in the middle distance, but payed no more attention to the peril of their offspring than as if I had been a magpie coveting the crumbs from the royal table.

Whereas generations of gunfire have taught the eagle a wholesome respect for mankind, there is no doubt that their innate ferocity, goaded by hunger, still impels them to daring feats wherever their natural prey is concerned. Not only do the eagles capture foxes, raccoons, and all other creatures capable of inflicting injury in turn, but they brave the brute force of some of the larger animals, sheep, goats, and even bucks. Mr. F. C. Willard reports a case from the Chiricahua Mountains where Golden Eagles attacked a four-point white-tailed deer, as it was floundering in the snows, and killed it by sinking their talons deeply into its back. Fawns frequently fall victims to the eagle's claw, and a successful attack of this sort often involves keeping the mother deer at bay. It is for this reason that eagles usually hunt in pairs; and I have been told, on what I consider good authority, that calves are sometimes killed by the combined ferocity and cunning of a robber team.

It will be difficult then, for us to make out a brief in defense of this royal brigand. Certainly, we cannot do so upon purely economic grounds. But there is robber blood enough in all of us to make us cry "Brother!" when we hear the eagle scream. It is envy and wicked folly, and not just vengeance, which leads us to strike down this winged presence of the mountains, this watcher of the deserts, and fearless companion of the sun. It is good to have something with red blood among us—or over us. And if it takes expensive food to sustain such quality, let him have it. What are grouse and ducks and rabbits, fawns, even, before the dignity of this majestic symbol! I'll take eagles myself!

Southern Bald Eagle
Haliaeetus leucocephalus leucocephalus

THE PASSING OF THE BALD EAGLE is doubtless ordained by the same factors—bravado, recklessness and revenge—which have decreed the destruction of his Golden kinsman.* The human animal simply cannot abide the presence of any bird larger than a pewee; and if the natural instinct to burn up gunpowder lags, it is possible to unearth or invent a hundred tales of evil-doing on the bird's part, each quite sufficient to bolster up murderous purpose.

We will grant without debate that the Bald Eagle is a bad actor. He eats fish—a most reprehensible practice—and he occasionally captures game birds, which we would prefer to do to death by our own peculiar artistry. Worse than that, he sometimes—not often, mind you—attacks *lambs*, and has been known to kill fawns. He has assisted sick sheep in their effort to shuffle off the mortal coil; and, worst of all, he has been known to carry off babies—say in two or three really authenticated instances in our entire national history. We will not even plead that dead and dying fish have been consumed by thousands of tons to the great benefit of the national health; that birds and mammals of neutral importance are captured as often as those of economic benefit, or that distinguished services have been performed by the eagles in freeing the land from weasels, marmots, squirrels, and other injurious species of mammals. It is idle. If the venerable dignity of the white-headed eagle posted on a sea-cliff excites only the itching of trigger fingers; if the prowess displayed by the eagle in pursuing and capturing swiftest-winged birds excites only a malignant envy; if, indeed, the murderer of an eagle is to be proclaimed a hero, and allowed to bask in the sunshine of local approval; the case is hopeless. We who enjoy Nature's variety, we who appreciate Nature's splendors, we who love the thrills of Nature's own choosing, we who do obeisance to the Creative Infinite expressed in Snowy Egrets and Birds of Paradise and swans and eagles and condors, we are a pitiful minority. Do not mind us. Kill, rob, devastate, poison, and utterly exterminate all who lift their heads above the common ruck. We shall still have left—Linnets.

---

* Editor's note: The Golden Eagle was nearly extinct in the eastern United States, and the Bald Eagle was approaching extinction in the 1960s. Although factors such as environmental degradation and poaching are continuing threats, populations of both species have been on the increase since the pesticide DDT was banned.

Nothing, outside of human woes, could be sadder than the sight of an eagle in a cage. Captivity is irksome at best, and the contemplation of it is seldom edifying. Yet the sight of a monkey is not so bad. Ropes and sticks and wire nettings are sources of infinite amusement to Jocko, as to his spectators. Bruin enjoys his fare of peanuts and bonbons, and might not wish to exchange his snug pit of concrete for the vicissitudes of mountain life. Caged song birds, even, have always artistic relief for their wounded spirit. But for the captive eagle there is no consolation whatever. Befouled, disheveled, sick at heart, and aching with imprisoned forces, he can only scowl in sullen disdain at his persecutors, or mope in abject misery before them. The sight of such a captive degrades the onlooker, as it outrages every sentiment of justice and fitness. We have no right to imprison creatures whose lives we cannot make reasonably happy.

California Condor
Gymnogyps californianus

IF WE WERE TO PROPOUND THE QUESTION "Where is the heart of California?" there would be a dozen instant and clamorous voices, each with a valid claim to urge. The heart of California? It is the Golden Gate, most romantic of portals, through which the Argonauts entered the land of dreams, thronged now with the roaring traffic of Occident and Ind. It is San Francisco, the passionate, the beloved, the furnace-tried, the unconquerable, now conquering herself and bearing rule with the imperiousness of self-possession. It is the desert, weird, empty, forlorn—or God-filled—according to your mood. Surely it is the desert where, if but a horned toad scuttles, you are startled; where, at the least, your own heart's beating fills you with a nameless terror, or else an exalted joy—according to your kind. It is the Sierra Nevada, heart of the world, where lightnings vie with cold snows to crown the dauntless monarchs of space and time.

Here is sanctuary and surcease of sorrow, and a world brought near to its Maker.

The heart of California is here. Aye, and in a dozen places more; for the heart of California is very large, and it is indivisible. But for me the heart of California lies in the condor country. And for me the heart of mystery, of wonder, and of desire lies with the California Condor, that majestic and almost legendary figure, which still haunts the fastnesses of our lessening wilderness.

It was with a happy heart, then, that the writer accepted, early in April 1911, an invitation to visit a condor's eyrie hidden in the heart of eastern San Luis Obispo County. My guides were interested to prove that condors, or at least *a* condor, laid a white or creamy white egg, instead of the stereotyped pale bluish green of scientific repute.

A night on the ground and a dip in a brawling stream makes us fit for condor-gazing an hour before daybreak; but the morning is foggy and we cannot see well. By and by Kelly descries a condor some two thousand feet above, distinguishable rather by sturdiness of motion than by size from the nearer "buzzards." The great bird is soaring over the heights of his ancestral castle, but he soon settles on top of a pine tree where we can study him with binoculars and telescope. Soon he is joined by another bird, and as they wheel and pitch in the clearing atmosphere, we note unmistakably the great white patches under the wings and the golden head of each. The unfulfilled desire of decades has been met. We have seen the fabled bird and pronounced him genuine. But there is business afoot and scant time for reflection. The birds drift over toward us, undoubtedly upon a tour of inspection. And there is a pretty passage at arms between them, a discussion of our demerits, perhaps, in animated sign language. They retire to a pinnacle perch and cogitate; but not for long. The morning advances, and duty rides the Gymnogypsian conscience. A saucy Prairie Falcon pursues each ancient bird in turn, but the condor always avoids the stroke by a downward swerve which seems absolutely beyond the falcon's power to judge or speed to follow. The falcon's stroke is lightning itself, and I have seen one punish a Golden Eagle unmercifully, but there are three birds that he cannot touch, a raven, a turkey vulture, and a condor.

As we watch the evolutions of this pair, they are suddenly joined by another bird, an all-black fellow, as large, to all appearance, as a condor—a youngster, perhaps, only a decade or so of age. These three gyrate together amicably enough at first, but presently the stranger (?) is hustled off the stage. The father recalls that an elder son has no proper place in contemporary family life. Later, one of the original pair is lost to sight behind an angle in the cliff whose recesses we cannot discern, although we see the wall beyond. We hold our breath. But no; he, or she, soon emerges, and there is more gyration, a little tedious now. O La! La! When will they get down to business? They disappear over the mountain instead.

But later, one returns—makes straight for the recess already noted in the cliff, and is lost to view. One minute, two, three, elapses. It has happened! She's on, boys!

Only two thousand feet above us; but if I were to stop to rehearse to you the arduous details of that climb, and of our sufferings, camera-laden, poked, prodded, buffeted, and gouged, as we made our way upward through an all but impenetrable thicket of buckthorn, you would chuck this volume into the fire-place and bolt for the door. It is yours to gather only the sweets. The actual foot of that rock-wall was sweet. We could have kissed it or bathed it with our tears.

Kelly now addressed himself to an examination of the nest, which could be best reached by a circuitous course from above; but while he was busy aloft with the tackle I heard an ominous sound, something between a hiss and a squall, proceeding from the depths of the rock. "Too late!" I shouted. It was even so; for a squab of *Gymnogyps*, instead of a white egg, occupied the cave. I examined the situation a few minutes later. The aperture of the nesting cave was midway of the face of a sloping stretch of sandstone, not too steep, perhaps, for inspection without the aid of rope, but too steep for comfortable work. The floor was of a fine dry sand and several inches in depth, and upon this at the remotest distance a baby condor hissed and roared. The infant was perhaps four times as large as the egg from which he had emerged, and since he held his head up well, we judged that he might have been ten days or perhaps two weeks old. He was clad in a downy jacket of sordid white, and his bill and forehead were of a yellowish flesh-color. The place was somewhat odoriferous, but not excessively so, and I should judge that the nature of the floor, dry sand, would ensure an exceptionally sanitary condition.

The fragments of the shell were examined, and these were certainly of a creamy white color, not pale niagara green, as is usual with this species.

The mother bird (supposedly) sat quietly, but not indifferently, through all these proceedings. There was an air of gentle breeding and dignity about this bird which not even the bizarre coloration of her head-dress could destroy. Indeed, the head with its orange-colored beak and frontal plate, crossed at the eyes with a black band, sits rather like a jewel in its setting of a shiny black ruff; while the feet and legs, of a shining flesh-color, stand out again in high relief as the bird perches. Although the bird fled at our closer photographic approach, she did not quit the neighborhood nor did she attempt to enter the nest. Instead, she gyrated about, or swept to and fro near the entrance in solicitous fashion.

The foregoing account of a condor's nesting is confessedly a rather prosaic affair. Nothing very spectacular happened. We returned *sans* egg, *sans* skin (thank God!), and, as the event proved, *sans* photograph, but we brought the condor away in our hearts. I am not ashamed to have fallen in love with so gentle a ghoul; and though I should not choose to dine with him, I am assured that if I did, my brother would not crowd me nor cheat me of my portion. And who are we that we should sit in judgment upon a brother who takes his meat a bit rarer than our own? A dead cow is, after all, a dead cow, is it not? And what if he does not kill his own meat. Do you? Or do you, like him, meekly accept from the gods of circumstance the meats which have been provided?

TURKEY VULTURE
Cathartes aura septentrionalis

IN THE FOG-BELT, THE VULTURE'S DAY may not begin before eight or nine o'clock in the morning, but once a-wing our sable hero enters upon a quest the most active and tireless, the most patient, and the most often unrewarded of any which mortals know. Eternal hunger is a-wing, and when the buzzard sweeps low to bend upon you an inquiring eye, you shudder. The passing shape casts a shadow as of death, and it is really the grave which appraises you in that deferential, hopeful gaze. But do not be dismayed! It is a gentle ghoul. He has not in himself the power of death for so much as a toad; and as for death's debris, why should not our thrifty mother feed her other children at our expense, if we are careless enough to get left around?

It is as an aviator rather than as a sexton, however, that one should think of the Turkey Vulture. His performances in the air are such as to awaken unqualified enthusiasm; and it is interesting to note in this connection that *Cathartes aura*, the species, is the oldest living performer among that highly specialized group of stars, the Cathartidae. While he did not actually invent the heavier-than-air machines—gracious, no!— the Turkey Vulture was calmly practicing the aviator's art at least half a million years before the Wright brothers waxed ambitious.

Be that as it may, the crowning touch of a summer day, A.D. 1918— 28—38—is afforded by the sight of a small company of Turkey Vultures lazily drifting across the middle distance, soaring, shifting, wheeling, weaving endless circles, in restful monotony of midsummer content. Lost in admiration and in envy of their powers, we may well forget that these gifted aviators are repulsive in presence or abject in demeanor. As a decorative feature in the landscape, the vulture possesses an irreplaceable value. And if you add to this the wonder of wings, the mystery or the incomprehensible adroitness of gliding flight, you have just grounds for respect.

Quail and Grouse

Mountain Quail

Oreortyx picta picta

THE MOUNTAIN QUAIL'S IS THE AUTHENTIC VOICE of the foothills, as well as the dominant note of Sierran valleys and of bush-covered ridges. Spring and summer alike, and sometimes in early autumn, one may hear that brooding, mellow, slightly melancholy *too' wook*, sounding forth at intervals of five or six seconds. Now and then it is repeated from a distant hillside where a rival is sounding. This note is easily whistled, and a little practice will enable the bird-student to join in, or else to start a rivalry where all has been silent before.

The nesting of the Mountain Quail is conducted at the higher levels of its range. Ten or a dozen eggs, of a rich buffy hue, unmarked, line a scanty shakedown of grasses or pine needles, which almost invariably enjoys the shelter of a projecting rock, an arching tree-bole, or a thicket of brush.

When the berries of the upper levels have been gleaned, the Mountain Quails begin a stately migration *on foot* to the lower levels in order to avoid the heavy Sierran snows. At such times they are said to be unwary, and even prefer the good walking of the open road to a laborious threading of the sage-brush. Hunters used to take advantage of this fact, and took excessive toll along certain well-known valley routes. Since market hunting was abolished, however, the Mountain Quail population has been picking up. Although their broods are smaller than those of the Valley Quail, their enemies are fewer and their cover better.

Catalina Island Quail
Lophortyx californica catalinensis

GLAD SUMMONER OF SPRINGTIME! Gallant pensioner of our lawns and hedges! Brave elf o' the nodding plume! Is there a heart in California that loves you not? Or an ear that does not thrill anew when it hears your sturdy call? What can we do to repay the kindness of your daily cheer? What less, indeed, than to give you the freedom of our premises, to let you glean for us a thousand seeded evils, and to let you parade, uncoveted, your saucy beauty? Stay, beautiful bird, and trust us, us whose tongues have never tasted your brothers' blood; us who would as soon frighten children as to violate your confidence. Woe is us that you must scuttle to the nearest cover and deliberate in anxious accents whether to fly or no. Woe! I say, and a plague upon the cause that brought you to this pass.

There! that is a very bad beginning for an account of "California's leading game bird." For ten years the author of *The Birds of California* has faced the task of expounding to his "fellow sportsmen" the glories of quail shooting. Duty is written large in the expectation of a hundred thousand owners of guns. "Come," they say, "glorify for us the ardors of the chase, the rustle of expectation, the sudden hurtling of winged rockets, the quick eye and the accurate finger that stops the hurtling mid-sky, and the limp form retrieved from the sheltering bushes, the count of the bag at the day's end. Recall to our pleasant recollection the skill of the cook who serves our birds and the daintiness of the white meat, an ounce or two to a portion, that graces our banquets."

Gentlemen, I cannot do it. I wouldn't eat one of those pitiful remnants of departed glory, unless I were starving; and I never was anywhere near starving, were you? Did you ever really *need* the flesh of a little bird, a beautiful, happy bird? Forgive me and let me pass.

The Valley Quail's day begins in some bush or tree—a live oak, as like as not—where, in company with his fellows, he has spent the night secure from all anxiety as to foxes and coyotes.

After a visit to some spring or running stream where water is copiously imbibed, the chief business of the day, if in spring, is foraging on grass and other tender herbage; if in autumn, the gleaning of fallen weed-seeds; or it may be a bit of grain, together with such crawling insects as come incidentally under review. If the day is warm, the middle portion is spent in retirement, again in the thick foliage of a tree. The siesta finished, the birds venture out again to provide another grist for their insatiable seed-hoppers, and to indulge a dust-bath, such as all fowls dearly love. As the twilight hour approaches, there is much scampering and calling, with some sportive pursuit, and a night-cap drink before the company is bedded again under its coverlet of thick green leaves.

The Quail's year begins sometime in March or early April, when the coveys begin to break up and, not without some heart-burnings and fierce passages at arms between the cocks, individual preferences begin to hold sway. It is then that the so-called "assembly call" *ku kwak' up, ku kwak' uk, ku kwak' uk-ko*, is heard at its best; for this is also a mating call; and if not always directed toward a single listener, it is a notice to all and sundry that the owner is very happy, and may be found at the old stand. Although belonging to a polygamous family, the Valley Quail is very particular in his affections; and indeed, from all that we may learn, is at all times a very perfect model of a husband and father.

OREGON RUFFED GROUSE

Bonasa umbellus sabini

PERHAPS THE MOST EXQUISITE PRODUCT of our somber western woods is this "Oregon" Ruffed Grouse with his plumage of warm browns and woodsy buffs, relieved by touches of white, and set off by the glossy black of neck ornaments, or ruffs. Nature has painted her favorite to match the moldering logs of red fir, cross-hatched as they are by the infinite traceries of the under-forest. When he steps forth at the sound of your footstep into some woodland path, alert yet curious, with ruffs half raised and tail partly opened, you feel as if the very beauty of nature had found concrete expression, and that the vision would fade again if you breathed too heavily.

If not pressed, the bird will presently hop up on some fallen log, the better to see and be seen; or else trip away, satisfied, into some mossy covert. Or it may take suddenly to wing, with a roar which you feel to be quite needless, especially when exaggerated by a series of grunts which must be decisive.

In the latter part of February the mating season commences, and from that time until well into May the rolling drum-call of the cocks may be heard at any hour of the day and sometimes far into the night. Every cock has some particular fallen tree which he has chosen for his private drumming ground, and he very rarely resorts to another situation. A favorite log becomes worn in the course of a season, so that an experienced hunter may locate the trysting place in its owner's absence. In executing this manoeuver the bird stands to its full height and beats its wings swiftly downward toward its sides, in this manner rendering sounds which closely resemble the syllables *bump-bump-bump, bumperrrrrr*.

A noisy surprise is in store for the person who comes upon a mother partridge with a brood of tender chicks. With a great outcry the mother bird charges up in front of the intruder, or dashes into his face; then stands before him with flashing eyes and ruffled feathers, looking fierce enough to eat him up. Thus she holds the enemy at bay for one bewildering moment—a precious moment, in which her tiny darlings are finding shelter. Then she collapses like a struck tent and vanishes in a trice.

Sage Grouse

Centrocercus urophasianus

As bamboo to the Oriental, or as the coconut palm to the South Sea Islander, so is the sage-bush to this Cock of the Plains. It not only provides him shelter of a sort, but food and probably drink as well. At least, from the fact that the Sage Cock is found at such distances from water, we are forced to conclude that the dew-covered browse of the *Artemisia* must often serve the bird in lieu of water. As to food, this grouse has so long depended upon the leaves and tender shoots of the sage-brush and greasewood for subsistence, that it is incapable of digesting grain when it is offered. The bird's gizzard, unlike that of other grouse, is not a strong, muscular grinding organ, but a membranous sac capable of great distension, but unequal to the task of reducing seeds, grains, or even hardshelled beetles. The bird's spring diet is varied by many kinds of tender herbage, and in summer it consumes quantities of crickets, grasshoppers, and other insects, but sage is eaten at all seasons and forms its exclusive ration in winter.

In the courting antics of this valiant son of the desert, Nature has indulged a fresh fancy. Indeed, it is to be suspected that the Dame takes a special delight in making some of the most staid and prosaic of her male progeny appear in a ridiculous light, when under the influence of the tender passion. This grizzled veteran of the wormwood does not express his sentiment with either dignity or grace. No; he first inflates the air sacs which line his neck until they assume alarming proportions, meeting in front and frequently engulfing his head; the tail with its spiny feathers is spread to the utmost and pointed skyward; then the gallant pitches forward and casts off for a bellybuster slide over the ground, not without much assistance of propulsive feet in approved "kid" fashion. As a result of this ridiculous dryland swim, the feathers of the breast are worn off at the tips till only the quills protrude. These ragged quill ends, in being forced over the earth, produce a mild roar which passes for an aria by Caruso with the gray lady in the sage-box. La! but it is absurd! Do you suppose—now *do* you suppose we ever make such fools of ourselves?

Cranes, Rails,
and Coots

Little Brown Crane
Grus canadensis canadensis

SPRINGTIME IN CALIFORNIA IS LIKE the gradual unfolding of a flower, a little more perfect each day. In the East it is either a gift or a conquest, a tropical favor or a disheveled bouquet, a something to be striven for, now flung in lush promise at the feet of expectant humanity, or suddenly snatched away again, according as Boreas or Flora wins each swiftly succeeding bout. In the West it is not so; and there be those of us who sigh at times amid the fragrant and inevitable orange-blossoms for the *Sturm und Drang* of a grosser passion. To such comes the multitudinous croak of the passing cranes as a blessed relief. "*Krr—kr—r, kr—r, kr—oo, Kr—r, kr—r, kr—r, kr—oo,*" shout these winged barbarians as their cohorts press northward. "Come with us," they challenge, "flee these soft enticements of the Southland. We will show you how to mock the gnashing teeth of retreating winter. Come where bitter winds provoke hot blood. Come where the owl and the lemming hold sway over vast tundras. Come where Aurora paints the sky with unimaginable splendors. Come—O ye gods!—where man or bird may breathe without the rebuke of jostling elbows." *Kr—r, kr—r, kr—r, kr—r—oo.* Oo aye! It is harsh, discordant, and all that. But it comes with the authority of bagpipes, or bugles. Our herts are wi' ye, birdies!

SANDHILL CRANE

Grus canadensis mexicanus

IF THE PIONEER WEST WERE TO CHOOSE a bird symbol, none could be more fitting than the Sandhill Crane. Like the buffalo, and the Indian, the crane stands for that type of the wilderness which the white man may obliterate, indeed, but cannot subdue. He is the typical child of the desert, and between him and civilization there is a gulf fixed, a gulf which shot-guns and reclamation projects have done much to widen.

Alert, wary, and sagacious the Sandhill Crane has always been, for even the hand of the Indian was against him. But these qualities have attained their highest development since the advent of the hungry whites: so that a study of these birds is no longer to be classed as natural history, but only as morbid psychology. In watching against enemies the Crane makes the most of his commanding height; but since he must stoop occasionally to the ground to feed, he requires to be further protected by a surrounding of level stretches in which no possible foe may lurk. In winter the cranes show a marked predilection for islands or river bars. Here, although vigilance may be safely relaxed by the majority, there are always sentinels kept at lookout.

The approach of an enemy is marked by a sonorous challenge—a mellow, penetrating, powerful note, which seems to hark from the elder Eocene. If this warning is not respected, the bird makes a quick run and springs into the air with a prodigious flapping, which presently smooths out into rhythmical flight, with neck and legs outstretched to the utmost. Meanwhile the bird is blowing his bugle frantically, and if many birds are at it, the syncopated chorus which ensues is one of the most impressive in Nature's oratorio.

In spring these gracefully ungainly birds indulge in curious antics of courtship. The male bows with outstretched wings and nearly touches the ground with his beak in the extremity of his devotion. The female returns the bow with respect quite as profound, and then they indulge an absurd minuet, swaying, dancing, leaping, and executing high kicks with an entrancing degree of awkwardness. There is no privacy about this phase of courtship, and twenty birds at once may join the giddy whirl which seals the fate of so many young hearts.

CALIFORNIA CLAPPER RAIL
Rallus obsoletus

SAN FRANCISCO IS A COMPARATIVELY CLEAN CITY, as cities go; but San Francisco Bay mud is the deepest and the blackest and the stickiest—in short, the muddiest that ever vexed a poor bird-man wanting to get from here to yonder across a half-filled tide-gut. The distance across may not be over a dozen feet—just a little long for jumping, with an uncertain foothold on either bank. What's to do? It is miles around this absurd little artery of the salt marshes. Shall we try wading? Only once! And never again! The mud is unfathomable; and the scuttling crabs, who say it is easy—well, they lie. What would tempt an honest bird-man to tramp these interminable acres of "pickle weed," and to flounder across these interminable mud sloughs, anyway? Obviously, only the presiding genius of San Francisco Bay, the California Clapper Rail. Here comes one of these dandies of the mud, now, a symphony in browns with insertions of white. Stepping forth from the curtain of salicornia, which leans over the sloping sides of the slough, Sir Clapper plants a careful foot, and eyes you quizzically. If passably reassured, he moves over the mud in a gingerly manner, hitching his head and jetting his apology for a tail. He is like a horse with a tight crupper, and his under-tail coverts flash a white distress signal each time he hitches forward. But he is only putting on airs. Let a worm appear on the mud and the rail seizes it by a nimble dash, in which dignity is utterly forgotten. The worm he bolts on the spot, or else retires to shelter if the victim requires disciplinary measures. If the bird, also, has business on the other side of the slough, he will swim the salty stream, also with a hitching motion; or else he will rise heavily, dragging his reluctant feet ostentatiously through the air, and drop to cover as soon as may be.

For all that we can see, the life of the Clapper Rail is passed in these humble surroundings, amidst endless acres of salicornia (*Salicornia ambigua*), broken only by occasional patches of "greenbush" (*Grindelia cuneifolia*). Nothing more exciting offers in the round year than a drenching storm, or a high tide which floods his meadows, and leaves the birds to swim about disconsolate until the waters are abated.

Virginia Rail
Rallus virginianus

GIVEN AN OASIS OF WATER OF, say, two acres extent, in a pasture desert of barren green; crowd a company of willows into one end; add a half-acre of bogs crowned with rose bushes; then a little space of clear water; then a jungle of cat-tails at the other end; surround the whole with a thirty-foot border of sedges and coarse grasses cropped close on the desert side, and you have an ideal home for the Virginial Rail and his kind. Poke about carefully in the edge of the rose-bog and you will soon start him, a sly reddish bird with a red eye and a longish beak. See him some ten feet away standing at the edge of cover, all alert, one foot uplifted and with claws curled down; or when he plants it gingerly, he alternately perks and lowers his head, as though divided in his mind between darting away and facing it out with you. Simultaneously he cocks his tail forward and relaxes it nervously. If you succeed in looking sufficiently disinterested, he will snatch a slug hastily and watch you furtively with a blood-red eye, to note whether you approve of such actions. If you pass all the tests of good behavior during the first five minutes, the gentle bird will relax his vigilance and show you how he can walk over half-submerged vegetation without sinking very deep himself, or if in the passage from bog to bog he comes to a space of clear brown water, he will swim as lightly as a duck, but with that odd bobbing motion peculiar to his race. A single false motion, however, will send him scuttling off through the plant-stems and out of sight in a twinkling, cackling in alarm and dudgeon.

AMERICAN COOT
Fulica americana

WHEN A CANVAS CANOE PROPELLED BY a double-bladed paddle grows big upon the horizon and then brushes noisily against the weedy outpost of some tule swamp, an ominous hush falls over the scene, a silence broken only by the rustling of the arum tops. You saw birds from the distance, but every man Jack of them has fled. The reeds will tell no tales. Presently a grebe relieves the tension by snorting—that is the word—then dives suddenly to quench his ill-timed mirth; next a leaden figure steals from behind a distant clump of reeds and glances this way and that apprehensively. It is only a man in a boat—perhaps— she *did* want to visit that snail-bed before the sun got too high. So she advances, not without many misgiving hitches of the head, across an intervening stretch of bare water, and disappears behind a screen of reeds. The passage successfully accomplished, another Mud-hen [Coot], and another, ventures forth, the last one sniffing scornfully over the alleged danger. Confidence restored, the invaded precincts begin to re-echo to their wonted sounds of life, splashing and noise of pursuit, and mellow notes of several sorts. Only sit quiet and your stranger presence will soon be accepted as matter of course.

Where unmolested, Mud-hens fill about as large a place in the economy of a well-conducted swamp as do chickens in a barnyard. Especially in the breeding season, the sound of their gulping call, *pulque pulque pulque pulque*, is the prevailing note of the swamp. These notes are rendered with the head close to the water, and seem to afford a prodigious relief to the bird's feelings. The Coot, on fatigue duty, is a very prosy-looking fowl, for the bird ordinarily sits half submerged, with lowered wings and tail both sloping into and under the water; but the Coot on dress parade is a very different-looking fellow, albeit his uniform is the same. When the ladies are looking, he sits high in the water; the wing-tips are pointed obliquely upward; the tail is held vertically or tilted forward; and two white patches of feathers, one on each side of the tail, are flashed into view and carried prominently.

Courtship is largely a matter of pursuit. In this both pursuer and pursued rise, or only half rise, from the water, with much floundering and splashing. And they proceed only a rod or two when both fall back exhausted, the female usually well in advance. This is mere gallantry on the part of the male, and exaggerated pretense on the part of both. When the male is in earnest, the pursuit is carried on under water as well as above it. Much time is spent by enamored couples in simply gazing into each other's eyes. A pair will face each other, beak to beak, with necks stretched out full length upon the water, and paddle about for minutes together in fascinated circles. The hinder parts, meanwhile, are carried high like those of a swan. This *vis-à-vis* pose is also a menace on the part of rivals, and is the inevitable preliminary of any cock fight. In this the birds appear to depend upon nail more than upon tooth, for they lean back upon the water, bracing with their wings, behind, and kick at each other most absurdly. After such an episode, which the female, as likely as not, has interrupted, all the interested parties float about with ruffled feathers and outstretched heads laid low, each apparently in a sort of trance of self satisfaction.

Shore-Birds

RED PHALAROPE
Phalaropus fulicarius

"SEA GEESE" THE ATLANTIC FISHERMEN CALL THEM, and if you can conceive of geese no bigger than your fist, scattered broadcast by thousands over the bosom of the ocean, you will have a fair idea of the general appearance, as well as of the confidence which inspires these remarkable birds. Albeit classed as a "shore-bird," this hardiest species of the Phalaropes spends its entire life upon the water, save as it is driven by stress of weather to seek shelter in the lee of some island or headland, or as it is led ashore by the promptings of the reproductive instinct. Inasmuch as the prevailing winds along our western coast are from the northwest during the spring months, and especially during May, no more favorable opportunity exists for the study of Red Phalaropes during migration than that afforded by the Farallon Islands, some twenty-five miles off the Golden Gate. Here in late spring thousands of these birds ride at anchor in the lee of the main island, along with other thousands of the other northern species, *Lobipes lobatus [Phalaropus lobatus]*. Of these some few scores are driven ashore by hunger and seek their sustenance in brackish pools, or else battle with the breakers in the little "bight" of the rocky lee shore. The date is May 23, and the company under survey numbers a few brilliant red birds in high plumage among scores in unchanged gray, together with others exhibiting every intermediate gradation. When to this variety is added a similar diversity among the Northerns, which mingle indiscriminately with them, you have a motley company—no two birds alike. Ho! but these are agile surfmen! Never, save in the case of the Wandering Tattler and the American Dipper, have I seen such absolute disregard of danger and such instant adjustment to watery circumstance. Here are thirty of these phalaropes "fine mixed," threading a narrow passage in the reefs where danger threatens in the minutest fraction of a second. Crash! comes a comber. Our little world is obliterated in foam. Sea-anemones and rock-oysters sputter and choke, and there is a fine fury of readjustment. But the phalaropes rise automatically, clear the crest of the crasher, and are down again, preening their feathers or snatching dainties with the utmost unconcern. Now a bird is left stranded on a reef, or now he is whisked and whirled a dozen feet away. All right, if he likes it; but if not, he is back again, automatically, at the old rendezvous.

Life goes on right merrily in spite of these shocking interruptions. Food-getting is the main business, and this is pursued with extraordinary ardor. The bird's tiny feet kick the water violently, and there is the tiniest compensatory bob for every stroke, so that their little bodies seem all a-tremble. There seems to be no difference of opinion between the two species, but there is time for a good deal of amatory play between the sexes of the Reds. It is always the bright-colored female who makes the advances, for the wanton phalaropes have revised Nature's order, and the modest male either seeks escape by flight, or else defends himself with determined dabs. Here is the authentic lady for whom Shakespeare's "pilgrim" sighed:

Oh would my lady had me thus at bay,
To kiss and clip me till I ran away.

The birds are perfectly aware of my presence, and they do not come *too* close, except as a wave breaks over the barrier and sweeps the whole company over toward me. In such case, several of the more timid fly, but most of them cast an eye upward in my direction and determine to take chances. When the birds climb up onto a rock, they totter absurdly and pitch forward helplessly, as if their bodies were surprisingly, as they undoubtedly are unexpectedly, heavy. Not infrequently they fall in this fashion, always pitching upon their faces.

One modest gallant is just taking a bath. Mere sousing by surf is evidently inadequate for this important function, but it needs must have personal attention. The bather therefore tips first to one side and then the other, kicking into the air with the upper foot and scattering spray with the upper wing, while he dips the under one. He changes with incredible swiftness until, his ablutions completed, he rises three or four feet into the air and shakes himself thoroughly.

We are told that these birds breed in immense numbers within the Arctic Circle, and that they are invariably found among those breeding farthest north. Their presence, also, is characteristic of open water anywhere in the Arctic Ocean; and it is hailed with delight by whalers as being a good indication of the near presence of some large cetacean, especially of the bow-head, or right whale (*Balaena mysticetus*), since the birds delight in the same sort of sea-forage as that upon which the whales subsist.

Northern Phalarope
Lobipes lobatus

NOTHING CAN EXCEED THE EXQUISITE GRACE of this delicate bird as it moves about, not at the water's edge, like other waders which it so closely resembles in appearance, but upon the surface of a pool or even on the bosom of the deep. As it swims, it nods with every stroke, turns at a thought to snatch some floating sea-morsel, or flits away with as little provocation as that afforded the bursting bubble of foam, its late brother. We who dwell by the sea wait eagerly for the reappearance of our confiding little voyageurs, in April or early May, and though our files are already bursting full of "negatives," we shall not cease to pursue this dainty apparition as often as he condescends to visit our brackish pools and shallows.

Truth to tell, the enthusiasm of photographic pursuit often leads the camerist into sorry places. Accustomed though it be to gleaning a living from the surface of the ocean, where everything is "clean," a phalarope's interest in backwater lagoons or interior waters is directly proportioned to their impurity. Here at Santa Barbara we have a most conspicuous example in the "Estero," which is a stretch of low-lying, flooded barrens near the car shops and the beach. This watery waste receives not only the contributions of ancient springs now polluted by civilization, but also the frustrated waters of the city's outfall sewer, when the tide is over-high. The combined result is a culture medium of a potency to daunt any but the most hardened human explorer, as well as to compel the attendance of even the most wary of avian gourmets. Here on a day during the August migrations I have seen the tepid waters teeming with "insect" life to a degree almost unimaginable. The upper strata of a six-inch shallow held bugs or wriggling creatures of at least twenty sorts visible to the naked eye; and of these, ten kinds might be distinguished in a single cubic inch. The lowermost stratum seemed a solid mass of living creatures, while the spaces between, though comparably clear to the eyes, must have been crowded with bacterial life adequate to the support of the visible hosts. Into one of these channels of liquid aliment, huge earthen platters containing soup of a richness beyond human desire, come the phalaropes to feast and fatten. They come after long fasting, perhaps, and as they settle upon the water they begin to rush about like excited schoolboys under a chestnut tree. Each bird gives a grunt of greedy satisfaction between mouthfuls, so that a curious gabbling chorus, or plunder song, rises. This strange music of the chase is instantly hushed at the approach of danger, and it can be heard to advantage only from behind a screen of reeds or salicornia.

BLACK-NECKED STILT

Himantopus mexicanus

AFTER ALL, TO OUR HUMAN JUDGMENT, the outstanding feature of bird life is its marvelous diversity. From the Hummingbird, which weighs a few scruples and is so adroit of wing that it can fly backward, to that waddling avian pig, the Dodo, which weighed six stone and couldn't fly at all, is indeed a far cry. But the contrast afforded here is no isolated example of difference in the bird world. Indeed, there is no single feature of avian anatomy which Dame Nature does not, in one place or another, seize upon and play up to the limit of imagination. Is it feathers, that distinguishing characteristic of the bird? Well, then, the whimsical arbiter of fashions will snatch a handful anywhere, and if she does not pluck it off outright, she will tweak, pull, twist, exaggerate, and distort until we have such creations as the resplendent trains of the Quetzal and the Peacock, or the absurd headgear of the Six-wired Bird of Paradise, into which six enormous hatpins have been thrust. Is it color? Some, like the Crow and the Drongo, she plunges into dye-vats filled with steaming logwood; some, like the Titmouse or the Brown Towhee, she covers with dust; some, like Poorwill, she drapes in lichen-hues; and some, like the Wood Duck, she clothes with the rainbow. The Ptarmigan is purest snow, while at some of the Lories this jesting dame has hurled her palette, paint, brush, and all, and has achieved thereby a very tragedy of color. Nor are major organs spared in the craze for variety. Wings may be like sails, or scimitars, or flippers, or else suppressed outright. Beaks are Nature's special plaything, as witness the Avocet, the Toucan, and the Pelican. But for the subject of this sketch has been reserved Nature's special humor as to legs. A creature actually only four inches long as to body—exclusive, that is, of neck and tail—has legs eight or ten inches long. The Stilt's tarsus, or "instep," is alone longer than its body. The Stilt is, therefore, the wader *par excellence,* and we shall see that it makes out very well with its extraordinary equipment.

I know of nothing which admits a man more surely to the intimate

wild of nature than the sight of a company of Black-necked Stilts
feeding quietly along the sedge-grown margins of a shallow pond. One
feels a delicious sense of privilege, as though he were being permitted
to gaze upon some assemblage of antedeluvians. Concealment on the
bird's part is impossible, for his plumage is highly advertising. Better,
though, if the observer have a blind or a tent or, at least, a covered
automobile. Fancy automobiles at a Miocene spectacle! The birds are
impossible; you have settled that in advance. This will be a clownish
performance with many a mishap of broken stilts or of damaged shins.
But as we watch the deft celerity and alert confidence of these gifted
waders, incredulity changes to wonder, and wonder to admiration. If
the water is only knee deep (and we always mean "heel" when we say
"knee" in bird-lore), then this bird threads the mazes of the budding
sedges adroitly, snatching now a larva from a plant stem, and now an
insect from the surface of the water. The foot is withdrawn backward,
with a deftness which scarcely disturbs the water's face, and does not at
all roil the oozy bottom. The Stilt will wade about belly deep, if need
be, and stoop to secure dainties off the bottom at that. It is quite at
home, also, on dry land, and will snap with unfailing dexterity at the
insects which rise bewildered from the ground.

Stilts are a commonplace of migrations in California, arriving
from the south about the middle of April. They visit all the wayside
ponds and plashes left by the rainy season, or created by the overflow of
irrigation. They are usually silent and not too wary at this season, and
their frank enjoyment of our wayside fare is one of the gladsome sights
of the season. Once, on the beach near Gaviota, I saw a company of
Stilts breasting the ocean waves; but it must have been a rare experience
for them, as it was a rare sight for us. They are poor swimmers, and
their frail pipe-stems were hardly made to withstand the suck of the
"hurryback."

It is to the breeding home, therefore, that we must go to see the
Black-necked Stilt at its best. Los Banos will be the first place thought
of, although the Stilt is much better distributed throughout the State
than the Avocet, and clings to many haunts which its larger fellow has

forsaken. It does not despise limited accommodations, and will tarry in small numbers, if need be, to utilize available forage space. Thus, according to Bradford Torrey, two pairs, or possibly three, raised broods successfully on the Estero in Santa Barbara in the summer of 1912.

But on the flooded plains of the San Joaquin Valley you shall see hundreds of them—hundreds at once, if you wish. The invasion of their haunts in May is the signal for wild alarm. Every individual in the local colony sets up a harsh outcry, which consists of a single note, *pep pep pep*, or *krek, krek, krek,* incessantly repeated. The din is so great and so constant that, if obliged to work in the swamps all day, one's head fairly aches with the clamor before the day's end.

The importance of those oft-mentioned members, the stilts of the Stilt, is again emphasized by the appearance of the young bird. While a newly-hatched chick exhibits the familiar pattern of black and tawny which is common to the entire Laro-Limicoline group, its feet and legs have already undergone an extraordinary development. In fact, to the excited fancy the chick appears to be all feet. The infant can make shift to shuffle away from the nest and into cover within the hour, if need be, but he cannot negotiate his stilts until several hours have elapsed after hatching; and he feels decidedly pale and tottery, like a young colt, until the day after.

As with the Avocet, the nest of the Stilt may be very simple or very elaborate. Many eggs are laid in mere hollows scratched in the dry earth, with a few twigs or bits of cow-dung to mark the site. Others occupy a substantial platform of dried grasses or felted water-plants. It is when the water rises that the birds rise to the occasion, and get busy with nest-building. Sedges, sticks, water-plants with clinging soil, anything movable, is seized and forced under the threatened eggs. Indeed, so apprehensive is the bird of the growing necessity, that as often as she leaves the nest she will seize loose material and fling it over her shoulder for future use. The eggs themselves, protectively colored in bister and black, are mauled about and soiled in the mud; but the day is saved. I have seen a Stilt, painfully conscious no doubt, squatted on a truncated cone of vegetation eight inches in height and as broad across the top—a veritable Noah's ark of safety.

Long-billed Dowitcher

Limnodromus griseus scolopaceus

THE DOWITCHER IS A SORT OF UNSOPHISTICATED country cousin of the Wilson's Snipe. No doubt his flesh is just as good to eat, also, but his manners are so unwary that his pursuit has, fortunately, never been rated good sport. Dowitchers, indeed, are such friendly, sociable chaps that I, for one, hope their names will never be removed from the protected list. In lieu of a shocking record of slaughter, I respectfully submit herewith a rather liberal gallery of portraits, record shots some of them, which in every instance left the birds unharmed and fully reassured.

Viewed simply as sport, the author can recommend the photographic pursuit of the shore-birds as among the most thrilling of human pastimes. Given a "reflecting" camera and a lofty disregard for personal appearance, one may have no end of fun—unforeseen difficulties, breathless suspense, sudden disappointments, increasing facility of approach, stupendous moments of opportunity, brilliant achievements—these are on the daily program of the bird photographer. And the trophies secured! They cause no one a pang, not even the bird; and are they not a joy forever?

My most regal hours with the shore-birds have been spent on the upper reaches of the tidal lagoons at Sandyland, near Santa Barbara. If the tide is out, the flats are fairly a-crawl and a-clatter with shore-birds of six or seven varieties—Western Sandpipers, Least Sandpipers, Baird's perhaps, Semipalmated Plovers, Killdeers (worse luck!), Wilson's Phalaropes, a Willet maybe, and most certainly a scattering company of Long-billed Dowitchers. To approach these birds in the open one must move always with extreme deliberation and get as low upon the horizon as possible. I go to it barefoot and hump over the camera until I look like some amiable tortoise. Plowing along knee-deep in muck in such fashion involves some little dexterity, and it is very tiring. The exertion is not unlike that required by a slack-wire performer, for the foot penetrates the black depths in such irregular and unpredictable fashion, that one must constantly strain to maintain a reasonable balance. Now and then one encounters a soft seam, the filling of an ancient mud-crack, and goes down so irresistibly that dignity is quite forgotten, and the outraged birds flee as from a scare-crow with suddenly brandished arms. Quietness, too, is *de rigueur*, and the author quite prides himself, now, upon being able to withdraw a foot from the depths, all silently, instead of with a sound like elephantine osculation.

Meanwhile, the sights visible on the plates are all of "Rewards and Fairies." Tiny "Peeps" are pattering over the glistening surface of the mud and gladdening the ear with Puckish chatterings. Their little bodies and roguish glances, displayed at minimum range, challenge another shot, even though the cabinets at home be already groaning with Peep negatives. Killdeers in the offing are shouting their imprecations and warnings, for nothing so delights the Killdeer's heart as to stampede the small fry in the face of pretended danger, and so be looked up to as a leader and a savior. But among those who wait and heed him not, the gentle Dowitcher is preeminent. He is very much occupied just now in jabbing holes in the soft muck. I had the curiosity one day to count the number of jabs made per minute: one bird delivered seventy-five, and another a hundred. This count included the minor thrusting motions made in each hole, as well as new prospects started. But the minute, as reckoned, was elapsed time, and included, besides the hundred thrusts, all moments spent in devouring prey and in pausing to take new bearings. Another bird drilled thirty new holes each minute.

When more closely pressed, the Dowitcher pauses and gravely considers, with motionless beak. He remarks, *Quit up* to a fellow, and scuttles away a foot or so, pausing again, or resuming busily. If driven to flight, the Dowitchers close ranks instantly and move off in unison like sandpipers, now wheeling sharply and flashing white underparts, now tacking so that their brown backs are scarcely visible against the dun wastes of salicornia. While never a noisy bird, there are always a few in a flock to make mellow comment or protest, *clip r teeoo* or *cleeu koo, koo*, unexpectedly Tattler-like.

LEAST SANDPIPER
Pisobia minutilla

LITTLE CHILDREN OF THE MARSHES! Dainty, lisping, pattering pipers! Confiding fairies, heritors of an elder world, left stranded on the roaring shores of time! How may we, whose eyes are inflamed with covetous passion, whose ears are deafened with the sound of our own instruments of destruction, and whose hands are red with blood, how may we face your gentle innocence? And how may we endure the light of confidence in your mild eyes? God made you to rebuke our follies, and God has kept you tender and trustful in order that we may mend our ways.

In sober truth, a man does well to approach a company of these tiny pipers on bended knees. He cannot deserve such good fortune as to be taken into full fellowship, but by a proper show of humility he may at least be permitted to see them in their innocence, dainty and unconscious; and he may guess for himself what influences have wrought to preserve so exquisite a thing in a world that reels with shock and countershock of human strife. Down upon your knees, then, or down on hands and knees to try if they will have you. You will suffer first, besides certain physical discomforts of untried muscles, pangs of conscience, that your fellows, or yourself, perhaps, have ever betrayed these innocents. For the uneasy shiftings and incipient retreats which you see are manifestly no part of *minutilline* nature, but only an aftergrowth wrought by centuries of gunfire. Then, mayhap, the Killdeer, remembrancer of our ancient sins, though evil-minded himself, will rehearse the danger and urge the little waifs to flight. But they, confiding souls, though swept off their feet by a sudden onslaught of evil counsel, will return presently to the same spot, forgiving, or else loth to believe so monstrous an accusation. A momentary pause, and then a babel of tiny sounds ensues. Life in all its varied functions breaks out afresh. Toilets are made with many flashing strokes of that factotum tool, the bill; wings are stretched, and their filmy draperies are rearranged to a fairy's taste. If you have been discreet, you are either forgotten by now, or else accepted as a part of life's gracious horizon. If it is mealtime, you shall see a thousand rapier thrusts into the sand for "fleas" or tiny crustaceans, which are swallowed at a gulp. Or you shall see bright eyes, which spy tid-bits and unguessable delicacies in the shallow water of a brackish pool or on its oozy bottom; and the peeps will wade about belly-deep, thrusting their heads under water as fearlessly as ducks. Or if it is the siesta, most privileged of hours, you shall see little beaks thrust under wing, and slumber at a rod's remove as sweet and perfect as though conducted under the shimmering canopy of an Arctic sky.

According to those who have made a close study of this species, as in the Canadian and sub-Arctic regions, it is not easily possible to exaggerate the confiding nature nor the winsome grace of the Least Sandpiper at home. The female who, for a season at least, has sole care of the nest, will patter about the very feet of the intruder, or else return to the nest at any cost, even under the threat of an overarching hand. On such occasions, also, she indulges in a song, remarkable not alone for its pathos, but for its variety and musical quality as well. This song is heard at its best in mid-air, and the ecstasy of the song-passion sometimes takes the performer out of sight. But what is this? She has pleaded, she has confided, she has even offered her body with its little spoonful of meat as a ransom for her little ones. Is it not enough? Then she will sing you a song, full-hearted, exultant, sacrificial; she will win you from the flesh with its paltry lusts, and summon to a like high-minded sacrifice—to *faith*, in fine. O joy of trust! O victory of sacrifice! O anthem fitly echoed in the human heart!

WESTERN SANDPIPER
Ereunetes mauri

"SAND PEEPS ARE ALMOST TOO WELL KNOWN to require comment—and as a consequence, comments upon the Western Sandpiper are few, and our knowledge of the species is a little hazy and lacking in detail. Yet our mud-flats and sandy shores are visited in fall and spring by myriads of these confiding voyageurs. While they are most abundant in late April or early May, and again in August and September, we yet have a little sprinkling of them throughout the year, so that ignorance of them is without excuse.

No better opportunity is afforded to study and speculate upon the mystery of flock movement than in the case of these gentle peeps. In flock flight they weave and twist about, now flashing in the sunlight, now darkening to invisibility, charge and recharge, feint and flee, all as a single bird. And because they keep up a dainty chattering, like a fairy rattle-box, one cannot decide whose voice in the babel has authority. Upon alighting, they first pause in absolute silence, absurd little Platos, done in plaster and sown broadcast over the sandscape. This, that they may note whether their coming may have provoked hostile notice. Reassured upon this point, they become animated, and begin to patter and pick and probe and peep, as though there were nothing else in life. There is something so detached about their happy chatter, that the bird-man feels like an uninvited cow whose hulking presence the banqueting fairies are politely minded to ignore. The flock moves slowly forward and successive platoons rising from the devastated rear pass over their fellows to take turns at the front. All is as merry as wedding bells, and the bird-man with his camera is trembling with excitement. But suddenly one of the little soldiers is smitten with a fear-thought. Like an electric flash it is communicated to all his comrades. Instantly, in the dreadful hush which follows, the flock takes wing as one bird, and they pass out of hearing, arguing excitedly. Ten to one, after they have swept the horizon two or three times, the panicky member is outvoted, and the peeps troop back confidingly to resume the pastures which they have just deserted.

At high tide the little fellows retire to the edges of the flats, where they either prepare elaborate toilets or else engage in one-legged slumbers. If the tide is too insistent, they do not mind standing in an inch or so of water. But it is delightfully absurd to see them economizing strength by the use of only one leg. Perhaps they want to keep one foot dry, for I have seen them hop about in a lazy tide pool, clearing the surface of the water at every jump, but never disclosing the missing member in the process. Or perhaps one of them had started a boyish dare, with a baby limpet as a prize to the one that held out longest. Anyhow, I think they all won, for as nearly as the eye could judge the birds hopped to wing without the assistance of the elevated foot, when startled from this position.

These little peeps, by the way, swim as gracefully as phalaropes when they are put to it. But they swim, apparently, only when tempted beyond their depth in pursuit of some escaping *edenda,* or when surprised by the inequality of the bottom.

It is a source of perennial interest to see how close one can get to a company of Western Sandpipers. If one has patience to lie motionless beside some salty plash, the birds will sometimes venture within touching distance. Nothing, to my mind, could exceed the flattery implied by the near approach of these trustful creatures. If the compliment were really deserved, the cunning little souls would undoubtedly respond to the most familiar advances short of actual handling. Slaughter in the name of science may be justifiable, though there be those of us who have passed up the solution of many nice problems here; but slaughter of these innocents in the name of sport is mere Philistinism. The Italian method of hunting is to shoot everything in sight. As a result, sunny Italy is a birdless desert in summer, and a nightmare during migrations.

Fortunately, the camera is superseding the gun. Pressing the button is not only more humane than shooting; it is more fun. Measured by its devices, its strategies, its hopes and fears, its tantalizing failures and its crowning triumphs—in other words, by its thrills—bird photography is ten times better sport than gunnery. Its trophies, moreover, are permanent and satisfying. In place of an emptied plate and an endless regret, the camerist retains a record which delights the eye and ministers to the spirit unceasingly.

But do not envy the bird photographer overmuch. He, too, has paid a price. If he has seemed to fellowship with the birds, it was only that he might get their images; and in getting these he has not seldom missed the birds themselves. The technique of photography, even snap-shottery, is quite exacting. One cannot both study and photograph birds at the same time. The camerist may score a success, and come away after an exciting brush with a rare species, flushed with triumph, yet knowing little of the bird's characteristic behavior and psychology. It is for your sake that he has wrought, and sacrificed mayhap his very opportunity to acquire that intimate knowledge of character which only the notebook may record. It is thus, I fear, with the Western Sandpiper. He is as common as mud, and as fascinating as a kitten; but, alas, he is photographically irresistible. We have forty-five negatives of the Western Sandpiper—and a flat notebook.

Black-bellied Plover
Squatarola squatorola

IN THE APPRECIATION OF NATURE everything depends upon the point of view. Thus, our attitude toward the Black-bellied Plover may be that of the artist, the sportsman, the farmer, the economist, or the scientist. It may be each of these in turn, or all together, or it may be something better still. It may be the friendly, sympathetic, penetrative attitude of the bird-lover. The scientist acquires facts; the sportsman, experience (of a sort); the artist, impressions, or visions of beauty; the economist mediates between them all and passes sentence of life or death; but only your bird-lover *lives* his birds. He it is who enters by an effort of sympathy into all the aspects of nature, and pronounces them good. He knows.

The artist, I submit, ought to have the first chance to pass judgment on the value of our plovers. Be the waters of Santa Barbara channel never so blue, as on this September day, the shore golden, and the air vibrating with conscious purity after two thousand leagues of matchless ablution, there yet lacks something in the vision unless a flock of Beetle-heads, splendid, tumultuous, is hurrying across the sky.

The strand, glistening though it be with each fresh silvering of the refluent wave, is a barren mockery unless it may reflect the beauty of some shore-bird. And what more haughty image may it give back than this plover in his nuptial panoply of black? Or what more modest and demure than the dove-like "grays" of autumn? If it were to paint a portrait in the narrowest sense, the painter could hardly do better than depict that large, gracious eye, that "beetling," capable brow, or that expression, half naive, half stern, and altogether powerful, which greets the fortunate student on an unexploited shore.

But the sportsman has long claimed this bird for his own. Its numbers mark it for the pot, while its increasing wariness invites genteel destruction. Sapid its meat unquestionably is, tender, and well-conditioned in the early fall. Its northern residence has assured the bird a heavy blanket of fat, a traveler's larder, which supplies the needful caloric consumed by the powerful pectoral muscles until the bird is safe within the tropics. These plovers respond to decoys, and may be "tolled" in by the easily imitated whistle. It is, however, one of the wariest of birds to eye, under persecution; and from the circumstance of its migrating chiefly along the sea-coast, where it is able to put out in case of danger, it has measurably escaped the doom which has overwhelmed many of our shore-birds.

The economist finds nothing to condemn in the habits of the Beetlehead, and something to commend in that it feasts heavily upon grasshoppers as often as it visits the uplands. It is with us, however, chiefly a beach bird and, according to Knight, its food "consists of small mollusks, worms, small crustaceans, brittle-stars, small holothuria, and similar material left by the ebbing tide, varied by more or less insects and larva picked up in the marshes at high tide." I have myself seen them seize pieces of kelp stranded upon the beach and thrash them about, apparently for the purpose of dislodging clinging mollusks. At other times they will feed furtively, by little snatches and quick recoveries, as they retreat along the beach.

The scientist knows that *Squatarola squatarola* is nearly cosmopolitan in its range, although it breeds only in the Arctic zone; that it is closely related to plovers of the *Charadrius* group, from which it is separated only by the trifling circumstance of having a tiny hind toe; but he does not know, apparently, any good reason why it should ever have been called the Helvetian or Swiss Plover, since it neither breeds nor winters in that tiny republic of glaciers.

Many other things the scientist is ready to offer, but we are anxious to reach the accepted domain of the bird-lover, and to declare that the bird belongs to us and to us alone, by right of sympathy. Only by the give and take of friendly pursuit, or by quiet observation, may one come to feel really acquainted with any bird. The Black-bellies are very wary with us upon arrival from the north, during the last week of August or early in September. A hat-brim thrust over the edge of the sea-cliff will send the flock scurrying seaward. They are somewhat more tolerant of an unconcealed approach along the beach, merely taking the precaution to quit the upper beach and to draw together. At times they will gather at the water's edge and endure some buffeting by the waves before taking flight. On wave-swept ledges I have seen them rise before the wave and settle again, after the fashion of Turnstones, quite determined to hold their own.

Purposeful pursuit makes the birds suspicious, and I have spent a half day with the camera without getting nearer than thirty yards of them; while my boys, engaged meanwhile in excavating a sand fort, declared the birds came within ten feet of them. I got even with this bunch of birds, though. Noting a considerable flock resting at a distance along the lower sands, I stripped off and went into the ocean, paralleling the shore until opposite the plovers, and then letting the waves wash me in like a stranded seal pup, until I lay within twenty feet of the nearest birds. I was near enough to catch the gentle curiosity and apprehension in their eyes. Some actually drew nearer to this plaything of the billows; but most of them held back haughtily, as though divining a disguise. There were other species of shore-birds in the flock, and it was the Snowy Plover who, as host and rightful guardian of the beach, felt the most responsibility, and pressed close to riddle my Neptunian sham. Never a merman so blushed before a court of kelp maidens—blushed and gloated.

KILLDEER

Oxyechus vociferous vociferus

OXYECHUS VOCIFERUS VOCIFERUS EARSPLITTERUS ANANIAS! The books concede only the first three epithets: we add the others upon our own authority. *Oxyechus* is the noisemaker extraordinary, the professional scold, the yap yap artist, the irrepressible canine of the bird world. In season and out of season her (or his) shrill cries arouse the countryside to attention, and in nine cases out of ten the object of her vociferous spite is a human being. *Vociferus* is the arch accuser of the human race, and as sure as a mere man sets foot upon a portion of the domain which she counts her own, every ingenuity of alarm is brought to bear upon him, every passion and prejudice of the wild things is appealed to, and the miserable son of Adam is denounced as a wrecker of homes, an ogre and an outcast. This is unfortunate, whether one's intentions happen to be honest or not. Nobody enjoys being barked at. But be you Beauty's self, or a burglar, it is easier to placate a barking cur than it is to silence the clamorous guardian of the meadows, this self-constituted tutelary of all lesser fowls.

The case is bad enough when the bird has real interests at stake. If you are actually near the nest there is some excuse for alarm, and the female does not fail to try every ruse in the endeavor to lure you away from the dangerous spot. First she rolls and flounders away across the ground, screaming with agony, as though she had been stepped on.

But if you are simple enough to follow, the bird gradually recovers, and is soon able to patter along ahead of you with tolerable celerity. The male, too, is no indifferent spectator. He comes as near as he dares, and shrieks, *"Dear, dear, dear, dear, dear,"* until the wonder is that he does not burst a blood vessel or split his vocal cords. Interested neighbors add their frenzy to the din, until in desperation you are almost ready to believe yourself the frightful villain they are all accusing you of being. If you are willing to quit the place, a bevy of fathers will pilot you out of bounds. One will patter ahead of you with breast pushed forward and legs incredibly nimble, only to pull up presently with a jerk and a compensatory bob to ask if you are following. The others describe a great half-circle about you with graceful wing but unceasing stridor, and take their places in the van. The birds believe themselves extremely clever as they lead you off by alternate flights and sprints, and you may hear them indulge from time to time in a low rapid titter, *teeeee-t*, which you may be sure is quite at your expense. All this racket is bad enough at best, and one may be really sorry to have intruded, at first, but when the whole operation is gone through with again the next time you happen that way, and when you know that the young are long since flying, all this fuss and outcry is distinctly annoying. One feels as if the Killdeer had contracted the habit of yellow journalism and couldn't let go.

As a matter of fact he has. He has become obsessed with a passion for denunciation. The excitements of the nesting season have spoiled him. He has racket and objurgation upon the brain, and long after his own chicks have joined the howling chorus, the Killdeer warns and hectors and incites sedition generally throughout the rest of the bird world. Or, in scientific parlance, the normal reactions of the breeding cycle persist, and are transferred to a broader field. Sportsmen hate the Killdeer and shoot him on sight as a marplot and general nuisance. Stalking game is impossible with such an alarmist on the job. Nor is the case any better with the bird photographer, that most innocuous of mortals. My final and overwhelming lesson came when, on October 11th, 1913, I had sighted on the grounds of the Empire Gun Club a small company of the rare Pectoral Sandpipers *(Pisobia maculata)*. It was the opportunity of a lifetime hereabouts, and left to themselves the birds would have proved amenable to those methods of gradual approach and disarming of anxiety which are usually so successful with the shore-birds. But in this instance an officious Killdeer set himself the task of thwarting all my plans. Not content with effecting his own escape, noisy enough in all conscience, the Killdeer turned back to warn his neighbors, and if a single one of the Pectorals did not dutifully heed the first alarm, the Killdeer returned forthwith and dived menacingly at the delinquent's head. He did this not once or twice, but persistently, insomuch that the "Kriekers" became wilder and wilder, and my last hour's effort with them was more fruitless than the first. And such conduct on the Killdeer's part is perfectly habitual. Speaking soberly, I believe the shore-bird portraits in *The Birds of California* might have been twice as numerous and much more excellent, if it had not been for the pharisaical machinations of the Killdeer. Is it any wonder, then, that the author is "sore"?

The Killdeer favors open situations wherein convenient access to water offers, be they pastures, meadows, fallow fields, virgin prairies, lake beaches, or mud bars. Being a plover and not a snipe, the Killdeer requires a firm footing. Though they haunt the edges of pools and wade belly-deep in water, on occasion, they neither dabble nor probe, but only snatch and glean—and "holler." The Killdeer nests on the ground in the most exposed situations, preferably, but not invariably, those devoid of vegetation. The four eggs are always placed with the little ends inward, and are so closely crowded together into the deep hollow that the major axes incline as much as 45 or 50 degrees, and the larger apices measure sometimes only an inch and a half from egg to egg; this, of course, that the parent bird may have the maximum of covering power over the relatively enormous eggs.

The nest, at times, consists of little more than the supporting earth or gravel; but oftener the nesting hollow is carefully lined with weed-stems, bits of bark, chips, or fragments of cow-dung. On one occasion I found a Killdeer proudly ensconced in the midst of a large dried "cow-flop" whose center had been carefully chiseled away for the reception of her eggs.

SNOWY PLOVER

Charadrius nivosus nivosus

THE SNOWY PLOVER IS PART AND PARCEL of the sand. His clothes assimilate its hue so perfectly that a crouching bird may be invisible from shore; and if a moving bird is glimpsed as he patters from the shelter of a footprint, one will hardly guess, at first, that a score of his fellows are also moving. Nor is a sitting bird's breast any such landmark as one might suppose, for the white breast might be a clam-shell, one of a thousand, and the interrupted black bar of the chest—what is that but a broken piece of charcoal tossed up by the tide? Anyhow, the dainty birds trust to their protective coloration quite implicitly, and it is not till you are approaching the edge of a given area and the birds begin to break from cover to run trippingly down the steep tide slope, or to flit with little cries of dismay, that you suspect the havoc of inconvenience you have wrought.

Snowy Plovers are resident upon our southern beaches. They are not distributed along over the entire stretch of shoreline, but occur only in most favored situations, usually those which are backed by sand dunes, or which give easy access to a hinterland containing brackish lagoons or a quiet-flowing river. In such places, they assemble in colonies numbering from half a dozen to a score of pairs, and if the annual crop of babies is a good one, one may see a hundred birds in August on a given stretch of beach. The Plovers show no jealousy of other birds, and mingle on occasion with such visitors as Sanderlings, Semipalmated Plovers, and Killdeers, or with the lesser sandpipers.

Some of their food is obtained at the water's edge or on the wet sand, and some is taken on the saline flats which border the lagoons; but more of it is found along the dry sand levels which lie above the ordinary mark of the tide. The Snowies scatter widely in pursuit of food, and spend much time apart, with a decent observance of "sea-room." When disturbed, however, as by a heedless stroller of the upper beach, the birds will muster rapidly at the water's edge, and when all are accounted for will make off in a compact flock, which is for the moment indistinguishable from a bunch of peeps.

For a nest our sand plover requires only the slight depression which may be formed by the pressure of her own breast. The choice of a location is, however, a matter of some solicitude. Several hollows may be formed of which only one is eventually occupied. For one thing, the bird requires a slight elevation—three or four inches will do—so that she may command an unobstructed view of approaching danger. The bird takes good care not to be caught at home, quitting her charge sometimes at a hundred yards' remove; and it is no easy trick to find the eggs, unaided. If incubation is advanced, or discovery indubitable, the anxious mother may return to practice decoy ruses, trailing a broken wing, grovelling, and the rest. The male meanwhile is describing anxious circles in the offing; or else, by way of distraction, he patters forward until he is sure that he is commanding attention, then stops abruptly, bridling the head, and by repeated bobs challenges your right to intrude. It is rather good sport, too, once a location is made, to return by stealth and watch the female making that long-range sneak from her eggs. Her attitude is eloquent of secrecy. She hugs the sand as closely as is consistent with lightning speed. The tell-tale marks of head and chest are averted, so that only the sand-colored back may be presented to an eye presumably undiscriminating. Pauses are made now and then to note the bearing of the stranger, but the glance is covert and the sandy flight is hastily resumed.

In still weather the vicinage of the nest is enveloped in a network of intersecting tracks; for the bird never leaves or approaches the eggs save on foot, and the male comforts his mate by many solicitous trippings to and fro. These tell-tale footprints sometimes aid the curious investigator; and it is not inconceivable that the birds themselves require some guidance in these wastes of shifting sands, for they sometimes select a site which is marked by some feature of minor prominence—a stranded snail-shell, a whitened bit of driftwood, or even, as in the case of one in the M.C.O. collections, an encircling piece of dried kelp. The nesting hollow, moreover, is often carefully lined with broken bits of shell, a mosaic in white which serves to throw the eggs into relief. The eggs, unrelieved, are protectively colored to the point of invisibility; and those very traceries and hieroglyphics of black which might serve to distinguish them from sand, make them resemble the weather-stained kelp balls, which outnumber them upon the beach a thousand to one. Indeed, the writer has not yet recovered from the self-satisfaction attending the discovery of a waif plover's egg in a drifted bed of these curiously simulant objects.

Hatching day is a day of manifold anxieties in ploverdom. The old nest, which may have attracted unwelcome attention by now, is forsaken as soon as possible. One by one the babies are spirited away in different directions, and when they are left under some sort of cover they are sternly enjoined not to move a muscle—no, not so much as an eyelid. No one but a fiend would want to harm such cunning bits of mortality, mere fluffs of sand-colored down, spotted and streaked with black, after the approved model of a weathered kelp-ball. But a dog is just such a fiend, and the life of the chick often depends upon its willingness to stay put while its parents are luring the frenzied brute to a fruitless chase. Although I have seen infants crouching momentarily on the open sand, the presence of cover, real or supposed, appears essential to the maintenance of the freezing posture. Otherwise, even under close surveillance, the baby will presently shift at any risk. On a blowy day at Monterey we once startled a baby Snowy which scampered away under the lash of the driving sand. It was looking only for cover, and crouched under the first apology which offered, a bare stick not an inch in diameter which stuck up out of the sand. *Here with eyes wide open* the bantling was presently half buried. Most pitiful of all was the accretion of sand which, moistened by the tears, gathered over the exposed eyes and sealed them fast. Of course we made haste with the camera and did what we could for the infant's comfort before hurrying away.

Black Oyster-catcher

Haematopus bachmani

Prosy hedgerows and quiet duck ponds for such as like them; but roaring reefs and a pounding sea for the Black Oyster-catcher! And what more romantic spot to charm the eye and fire the imagination than a bird rock in the blue Pacific! The fog, it may be, shrouded the entire scene at daybreak, but as we launch out from the surf at nine o'clock, it is clearing away, and only stray wisps of mist cling about the battlements of the promised isle, a league offshore. As we approach, uneasy gulls and inquiring puffins pass near us overhead, the former drifting up as though casually, but quavering suspiciously; the latter including us upon the rim of great circles several times repeated, and checking their flight each time sufficiently to survey us with grave and careful curiosity. The cormorants begin to shift uneasily upon their nests, while disengaged members of their company join the increasing ranks of scouts. Marauders are not so little known that the approach of mysterious strangers can be regarded calmly.

But the official greeting of the motley host is extended by the Black Oyster-catcher, the self-constituted guardian of all sea-girt rocks. He has had his eye upon us from the moment of launching, and when we are within a hundred yards, mindful of his brooding mate or the secreted babies, he flies straight out to meet us and quavers a boisterous welcome, a welcome wherein anxiety is veiled by effusiveness. His effusiveness, moreover, is not unmingled with sarcasm, as who should say, "Good morning, gentlemen, good morning. Ah, you are officers of the law, I perceive, and armed with a search warrant. Quite proper, quite proper! Help yourselves, gentlemen. If I can be of any assistance to your worthy cause, command me."

And so the garrulous old marshal goes back shouting and chuckling. Once out of sight behind the rock, he repeats hurried instructions to his children to remain hidden in their crevices; then, ever mindful of appearances, he hurries forward again, beaming with virtuous importance, and vociferating shrilly, "No, gentlemen, there is nothing the matter. I have been clear around the island and there isn't a thief in sight. But help yourselves, gentlemen. Oh, yes, help yourselves. Doubtless you are experts."

Anon, birdlums! We are very much occupied just now with the problem of landing. Our island is nearly surrounded by rocky shoulders which are covered only at highest tide, and upon one of these, on the lee side, we hope to disembark. Albeit there is little breeze, there is a heavy swell running, and the boatman sculls cautiously as we draw near. Just as we prepare to leap ashore with the cameras we are swiftly upborne by a quartering sea. "Look out!" the oarsman cries sharply, and we crouch in terror as the dory seems about to be dashed in pieces upon the flooded reef. But the boat just clears in the recoil and we go down, down, while a swift pageant of mussels, barnacles, sea-urchins, and bright-hued anemones shoots past us, sputtering and choking at the sudden exposure to air. When we do effect a landing, we must scuttle for safety before the next wave reaches, with a dull chug of satisfaction, our recent landing place.

The lower levels of the bird-rock are sacred to the Oyster-catchers, and these engage our attention at once. Very diverting creatures they are at any time, but never more so than at close quarters. As large as domestic fowls, with sooty black plumage, they are provided with stout feet and legs of a pale flesh-color, and a strong chisel-shaped bill of a bright vermilion hue. The yellow eyes are surrounded by rings of carmine, which impart a droll appearance to these wags in feathers; and in the midst of most earnest floods of bombast, they cannot forbear tipping you sly winks, like auctioneers.

Now and then one will alight quite near and stand for a moment looking very big and bold. Then he will draw his head in and settle his body lower on the legs and sneak off, glancing furtively over his shoulder to see if his movements are being shadowed. Without question he is trying to develop the kind and degree of our interest. If the female was sitting upon eggs she slipped away too soon to be caught at home, and she spends the entire time of our stay arranging elaborate pantomines for our misguidance. Now she bends with quivering wing and dips her head up and down, as though inviting attention to her charming nestlings. "Aren't they darlings?" (She means a heap of mussel shells just before her eyes). Or again she settles down upon a barnacle-covered rock and broods virtuously—on barnacles.

And if, by any accident, one does become possessed of the real secret, it is great sport to devise a stealthy return and to watch the bird steal away from the eggs, slowly, painfully, in abject humiliation, hoping against hope that she is eluding observation, until a safe distance is reached. When the game is "all off" the birds cause the rocks to resound with their strident cries, and if there are neighbors, these join forces with the immediately besieged ones until our ears ache.

Left to themselves, the birds are no Quakers, and the antics of courtship are both noisy and amusing. A certain duet, especially, consists of a series of awkward bowings and bendings, in which the neck is stretched to the utmost and arched over stiffly into a pose as grotesque as one of Cruikshank's drawings—the whole to an accompaniment of amorous clucks and wails.

The eggs of the Black Oyster-catcher, normally three in number, are oftenest placed in the hollow of a bare rock, lined with a pint or so of rock-flakes, laboriously gathered.

In default, apparently, of suitable stonechips, the bird will utilize bits of shell, rounded pebbles, or, still more exceptionally, grass. The use of pebbles serves to connect, in thought at least, the chip-lined nests with those instances, comparatively few in number, where the eggs are deposited upon unmodified beach gravel.

Needless to say, these Spartan cradles are not considerate of their contents. Dented eggs are common in the nests, and many an unhatched *Haematopus* goes rolling over the steeps. But these chosen dangers are a bagatelle in comparison with the depredations of the Raven. Little escapes his sinister eye, and an egg once marked is doomed. Ravens abound on the Santa Barbara Islands, and if it were not for them we should have, perhaps, ten times our present population of Oyster-catchers.

The name Oyster-catcher is, of course, a misnomer. Oysters are not much given to sprinting anyway, and this bird is not at all interested in their ambulatorial powers; for he does not frequent sand-beaches, mud-flats, or oyster-beds. Even when visiting the mainland shore, which is not often, the bird confines its attention to the barnacle-covered rocks and high-lying mussel-beds. Its food consists of marine worms and crustaceans of various sorts, barnacles, limpets, and especially mussels. Its stout, chisel-shaped beak enables it to force an entrance into the most refractory mussel-shell, and to sever as by a knife the strong abductor muscles, which hold the valves together. Its feet, also, are large and strong, and the toes are provided with an elaborate set of pectinations which enable the bird to maintain a footing upon the most slippery rocks. If the foothold on a sloping rock is anywise precarious, the bird retreats backward and uphill by means of these convenient calls.

Gulls and Terns

GLAUCOUS-WINGED GULL
Larus glaucescens

ONLY THE SEA-FARING MAN may boast of acquaintance with the mighty albatrosses; and only the lucky adventurer may follow the fortunes of the sea-fowl amid their sea-girt rocky homes; but there is no man so humble that he may not know something of the gull, and from this knowledge guess something of the joys of ocean life. To the city man, especially, the gull is the one visible point of contact with the Great Beyond of Nature. Pray, consider what a benevolent miracle it is that these most improvident of God's creatures, the birds, are impelled to loiter for a season about the doorstep of a great city. These thronging docks, upborne by close-set piles, and housing the wares of Occident and Ind, what are they but the very ramparts of order, the symbolical breastworks of organized human industry now millenniums old! And yet, upon a wooden pedestal hard by sits a gull, serene, sedate, unhurried, a son of the wilderness gazing upon you with level eye, and rebuking by his very blue-gray calm the pomp and madness of men. This throbbing ferry-boat grimly intent upon the business of getting its human freight from shore to shore is still our best serviceable solution of the transportation problem. The gull furnishes his own conveyance, simple, subtle, compact, yet elegant beyond the powers of art, and adequate beyond the dream of engineers. Effortless, noiseless, tireless, he views from a thousand easy angles your muddled helplessness, and mocks by a thousand airy caprices your tedious destiny as freight.

To and fro, forward and back, in and out, up, down, and around, moves the restless multitude when the hungry mood is on—a twirling kaleidoscope of action. And, while the gulls are no songsters, not the least of their charm lies in the manifold cries, in the trumpet calls and croaks, in the barks and screams, with which the birds mark the progress of their quest. And when a treasure of floating biscuits is discovered, how the screams rise to a grand medley of stridor, fierce, exultant, like the triumph of Tritons over smitten reefs!

One marvels at the boldness these harbor gulls at times display, especially when a touch of winter has made us all akin. The man who minds his own business may sometimes pass within six feet of sitting birds—pass, not pause. For let him stop but that fraction of an instant necessary to adjust a focus, and the wary birds are off, their minds poisoned by dark suspicion. When the great hunger is on, it is possible to bait the gulls to the camera in many ways; but when that aching void is filled, all direct efforts at acquaintance are futile.

The gulls nest almost anywhere, save that they have not yet been driven into trees, as is the case along the Maine coast. Sloping, grass-covered hillsides are favorite places, and the seclusion of the underbrush is not despised; but the sculptured chambers of sandstone, hollowed by the high-flung chisels of the winter's storms, constitute the ideal setting for a gull's nest. The eggs, barring mishap always three in number, are in color and markings skillful epitomes of their average surroundings. The chicks, likewise, are marked for obliteration. They have, moreover, a faculty of absolute movelessness on occasion, which those of us who are parents ardently covet for our six-year-olds.

Gull discipline can be very stern while danger lasts; but once let the parents suppose themselves unobserved, and they will lavish every attention upon their offspring. The fish-laden bird, returning from the chase, first disgorges his catch of smelt or the like upon a convenient spot; then in a wheedling voice summons the chicks from hiding. They come skipping up like kids, and fall to, while the doting parents dance attendance and utter incessant blandishments. And after the youngsters have stuffed themselves to repletion, the mother still urges, "Can't Mama's darlings eat just one more fishy?" until the beholder, recalling the ways of his own kind, is almost nauseated.

WESTERN GULL
Larus occidentalis

MUCH THAT IS GOOD AND ALL THAT IS EVIL has gathered itself up into the Western Gull. He is rather the handsomest of the blue-mantled Laridae, for the depth of color in the mantle, in sharp contrast with the snowy plumage of back and breast, gives him an appearance of sturdiness and quality which is not easily dispelled by subsequent knowledge of the black heart within. As a scavenger, the Western Gull is impeccable. Wielding the besom of hunger, he and his kind sweep the beaches clean and purge the water-front of all pollution. But a scavenger is not necessarily a good citizen. Call him a ghoul, rather, for the Western Gull is cruel of beak and bottomless of maw. Pity, with him, is a thing unknown; and when one of their own comrades dies, these feathered jackals fall upon him without compunction, a veritable *Leichnamveränderungsgebrauchsgesellschaft*. If he thus mistreats his own kind, be assured that this gull asks only two questions of any other living thing: First, "Am I hungry?" (Ans., "Yes.") Second, "Can I get away with it?" (Ans., "I'll try.")

The ocean, to be sure, offers the gull an abundance of "natural" food. Surface-ranging fish, herring, smelt, and the like are staple objects of pursuit; and the birds quarter the sea at a considerable height until some indication of a traveling school is noted. Tell-tale haste on the part of any one bird is remarked by distant comrades, and all hurry to the scene of slaughter. Excited screams publish the news still more widely, if the prospect is a good one, and a thousand birds may join the feast before the bewildered fish realize that they are furnishing both mirth and meat, and go below.

When fish are scarce the gulls resort to the beach and strip every carcass, whether of fish, flesh, or fowl, which the sea has cast up. Once, after a storm, on a northern beach, I followed a high-piled windrow of dead tom-cods for miles. The gulls were in their glory, but in spite of the fact that meat was so abundant, I noticed that each bird stuck to his job, once it was started, and was willing to contest his rights against all comers.

Next after carrion, clams are a favorite food. These are gleaned from the surface, where they have been cast by the tide; or, in rarer instances, they are dug, most actively, from their burrows in the sand. The "razor-backs" are easily crushed and gutted; but the cockles require a most ingenious expedient. According to many witnesses, a gull will carry the clam aloft and drop it on the rocks, where the shell will be smashed and the contents released. Anthony tells of instances where birds had only half learned their lessons and dropped the clams upon the sand, seemingly much mystified that the pronunciation of the sacred formula, "Open sesame," had failed to effect the desired result.

It is at the breeding season, however, that the Western Gull accomplishes real mischief. While he effects a passable truce with his own kind at that season, it is that he may the better combine with his fellows and terrorize all other breeding sea-birds. As an egg-thief and as a kidnapper of infants the Western Gull is simply incorrigible. The only chance which the lesser fowl, petrels and auklets, have of escaping the rapacious beak is to burrow under ground or to file into crevices.

A pleasanter aspect of gull life is afforded by the sight of the birds a-wing. In a wind, especially, one may forget his grudge and lose himself in admiration of the consummate skill and grace with which the birds address themselves to the tasks of breasting the wind or coasting down the gale. Here is the original school of aviation—a forty-knot breeze blowing over "Maintop," the western eminence of the southeast

Farallon. Here, if ever, one will see bizarre postures and incipient shipwreck in the air. The highest speeds are made against the wind, and I am sure that the Baird's Cormorant can do 120 miles an hour in the teeth of a 45-mile norther. But the Western Gull enjoys the sport most of all. He passes and repasses the crest of the hill just for the fun of the thing. Now he lets the wind blow him up like a lost paper napkin, and now he cleaves it with the nicety of a descending razor. The most striking thing about these wind postures is the position of the feet. These are sometimes thrown violently forward, or else maintained in a perpendicular position to check speed or to cover flaws in the wind. Viewed from any angle, a gull or a shag with feet in full play cuts an odd figure. Regarding the situation in a cold, dispassionate light, as one may, seated on the side of a cliff, *it is not an easy thing to fly*. The birds can have the job for all o' me.

California Gull
Larus californicus

GULLS FILL A LARGE PLACE not alone in the "economy of nature" but in the affections and economics of men. Latterly the envy and despair of the automotive engineer, the way of a gull both afoot and aloft has always intrigued the admiration of human kind. Fishermen for a thousand centuries have alternately wrangled and fraternized with them, now brandishing an oar in impotent rage, and now flinging a largess of fish in wondering obedience to some higher law of pity. The picnicking tourist, lolling on a southern beach, marks the passing legions of the air with squinting eyes, or else bestirs himself to offer refreshment, a neglected sandwich or a surplus bun. The artist and the poet, too, chief of nature's appraisers, mark these fluent notes of white-and-flesh-and-gray and smear them upon canvas, or weave them into distiches, according to their kind. And last of all, plain mortals, who know not exactly why they are glad at the seashore, and care not so they are so, these borrow also of the gull the fuel of those unquestioned fires of average content. And though we may appraise the blueness of waters and the brightness of skies and the genial warmth of sands, it is, after all, the gulls and their kind who give the crowning touch of life to any littoral scene.

The Pacific shores in winter are highly favored by an abundant and a would-be friendly host of northern pilgrims, among them gulls of eight or nine varieties. And of these the California Gull is most closely attached to the ferry-boats of the Bay Cities and to the coastwise steamers which ply from Crescent City to San Diego. These gulls play pilot, hovering angel, and passenger, by turns; and often, for the sheer humor of the thing, trail doggedly behind, as though flying, forsooth, were hard work.

If you would cultivate gull society, fee the galley for a loaf of bread and smuggle it up surreptitiously to the hurricane deck, well aft. Now for some fun! The hungry horde weaves to and fro, forward and back, up and down and around, mewing expectantly like a litter of kittens at milking time. Hold up a piece of bread and the pace becomes furious. "Please! please! please!" they cry, until their mandibles fairly quiver with eagerness. But none snatches it from your hand; they are too well disciplined in the treacherous ways of men for that. When at last the bit is flung—instant silence. Every gray bolt is launched at the falling bread and the water where it must pause. Crash! And the clamor bursts out afresh, for the luckless many must voice their disappointment while the lucky one gulps down the prize and hurries back for more.

Gulls do not ordinarily dive, for they are light as corks. They snatch their food rather from the surface of the water. If there is plenty, as when the cook dumps the accumulated leavings from the captain's table, the gulls settle gracefully upon the water and throw the morsels down by rapidly succeeding jerks of the head.

The more experienced birds learn to catch bread on the wing, and the disclosure of such ability guarantees its owner a full meal. It is no small trick to catch a bit of flying bread in the teeth of the wind, for it is sometimes a nice fraction of a second between the bestowing hand and the bird's beak.

On the voyage, feet are useful only as the birds take turns at the masthead, pausing for a moment with wings gracefully outstretched until they have mastered the motion of the boat. These stations on mast and flagstaff are jealously coveted, and the gull that would hold one must be vigilant in defense, or at least ready to bluff the aspirant with a mighty scowl. Otherwise a quick dab from behind will upset the dignified Burgomaster, balance, dignity, and all. But who may comprehend by epithet or episode the unflagging charm of the white-winged fleet— now in the van leading away with brave impudence, now registering a retreat with far-flung shadows on the smoke-stack, now trailing laboriously in the wake, like faithful hounds in leash. What humility of supplication! What perfect independence! What condescension of grace! What boundless exultation of wings, wings, *wings!* Oh, who would not give hands and feet for wings! Is it any wonder that the lure of the air has caught us, and that we are still offering up the lives of our best and bravest upon the altar of progressive "achievement"?

Caspian Tern
Hydroprogne caspia

THE CASPIAN TERN IS COSMOPOLITAN; and Cosmopolitan Tern would perhaps have been a better name for it. A cosmopolitan species is necessarily a rigid, non-plastic species. It has arrived. Its habits are established. If it is no longer characterized by aggressiveness, it has at least nothing to fear. It has made its peace with varied conditions and has achieved a static goal.

It is impossible, for a sensitive person at least, to escape a sort of awe in the presence of one of these world travelers. He has seen so many skies, and weathered so many storms, and tasted so many viands, and thought so many thoughts. He is, as a consequence, as alert as he is placid, as independent as he is tolerant, and above all things, self-reliant and capable. This may sound like fanciful stuff for appreciation of a bird, but the root of it is there in the dynamic of the species, even if the individual escapes recognition.

In carriage the Caspian Tern does not differ especially from its fellow *Sternae*. It frequents lakes, ponds, water-courses, and brackish lagoons during the migrations, or else parallels the sea-coast in its major flights. It quarters the waters with down-turned beak, like any other tern, and it foregathers with its larine fellows on the sunny beaches, or at the mouths of estuaries. Surface fishes form its almost exclusive diet, these and a sample or two, during the breeding season, of baby terns of the lesser sorts.

Common Tern

Sterna hirundo

WHAT A PIECE OF WORK IS A TERN! How gentle in instinct! How untrammeled in discursion! In form and moving how elegant and admirable! In action how like the swallow! In innocence how like the dove! The beauty of the air! The paragon of sea-birds!

Terns are the animating spirits of summer seas. Not bluff and sturdy like the gulls, they have little place in winter's storm, but when the sun has re-established his dominion and only Zephyr pricks the caracoling waves, then the blue-gray daintiness of the Tern is as necessary to the scene as are the criss-cross mirrors of the amethystine sea. We hail with delight the appearance in the offing of a busy, happy company of the white-winged birds, weaving in the air by their incessant plyings a close-meshed fisher-net, wherein many a luckless minnow is entangled. Soon a lone straggler from out the company drifts shoreward, parting the air with graceful wing, now pausing critically over a suspected fish, like some pensive mosquito with his beak down-turned; now dropping with a splash beneath the wave, or making a nimble catch at the surface without wetting his plumage. Ever and anon the muffled undertone of the waves is pierced by a weird and half-petulant cry, *te-er te-erve,* childish, plaintive, yet somehow thrilling and exultant. And as the bird passes to rejoin his companions, you find he has borne away your fancy evermore to hover where blue skies laugh at blue waters, and innumerable wavelets trifle with innumerable sunbeams.

Brown's Least Tern

Sternula antillarum browni

THE DOVE IS OFTEN HELD UP TO US as the symbol of architectural indifference or of slovenly home-making, but the palm really belongs to the Least Tern. House-building for the tern has no other meaning or instrument than a pressure of the breast upon the sand. Home has no slightest connotation for her beyond that of locality, the place, perforce, where earth and sky must meet. For herself she would fainest linger ever in the air, descending only momentarily to seize her sustenance from the billow. But Nature in her wisdom has not seen fit to perfect a method by which such airy fairy creatures may perpetuate their kind, save by vulgar contact with the earth. And if it were not so, we should learn no more about them than we know of wandering comets. These Least Terns shall form no exception to the living line and they shall have no respite from the common lot. They must cease their tropical flutterings, their happy wanderings up and down the airy aisles which parallel a thousandfold the illimitable shores. Come, birdies, sea sprites, fog-fays, wisps of sunlit spray—howsoe'er ye call yourselves—get you to your knitting. Reproduce your sylphian, frivolous kind! Where? Oh, any stretch of sun-warmed sand will do, fronting the ocean. Oh, of course, the ocean. But better one where humans will not come, nor dogs, those boisterous marplots! Better, too, if you have a stretch of quiet waters to the rear, a lagoon or river or imprisoned pool, where fish will never fail you for the babies.

Truth to tell, the shores of California no longer offer safe asylum to these tender children of the tropics. They still nest with us, or try to, but the odds are against them. The playground of humanity, as we boast our southern shores to be, is no fit place for birds like these. The beaches belong to us. The sand is ours. We require it for the erection of cottages, casinos, bath-houses, and other important things—and to exercise our dogs, withal. The mermaids are gone, the Tritons are fled. Better that these birds go after them.

BLACK TERN

Chlidonias nigra surinamensis

THE BLACK TERN IS THE FAMILIAR SPIRIT of all fresh-water swamps in California north of the Tehachapi. Wherever water spreads itself not too deeply to encourage vegetable growth, whether of sedge or typha or tule, this restless, petulant, graceful water-sprite harries the face of Nature, pursues insects, chides intruders, builds adventurous rafts for the use of his offspring, and otherwise conducts his Chlidonian business.

The food of the Black Tern consists very largely of insects. These are obtained a-wing, and in securing them the bird exhibits great dexterity—now towering to a lofty height, with a single stroke against the wind, to make connections with a drifting moth; now following a bewildering zigzag through the reed-tops in pursuit of the agile dragon-fly.

In searching for the nests of the Black Tern, one must penetrate the oozy recesses of an undisturbed swamp, preferably in a flat-boat. Here in some secluded stretch the birds will hover about the intruder, fretting and screaming incessantly. If the water becomes too thick with mud and tangled vegetation to admit of easy passage, one must be content to strip off and wade through black water, say six inches deep, over black mud one and a half feet deep, and be prepared as well for occasional plunges into uncharted depths. When one gets "hot" in this ancient game of hide-the-thimble, the most interested pair of birds will single themselves out from the hovering throng and prepare for defense. Unless their advances are early discouraged, the boldness of these two will increase until they actually strike the intruder on the head, to say nothing of frequent salutations with flying shearn.

The nests are placed variously in the swamp, sometimes on a little raft of floating vegetation which the bird has brought together, sometimes on a truncated cone of fresh-cut herbage and twisted grasses resting upon the solid earth, but oftenest upon the ample expanse of some grebe's nest, new or old. The little tyrants have no hesitation in appropriating a grebe's nest of fresh construction, even though the rightful owner has already deposited eggs. The spitfires have the advantage in being able to strike from above, and it is to be feared they sometimes resort to mob tactics in case of serious opposition.

As a special instance of nesting in the cattle country, one cannot forbear to mention the frequency with which these birds are beguiled by the attraction of floating cakes of cow-dung for use as nesting-sites. These sturdy "cow-flops," raised by sudden floods from their ancient repose in the erstwhile pasture, offer all the requisites of stability, lightness, and convenient size which the birds admire—for a season. But the disintegrating power of the circumambient water is invariably more rapid in action than are the processes of incubation, and the end of that lowly cradle is inevitably tragic. But the birds will not learn, and the houses erected upon these deceitful foundations are as numerous as ever the following year.

WESTERN MOURNING DOVE
Zenaidura macroura marginella

WHEEEW HEWH HEEEEOOOO HEWH HEEEEOOOO. The tender, impassioned notes of the Mourning Dove are not only the most familiar, the most characteristic and commonplace, but the most lyric and soulful as well, the most romantically moving of any in the American chorus. Though the love-lorn swain blows but a single note, the sound sets a myriad chords to vibrating—hope, memory, and desire, no less than sadness. Gentle melancholy, the sickness of springtime, is really the budding of desire, the yearning of the Live One for his complement, the Also Living. Love-sick the bird unquestionably is, but who are we that we should affect to pity or to scorn? His is a voice of dignity and allurement, a voice of gentle compulsion which bids us also sigh and hope and aspire. Oh, there be those who call it doleful, and who profess a dislike for the solemn tenderness of the Mourning Dove, but they are such as have never loved, or who, having loved, have seen life's wine turned into vinegar. They do not wish to remember. For forgetfulness and indifference are alike impossible for those who listen. *Wheeew hewh heeeeoooo hewh heeeeoooo.* Voice of the heart! the heart expressive, yet forever unexpressed; achieving, yet forever uncontent; aspiring and forever aiming higher, higher, higher! Voice of the spirit art thou, O gentle bird! *Wheeew hewh heeeeoooo hewh heeeeoooo.*

These familiar, long drawn "mourning" notes are uttered only by the male, and for all their tenderness they have a penetrating quality, which makes them one of the most insistent elements in the chorus of springtime. Besides these the birds make no other sound, unless we count a musical wing-note which is made when suddenly taking flight, and which is so distinct that one can never be quite satisfied that it is not a vocal outcry. The same note, moderated, is heard in mid-flight, and also with renewed force when the birds are checking their flight or alighting; and it is so exactly timed with the wing movement that we must conclude its external origin.

The wild doves are model lovers and are chiefly known for their domesticity. During the mating season they sometimes vary the monotony of the ordinary whistling flight by sailing about in graceful curves on stiffened, noiseless wings. There is always an abundance of billing and cooing; and love-making, it is to be feared, often interferes somewhat with the practical side of housekeeping. At least the young wife is not a good house-builder, although she may be, and doubtless is, a kind mother.

A dove's nest is the symbol of frailty. A few careless sticks or straws are laid together in a platform, and lodged at a moderate height in the crotch or upon the horizontal limb of a tree or bush. Fence-corners, the tops of stumps, brush-piles, and overgrown stone-heaps are favorite places, and occasionally eggs are laid upon the ground with little pretense of a nest, or none. This is necessarily the case in sections given over to grain-growing; and in such regions, also, the danger from ground-haunting, predatory animals is greatly reduced. Sometimes, the dove builds in bush-clumps entirely surrounded by water, the purpose being, manifestly, to escape prowlers. In the deserts the dove has recourse to the cholla cactus, although, truth to tell, she is not an adept at this sort of thing, and chooses for her site the lower, weathered portions of the plant, rather than the "stickery" top. Again, old Thrashers' nests or those of Brewer's Blackbirds, Magpies, and Jays afford acceptable foundations.

When one of these is used, the tenant merely adds a few clean straws or twigs by way of lining. Now and then, however, a quite substantial nest is constructed, and one which reflects credit upon the gentle builder. The student of caliology, indeed, finds more to wonder at in the varying artistry of doves' nests than in the case of any other group of birds.

Road-runners and Cuckoos

Road-runner

Geococcyx californianus

WE HAVE ALWAYS CONTENDED THAT the Almighty has a sense of humor. Hence we point with pride to another of California's native sons, curious, conscious, and contradictory, the ingenu and adept of the desert, quaintest of feathered creatures. But we will not be understood as holding our favorite up to ridicule. Droll the bird is, even comic on occasion; but the humor of the Creator has been kindly, and he has endowed this desert masterpiece with endearing qualities, such as ought to assure him an enduring welcome. For, however grotesque the fowl may appear to be at first sight, I can assure the reader that he improves upon acquaintance; and as for myself, I confess toward the bird a good fellow feeling which is compounded of laughter and tears. The Spaniards called him *paisano*, "the countryman," and recorded thereby their appreciation of his uncouthness and worth—a diamond in the rough. More prosaically, we call him the Road-runner, the bird who tries conclusions, or else seeks escape, by running instead of flying. In the western portion of his habitat, where the running is not so good, we call the bird Chaparral Cock, and recognize his right to rule over that interminable half-forest which fills the landscape, and fills the eye, but never the pocketbook, of the Californian. *Paisano* makes his home here, but his heart is in the desert. For even where trees have become an accepted part of the Chaparral Cock's setting, he treats them rather as just so many rougher bits of desert to be gotten over, a-foot; and so he climbs, scrambles, runs, or leaps into and about a tree, instead of flying; and when he comes to quit it, he either leaps again, or volplanes to the ground. The bird is incapable of upward, or "earning" flight, but a clever sail from a treetop, assisted by some flapping, will carry him a hundred yards or so, if need be.

Since these are sadly civilized days, the chances are you will see your first Road-runner in a little hillside pasture dotted with trees. The bird stands at attention, eyeing you with mingled coquetry, mockery, defiance, and friendly curiosity. It is your next move—or would be if the bird had not just then caught sight of a spider and darted nimbly after it. Then, scrutiny forgotten, the bird proceeds to have as much fun in that commonplace pasture as a boy at a circus. The mere suggestion of a cricket brings this racing outfit all up standing with neck outstretched, crest erected, and tail raised to an angle of 45 degrees. It is a thrilling moment; and these thrillers recur in the active life of the cuckoo about once in every six seconds. The insect dispatched, the bird suddenly leaps six feet high to snatch a passing beetle. Bravo! Gusto! Avanti! *Mais non!* the bird recalls your gaze, assumes instantly a meek expression, tilts the tail sidewise in token of self-effacement, and makes as though to leave. As she goes, she minces in pretended fastidiousness, or reels in pretended intoxication, until—*psst!* the bird is faced about, head up, tail up, every outline filling the picture of clownish exaggeration. "Gracious! I nearly stepped on an ant!" And just as you prepare to dismount and bring your binoculars to bear upon the bird, she melts into a fringe of sage, and the exhibition is over for that day—mayhap for that month!

Seen on the desert proper, the Road-runner strikes you instantly as being the fitting thing. The purplish-blue and bottle-green of the upperparts, relieved by whitish edgings, fade before a background of glistening cholla or of fiery sand. If you are moved to pursuit, the bird laughs at you over giant strides, as, head down, tail depressed, it makes off with incredible ease. By a side swing of the tail the bird can round a bush with the utmost alacrity; or by a sudden expansion of that member, can put on the brakes instanter. With its long hooked beak the bird can deal out justice to centipede, horned toad, or lizard, even snake or scorpion; and it is interesting to note that the bird's head is protected against, say, the insensate lashings of a lizard's tail, by an array of stiff bristles scattered through its plumage. Those immediately over the bird's eye are especially sturdy, and there can be no doubt of their defensive purpose. As for the Roadrunner's legs, they are a marvel of speed and endurance, though a horse or a dog may tire them out. The footprints, two toes forward and two to the rear, are among the most characteristic sights of the desert; but we may not suppose that this double-toed arrangement makes for especial efficiency upon the ground. Indeed, it is altogether probable that this bird, whose ancestors were, and whose cousins are, strictly arboreal, is in so far handicapped. The hinder toes are weak; and, surely, three toes in front would give a better traction.

More probable, in fact well authenticated, are the stories that Road-runners destroy young birds, as well as mice and other minor mammals. These matters have been pretty well thrashed out; and while it is established that some damage is done to bird life, it appears to be a quite incidental and inconstant trait. Of more consequence is the bird's enormous consumption of grasshoppers and crickets; and these form more than one-third of its entire diet. Beetles, cut-worms, and caterpillars come next in order, and of the latter, hairy caterpillars, "woolly bears," which no other bird, save Cousin Cuckoo (*Coccyzus americanus occidentalis*), will touch. Beetles, crickets, scorpions, lizards, and small snakes are swallowed whole; and the bird boasts a digestion which our American Croesus, he of the bread-and-milk diet, would surely envy. The ten percent of vegetable matter with which the bird varies its regimen is found to consist almost entirely of "sour berries" (the fruit of *Rhus integrifolia*), and these evidently serve as sauce for snake and centipede *à la mode*.

In nesting the birds prove themselves very adaptable. If in the open desert, the lowly shelter of the cholla cactus will suffice; but if mesquite trees are available, the bird much prefers the security of a horizontal limb or trunk. In the chaparral, the cover of the densest shrubs is sought, or else the live oaks. I have found these birds nesting also in the convenient crannies of the sandstone cliffs. In one such station overlooking the Antelope Plains of western Kern County, the bird sat with her tail bent forward sharply by the rear wall of her niche. When disturbed, she did not fly directly, but scuttled nimbly along the face of the wall, then sprang into the air for a long sail which ended in the sage.

California Cuckoo

Coccyzus americanus occidentalis

Sumer is icumen in
Lhude sing cuccu!
Groweth sod, and bloweth med,
And springth the wude nu—
Sing cuccu!

SO SANG ONE OF THE EARLIEST of the English poets, of *Cuculus canorus;* but if we were to wait for the California Cuckoo to bring us summer we should lose our reputation for peerless Marches and full-blown Aprils. For the California Cuckoo is among the laziest of birds. When he does step in, surreptitiously, and hides in the greenery of late Maytime, the drama of summer has already reached the third act, and his services as enunciator are no longer required. Our bird comes silently, as well, and it is only after a week or two of residence, "getting settled," that he begins to sound the notes which will put him in touch with his fellows or, perchance, lead to him the lady love of the season. The song then is a series of explosive pouting notes: *Cuckookook ookookook ook kook kook kook,* first energetically then *rallentando et diminuendo.*

Although the bird enjoys a rather wide distribution throughout the forested lowlands of the Pacific slope, the sight of a California Cuckoo is one of the rarest; and save in some few favored places, recognized breeding haunts, his voice is the rarest of sounds. Although I have lived for twenty-five years in the West, and am accounted fairly alert of ear, I should hesitate to tell how few times I have heard this bird—say six or eight. Those more favored by reason of acquaintance with the birds' restricted breeding haunts tell us that upon arrival in the north the birds keep to the higher woodlands for a period of two or three weeks, after which they retire to the willow bottoms to breed. After this their entire aspect changes. No longer shy and difficult of approach, they show themselves more or less freely, as those who belong to the country; while a bird found on the nest will almost suffer the caress of a hand before darting off quietly to be lost in the foliage. At such times, too, the loud challenge "song" gives place to a low guttural note, still "*kuk, kuk, kuk,*" with which the bird betrays anxiety, or signals to its mate. Then, too, a sort of exorcism is undertaken. The bird employs its ventriloquistic gifts and fills the neighborhood with weird unplaceable *kuk kuk kuk* sounds, which are intended to be for the intruder an accusing voice of conscience, or a reminder of avenging powers which haunt the woodland.

But apart, if possible, from its nesting anxieties, it is worth while to examine this genius at close range. Most birds prefer to face the enemy, so as to keep his every movement well in eye; but Cuckoo presents his back, a cold gray affair (save for russet wings), from behind which he peers now and then, turning his neck and giving you one eye in a lofty, well-bred way. I recall no other bird whose gaze is so calm, so direct, so fearless, yet withal so decorous. But nothing escapes him. He is not so vulgarly devoted to curiosity that he forgets business. Mercy, no! You may be within ten feet of him, but he plucks and swallows a caterpillar with as little ado or apology as if you were in the next county. But make a false motion, and the bird glides away into the deeper foliage with an ease and grace born of long practice. Silken, silent, sinuous are adjectives which you instinctively apply to this sober, sly bird, as he steals through the upper branches, scarcely seen, but not unseeing, to emerge at length from the opposite side of the tree, and to dart away like a little brown arrow into some distant copse. A close study of the California Cuckoo's breeding confirms the opinion gained elsewhere, that *Coccyzus americanus* is a bird of highly irregular habits. It nests in May—it nests in August. It builds a nest on a rush order and deposits three eggs therein all within the space of a week—it loafs and dodders for a month, so that fresh eggs and young are found together in a nest. It lays one egg and attends it devotedly— or five and deserts them. It erects a slovenly platform which would disgrace a dove—or it builds a sturdy nest which would do credit to a thrasher. Or, again, it does not build at all, but uses instead a deserted nest of some other bird, Mourning Dove or Black-headed Grosbeak. And, lastly, it is a model of the home-keeping virtues, rearing and tending its own as all virtuous parents should; or, yielding to the taint of cuckoo heredity, it inflicts its casual offspring upon a foster mother, and goes its way unheeding.

American Barn Owl

Tyto perlata pratincola

IF ABILITY AND WORTH ARE TO COUNT for anything, the Barn Owl, and not the Moon, ought to be the Queen of the Night. Whoever thought of calling the blear-eyed old man in the moon a "queen" anyhow? Not to mention the mistake in sex, his derelictions are notorious. He is off the job half the time, though he manages to keep the world in the dark as to his misdoings *in absentia*. He is an inveterate tippler—that we know. I have myself seen him "take a horn"—two of them, in fact. And that he goes on a spree and gets full every month is the scandal of the heavens. He rises at irregular hours, and for days after the big debauch his friend Phoebus has to help him to bed. Away with this tradition of moonly virtues!

But consider, I pray, the merits of the Barn Owl. She is on duty 365 nights in the year. Rising punctually when the sun is well set, she sallies forth to review and regulate her realm with tireless diligence. Softer than silk, or than any similitude, are her aerial floatings. All gentle things trust her, and none save mischief-makers have aught to fear from her gentle sway.

As for her beauty, who may say that in her robes of white, overlaid with filmiest laces of the dusk and set out with burnishings of ochraceous gold, she is not, indeed, the fairest of night birds, and entitled as such to unbroken rule? Though the populace hoots, as it always has, when confronted with claims which it does not understand, and dishonors this gentle bird with such a vulgar name as "Monkey-faced Owl," on those occasions, fortunately rare, when our heroine is dragged forth into the disabling light of day, we insist that this is Beauty's self, and Aphrodite's double, appointed for the rulership of Night.

But when the "Night-bird" sings—ah, there is pause, food for meditation and regret. For, like the lordly peacock, bird of Juno, the Barn Owl has been saddled with a most unmelodious voice. She does not know it, poor thing, and fills the night, therefore, with screeches which seem the very soul of petulance or hate. This challenge note of the Barn Owl is harsh beyond all expression, a snarling *churr*, ground out between clenched teeth. I do not know where Lewis Carroll thinks he got the name for his impossible animal, the "Snark"; but I suggest that it came subconsciously from the Barn Owl's cry, *snarrk*. By this sound we know that the Barn Owl is abroad, and by the sustained succession of these sounds, we judge that the Barn Owl spends more time a-wing than do any of the Strigine owls. *Aluco* is a tireless quester, the buzzard of the night, pausing only, and that very frequently, when its prey is spotted on the ground. The function of the *snarrk* cry is not exactly known, although the birds do hunt more or less in pairs, and may wish to keep in touch, however distantly. It is more probable, however, that *snark* is a joy cry, and expresses the bird's delight in the prospects of the chase, or its exultation over life lived under the tipsy beams of the swelling moon.

The Barn Owl is the most strictly nocturnal of all owls; that is to say, it "rises" later, and "sets" earlier, usually a good half hour before sunrise. It occupies by day, also, the darkest of available retreats; but the birds are so abundant and so well distributed that they must avail themselves of a great variety of hiding places. Buildings are in good demand, barns, attics, vine-covered porches, tank-houses, towers, and belfries. Niches and tiny grottoes in the cliffs are sure of attracting Barn Owls, no matter what their outlook, provided only that the local accommodations are convenient. For this reason *Tyto* occasionally figures as a sea-bird. Certain favored cliffs of sandstone in the inner coast ranges fairly swarm with Barn Owls, and their presence may be known by the generous smears of "whitewash" which decorate the skirts of long frequented ledges.

Of course the nesting places are in part identical with the roosting places. The first token of occupation, present or past, is the flamboyant whitewash—excrement wherein the calcium of unassimilated bone-stuffs figures predominantly. But the second token, the refuse heap, is more interesting and more instructive. Below or beside each nest is an accumulation, sometimes decades old, of mammal-skulls, fur, and feathers, in part rejected portions from the banqueting table, but chiefly pellets, or "casts," indigestible portions of food which are automatically ejected from the bird's crop when the edible portions have been released. Barn Owls are prodigious eaters, and it becomes important to examine their table and their garbage can, both qualitatively and quantitatively. As to quantity, I have seen dumps which contained not less than three bushels of material, with hundreds of skulls apparent on a superficial examination. Not even this represents the original mass, for in the older of the Aluconine kitchen middens, the lower strata have disintegrated and settled. The Barn Owl's table, too, is always set. The youngsters are not only fed diligently all night, but a generous store is laid by for daylight lunches. The poor dears are sure to need a "piece," you know!

Barn Owls' eggs are notably different in shape from those of other owls, being elongate or truly oval, instead of rounded, as in the Strigidae. The index is 76, as against an average of, say, 83.5 for the other group. This points strongly to an ancient separation of stock. The eggs are laid upon the bare floor of a cavity, or else upon whatever chance accumulation of disintegrated pellets, or other *incognoscenda* may offer. The place is sure to be filthy, and before the youngsters are done with it, the stench is likely to be overpowering. Eggs are deposited every other day, or irregularly; and incubation begins immediately, so that the youngsters arrive seriatim, and are most accurately graded in size. The parents try to be fair, but the youngest frequently arrives too late, for what helpless infant could hope to thrive after having been stepped on, whether purposely or no, by an eighteen-day-old brother! When intruded upon, the young family will hiss like a nest of snakes, and throw themselves in various defensive postures. The babes, in their close covering of white wool, are comical looking creatures, but they do not scruple to press home a set of claws which are sharp as needles; so perhaps it is just as well not to try to chuck them under the chin. The older birds will fight like demons when closely pressed, and one soon comes to see what a powerful as well as alert foe the wicked gopher has to fear. Their feeding habits, also, are not fastidious. The rending of a rat carcass would be a terrifying sight if the birds were, say, a hundred times as large. The head of the victim goes down first, probably because the brains are the most delectable morsel, and the rest follows piecemeal, "hide, horns, and hair." But the case is not hopeless, for punctual to the minute the skull reappears, and later the clothes of the late lamented, done up in a neat package. *Thomomys*, he of the tireless tooth, who loves our choicest vegetables and most expensive flower-bulbs, he shall have, thus, a befitting monument—the skull and bundle. Hail, beneficent deliverer! Queen of the Night!

Spotted Owl

Strix occidentalis

EVEN THE SIGHT OF A SPOTTED OWL is counted a bit of a rarity in these parts; and specimens taken are still dutifully reported in the columns of the "Condor," or elsewhere. Yet when the great day comes, the bird of mystery is likely to prove as obliging as a well-bred hen or shall we say as a sleepy rooster? It may be his favorite roost that we have blundered upon, all in a shady dell, unfrequented of men. There is no need for anxiety.

The bird is mildly curious himself, and not in the least alarmed. His aspect is anything but ferocious—benevolent, rather—and he looks for all the world like some patriarchal gnome disturbed at his slumbers, yet not resentful. We vote him handsome at the first breath, and admiration grows as we dwell upon the sleekness, the mellow rotundity, and the exquisite harmony of the figure, and especially of the costume before us. Spotting suggests the conspicuous, and this bird is spotted with white from head to foot, on a background the deepest of wood-browns; and yet the pattern blends in so perfectly, is so essential a part of the checkered sunlight falling upon branch and leaf beside him, that we say, "Why, of course. How could he be any different?" Whereas an object merely brown or merely white would stand out here like a sore thumb, this camouflaged statuette almost disappears under the searching eye. We must circle about him to coax an inclination of the head, or a tell-tale movement of the foot. Now and again the benignant creature winks prodigiously, and the ladies with us shriek with laughter. Silly things! The bird is not winking at *them*. He was up late last night and the sun hurts his eyes, that's all.

There is no clear-cut account of the notes, and especially of the mating "song," of the Spotted Owl. Clay enjoyed a midnight serenade wherein the birds produced a "ghostly racket," preceded by a long-drawn-out whining, which gradually increased to a grating sound. In this performance two birds, attracted, no doubt, by the light, ventured upon a limb within three feet of the inquisitive student. Peyton likens the call of the male to the distant baying of a hound, and Dickeys confirms this estimate.

Little is known, either, of the food habits of this rare owl. Dickey found rather scanty remains of mice and brush rats at the owl's nest, and saw feathers of crested jays which he attributed to a Strigine banquet. Curiously, however, two instances are on record where remains of Pygmy Owls, *Glaucidium gnoma*, have been found in the stomachs of recently killed Spotted Owls. Evidently there is scant courtesy among brigands.

HORNED OWL

Bubo virginianus

BY A FANTASTIC QUIRK OF HISTORY the grizzly bear *(Ursus horribilis)* has become the emblem of California. In justification of this early whim, we can only urge that the bear is enthusiastic in welcome and gets an everlasting grip upon the stranger who ventures within her borders. In presenting *Bubo horribilis*, the grizzly bear of the bird world, we shall not be able to offer anything beyond the above named characteristics in his favor. He loves the darkness because his deeds are evil; and after the protecting sun has set, woe betide the mole or rabbit, partridge, jay, or chanticleer who dares to stir where this monster is a-wing. When captured in a trap, as he sometimes is by aggrieved poultry fanciers, the ruffling of the feathers, the alternate hissing and fierce snapping of the mandibles, and the greenish yellow light which comes flashing from the great saucer eyes all give fair warning of what one may expect from the free foot once it gets a chance to close upon a victim.

Horned Owls in a state of nature do not pose for inspection unless forcibly detained. A steel trap is, of course, the surest method of detention, but a mob of blue-fronted jays ranks a close second. Nothing can exceed the joy of the jay upon the discovery of one of these grim death's heads secreted in the depths of a fir tree. Here is a day's sport cut out for one whose "sportin' blood" runs high on week-days and turns feverish on owl days. The whole jay countryside is aroused. To the number of a score they gather about the victim and throw all his sins up to him in a chorus of Billingsgate. The owl beams hate at them, snaps his mandibles fiercely, and makes now and then an ineffectual dab at his pursuers, which only seems to arouse fresh shrieks of laughter. When the din becomes unbearable, he may dash from cover, but the jays surround him at the next resting place, screaming sarcastic apologies for their past rudeness, and promising redoubled misbehavior.

One wonders that they dare do it, for the sullen object of mirth will assuredly wreak vengeance on them when his turn comes in the first watch of the night. It is difficult to exaggerate the rapacity of these freebooters. An observer in New York State, speaking, of course, of the eastern form, "states that in a nest he examined, containing two young owls, he found the following animals: a mouse, a young muskrat, two eels, four bullheads, a woodcock, four ruffed grouse, one rabbit, and eleven rats. The food taken out of the nest weighed almost eighteen pounds. A curious fact connected with these captives was that the heads were eaten off, the bodies being untouched." The brain of the victim is counted the tid-bit, and in seasons of plenty the bird will have nothing else. Thus, while the owl probably will not kill wantonly, it is notoriously wasteful, and the coarser portions of these choice viands of which we read, these bloody offerings to the infant Dinops, are removed periodically from the nest.

While a certain amount of "good" is undeniably accomplished by the Horned Owl in preying upon rats and gophers, it is more than offset by the relentless attacks upon birds, especially upon meadowlarks, quails, and grouse, and by the frequent, although not regular, depredations upon poultry. Other predatory species are not exempt, either. Crows and jays are frequent victims, and Screech Owl appears to be a regular item on the Bubonine bill of fare. Mr. Bowles relates, also, that during the fall and winter months on certain shooting preserves these birds make a thorough search every night for wounded ducks. So successful are they that out of hundreds that are wounded and lost by sportsmen, it is unusual to find one; while well-picked carcasses are common.

Horned Owls, too, are of commoner occurrence than is sometimes realized. Although normally bold and aggressive, the birds soon learn caution, and because their local attachments are very strong, they will forego the pleasure of song rather than desert the ancestral haunts. Where danger has not taught discretion, they are quite free with their nocturnal concerts; but they are known to nest in places where a single full-voiced *hoot* would draw the fire of the countryside. The mating song (save the mark!) is a succession of resonant bellowings in a single key—*Whoo, whoo, hoo-hoo, who*—quite variable as to length and form. Besides this the bird occasionally indulges in sepulchral laughter, *hoo*

hoo hoo hoo hoo hoo hoo, which arouses anything but mirthful feelings in the listener.

But these modest notes by no means exhaust the Horned Owl's repertory. As a young man, in Tacoma, the writer once lived in a house which immediately adjoined a large wooden church. My chamber window looked upon a flat kitchen roof, through which projected a brick chimney some ten feet away. At three o'clock one morning a horrible nightmare gave way to a still more horrible waking. Murder most foul was being committed on the roof just outside the open window, and the shrieks of the victims (at least seven of them!) were drowned by the imprecations of the attacking party—fire-eating pirates to the number of a dozen. Pandemonium reigned and my bones were liquid with fright—when suddenly the tumult ceased; nor could I imagine through a whole sick day what had been the occasion of the terrifying visitation. But two weeks later the conflict was renewed—at a merciful distance this time. Peering out into the moonlight I beheld one of these owls perched upon the chimney of the church hard by, gibbering and shrieking like one possessed. Cat-calls, groans, and demoniacal laughter were varied by wails and screeches, as of souls in torment—an occasion most memorable. The previous serenade had evidently been rendered from the kitchen chimney—and I pray never to hear its equal.

The early nesting of the Horned Owl is the marvel of those eastern states whose Februaries are given over to blizzards instead of roses. Fresh eggs have been taken in early February, with zero temperatures prevailing, from nests wherein all but the sitting bird was encrusted with snow. Here in California, where temperature cuts so little figure in nesting calculations, the Horned Owls hold pretty much to the ancient habit. February and March are the usual nesting months, and January 29th (1911) at Escondido is the earliest date I can discover. These owls never build nests of their own, in the strict sense, but either occupy some deserted nest of Redtail, Magpie, or Crow, or else make shift with the natural opening of some ledge or cliff cranny or steep hillside. Shelter is a minor consideration, since the bird fears neither storm nor prowling coyote; but some degree of elevation, a commanding lookout, is the prime requisite. The nesting hollow, whether of sticks or of earth, is lined casually with feathers from the bird's breast. And in this depression two, sometimes three, or, very rarely, four, white eggs are laid. These are subspherical in shape; in size about that of hens' eggs, notably small for the bulk of the bird; and they require the services of the mother for something over four weeks. During the period of incubation the male is in close attendance, feeding his mate faithfully upon the nest and keeping a sharp lookout for intruders.

When disturbed, the owners pose in various attitudes, grotesque or frightful, snapping their mandibles, and groaning now and then in a most dismal fashion. If the young are well grown, it is not at all safe to venture near, for an irate Horned Owl is incredibly swift in attack, and a raking shot from those powerful talons will leave at best a very sore head. One ardent investigator, presuming too much upon an acquaintance of two years' standing, attempted to remove the owlets from a nest for photographic purposes. The blood flowing from three scalp wounds was soon staunched and he recovered his cap from a treetop a hundred yards away, "a punctured souvenir of our last intimate contact with the local Horned Owls."

Pygmy Owl

Glaucidium gnoma californicum

SAVE TO THE FEW INITIATES, a meeting with this fascinating little fiend must come as a happy accident. Fiend he is from the top of his gory beak to the tips of his needle-like claws; but chances are you will forget his gory character at sight and call him "perfectly cunning," just because he is tiny and saucy and *dégagé*. Look your fill when fate brings him your way, for like the wind, his royal owlet flitteth where he listeth, and you cannot tell whence he comes nor whether he will come again this twelvemonth. When my moment of privilege came, this pocket edition of the powers that prey stood out boldly and unequivocally upon the topmost splinter of a wayside stub in a northern forest, and challenged attention. The gnome gave his back to the road, and now and then teetered his tail, which was otherwise set at a jaunty angle, nervously, as though there were something on his mind. But this preoccupation did not deter the Owl from bending an occasional sharp glance of scrutiny upon the bird-man. Then all at once the bird whirled backward and launched himself, like a bolt from a crossbow, at a mouse some sixty feet away across the road. Seizing the "wee, timorous, cowerin' beastie" at the very entrance of his hole, the bird maintained its grasp upon it with both feet, and supported itself against the rodent's struggles by wings outstretched upon the ground. Not until the squeakings of the victim had quite ceased did the captor rise and disappear by rapid flight into the wood.

A second meeting was more prosaic, but still illuminating. The *Zwerg* was out before sunset, but we never should have noticed him if we had not been looking upward, intent on early pussy willows, amongst which he sat, calmly, at the height of a dozen feet. There is always a curious impersonality about the gaze of this little owl. Even when he does look in your direction (and he does not flatter you by constant attention by any means), he does not appear to focus on you at all. Perhaps this is a trick of the eye, or else arises from its unlikeness to that of other owls. For although the atmosphere on this occasion was full of light, the bird's pupils were dilated to the utmost, and the irides were mere yellow rims.

When first put to flight, by approach from below, Owlikins did not flutter off like a soft shadow, as might have been expected, but pitched downward nearly to the ground and buzzed off like a young meteor, fetching up suddenly on another osier branch some fifty feet away. Thither I followed and clambered up to a point within six feet of him on the level. Even then the bird did not appear greatly disturbed, and he deliberately looked away from me as often as at me—affording an example of self-sufficiency which was really startling. In "bout facing," not a muscle of the body moved but only the grim little death's head went round and round. The Little Corporal was not greatly disturbed, either, by the noise; but when I reproduced the Screech Owl cry, he gave me careful attention and appeared so interested that when he flew again it was only for a space of ten feet.

Each time, a little before he shifted, the bird evacuated, with an absurd little stretch and recoil, apparently so as to be ready for eventualities. By the way, what a fierce digestion those little cannibals must have, for their excrement is always glistening white! I do not know how else to interpret this, save as the passage of the lime and phosphates of their victims' bones, which alone their voracious systems reject.

In spite of his insignificant size, the Pygmy is a dashing little brigand, and no bird up to the size of a Robin is safe from its clutches. So bold is he that upon one occasion, when Mr. Bowles threw a large stick at one, the owl charged at the passing missile with all imaginable fury. The diet descends not infrequently to insects, but squirrels of twice the owl's weight are promptly seized when occasion offers. Dark days are as good as night to them, and they are sometimes abroad on bright days as well.

The flight of the Pygmy Owl is not muffled by softened wing-linings, as is the case with the Short-eared and others which hunt much a-wing; it is rather pert and noisy, like a Shrike's. Like a Shrike, also, in extended course it dives with closed wings, then opens suddenly and flutters up with rapid strokes to regain the former level—describing thus successive loops of flight.

ARIZONA ELF OWL
Micropallas whitneyi whitneyi

A FEATHERED SOMETHING AT THE BOTTOM OF A HOLE! Not a very inspiring thought, you say? No; not unless you happen to have "the bug." Yet it is for this that the oologist will pack a ladder for weary miles over the desert. For this he will invade the haunts of the "side-winder" and the Gila monster. For this he will wrestle with tediously unending creosote and insinuating cat's claw. For this he will brave the cruel cholla, which looses its bunched lances at a touch, or pierces the feet of the passerby. For this he will ascend rickety heights of sahuaro; if need be, hug its spiny column to meet a flow of wind or to gain an objective just six inches higher. (The thorns can be removed from the knees and arms at leisure over the camp fire.) For this he enlarges ancient wounds in the venerable cactus, plying his hatchet in the slithery substance of the "giant's" flesh, until his arms are ready to drop off from weariness. And all that he may at last come upon a bundle of feathers at the bottom of one of the holes.

The bundle is elongated, supine, comfortable to the hand, all but non-resistant. Draw it forth, the drowsy little elf! Claws it has, and they clutch convulsively, but they are scarcely strong enough to hurt you. Eyes it has—yellow, saucer eyes, that might be wrathy if only the elfkin would wake up. Soft, weathered browns and streaky whites with touches of fawn make up a costume as proper as that of Scops or Bubo; but who can believe that this little midget, who may be entirely hidden in the hollow of your hand, is really an owl? Owl! your grandmother! Why, you want to nuzzle it and call it "pretty baby," and say its daddy ought to be proud of it. But hold! Let us see if there is anything else in that hole. One-two-three-*four* round white eggs, as big as a Flicker's, lying on the hard bottom of the cavity, without a shred of lining. This drowsy infant, this puny, pathetic pickaninny terror is a mother! Doubtless her little wits are working mightily under that mask of insouciance. Let us see. Relax the fingers. Psst goes the bird upon the instant and takes refuge in the nearest bush. There she glowers for a moment, and then takes wing for another sahuaro and dives confidently into another hole. It is the last we shall see of Mrs. *Micropallas whitneyi* today.

Truth to tell, Elf Owls are very difficult of observation. The lore which has grown up about them is scanty and not always consistent. They are strictly nocturnal in habit, are none too noisy, and live a life so secluded that we can do little better than catch them asleep, or note them under artificial conditions.

Examination of many stomachs has developed the fact that Elf Owls subsist almost exclusively upon an insect diet. Beetles, ants, grasshoppers, and moths are mentioned; and one observer finds that they make sallies into the air for flying prey, after the fashion of flycatchers. No instances of their preying upon other birds have come to light; and, indeed, Elf Owls appear to be on the best of terms with their feathered neighbors.

Elf Owls, chiefly males, are sometimes taken by surprise in thickets, and their behavior on such occasions is quite like that of large owls, viz., drawing themselves up rigidly with feathers "appressed," and looking like badly bored majors. We took a specimen, a male, from a hackberry tree near Tucson, who on this account looked a half size taller than he should. Stephens thinks that the male may be partially gregarious during the breeding season, for on one occasion he found two "sitting out" in a bush, and on another—five.

Goatsuckers, Swifts, and Hummingbirds

NUTTALL'S POORWILL
Phalaenoptilus nuttalli nuttalli

THE SUN HAS SET AND THE LAST CHORE IS DONE, all save carrying in the brimful pail of milk, which slowly yields tribute of escaping bubbles to the evening air. Sukey, with a vast sigh of relief, has sunk upon the ground, where, after summoning a consoling cud, she regards her master wonderingly. But the farmer boy is loth to quit the scene and to exchange the witching twilight for the homely glare of the waiting kerosene; so he lingers on his milk-stool watching the fading light in the western sky and dreaming, as only a boy can dream, of days which are yet to be. Every sense is lulled to rest, and the spirit comes forth to explore the lands beyond the hills, to conquer cities, discover poles, or scale the heights of heaven, when suddenly out of the stillness comes the plaintive cry of the *Poor-will, Poor-will, Poor-will*. It is not a disturbing note, but rather the authentic voice of silence, the yearning of the bordering wilderness made vocal in appeal to the romantic spirit of youth. *Poor Will! Poor Will!* you think upon cities, actions, achievements; think rather upon solitude, upon quietness, upon lonely devotions. Come, oh, come to the wilderness, to the mystic, silent, fateful wastes! And ever after, even though duty call him to the city, to the stupid, stifling, roaring (and glorious) city, the voice of the Poorwill has wrought its work within the heart of the exiled farmer boy, and he owns a reverence for the silent places, a loyalty of affection for the wilderness, which not all the enforced subservience of things which creak or blare or shriek may fully efface.

The Poorwill spends the day sleeping on the ground under the shelter of a sage-bush, or close beside some lichen-covered rock, to which its intricate pattern of plumage marvelously assimilates. When startled, by day, the bird emits a mellow *quirp, quirp* of protest, flits a few yards over the sage-tops, and plumps down at haphazard. If it chances to settle in the full sunlight, it appears to be blinded and may allow a close approach; but if in the shade, one is not likely to surprise it again. Even after nightfall these fairy moth-catchers are much more terrestrial in their habits than are the Nighthawks. They alight upon the ground upon the slightest pretext and, indeed, appear most frequently to attain their object by leaping up at passing insects. They are more strictly nocturnal in habit, also, than the Night-jars, and we know of their later movements only through the intermittent exercise of song. Heard in some starlit canyon, the passing of a Poorwill in full cry is an indescribable experience, producing feelings somewhere between pleasure and fear—pleasure in the delightful melancholy of the notes heard in the dim distance, but something akin to terror at the near approach and thrilling climax of the portentous sounds.

Taken in the hand, one sees what a quiet, inoffensive fay the Poorwill is, all feathers and itself a mere featherweight. The silken sheen and delicate tracery of the frost-work upon the plumage it were hopeless to describe. It is as though some fairy snowball had struck the bird full on the forehead, and from thence gone shivering, with ever lessening traces, all over the upperparts. Or, perhaps, to allow another fancy, the dust of the innumerable moth-millers, with which the bird is always wrestling, gets powdered over its garments. The large bristles which line the upper mandible, and which increase the catching capacity of the extensive gape by half, are seen to be really modified feathers, and not hairs, as might be supposed, for in younger specimens they are protected by little horny basal sheaths. With this equipment, and wings, our gentle hero easily becomes the envy of mere human entomologists.

Pacific Nighthawk
Chordeiles minor hesperis

THE NIGHTHAWK IS THE LAGGARD among the western migrants, and it is always something of an event when his pouting notes, *bayard, bayard*, first break upon the stillness of the evening air. We crane our necks, too, to catch the first glimpse of the season—in mid-May, or later, according to altitude. The way of the Nighthawk in the air is, perhaps, the most varied, certainly the most eccentric, of any of the feathered kind. He seems such a frail thing, as he goes tottering and careening across the sky. We half expect to see him collapse, like a broken butterfly, or else get blown out of bounds. Now he minces along, like a school girl; now he races to and fro in a frenzy; and now he glides along smoothly with the ease and stateliness of a gondola. He is a more dignified bat, graceful at times, but always a bit uncanny. But the "bull-bat" knows exactly what he is about, and he is playing the air game for the maximum of gastronomic profit.

With a mouth like the opening of a butterfly net, and a stomach to match, this winged bug-hunter is one of the world's most successful entomologists. Everything with a pinched-in waist is grist to his mill—chinch bugs, squash-bugs, June-bugs, any old bugs. One Nighthawk stomach under examination gave up seventeen species of beetles at one time. Another, nineteen entire grasshoppers. Another, parts of thirty-eight. But if the bull-bat has a specialty, it is flying ants. Dr. Grinnell took a stomach which held forty-three of our large-winged white ants (and of these some were still alive fifteen hours after capture); while Professor Beal took one individual whose crop was gorged with eighteen hundred of a small variety.

Nighthawks are not so strictly nocturnal as are the Poorwills, for they put a quite liberal construction on the word "twilight," and are sure to avail themselves of all cloudy days. In fact, they move about at will whenever the sun slants fairly. The middle hours of the day are spent upon the ground, or if in timbered country, crouched lengthwise upon a tree limb. For the latter situation nature has devised a special apparatus in the shape of a comb-like process along the inner edge of the middle claw of each foot. The feet and legs being, for lack of other use, very weak, this pectination of the middle claw must be of material service in enabling the bird to retain its footing on a rounding surface of bark. It is in these hours of the middle siesta that the intricate color pattern of the plumage makes the bird appear—or rather disappear—to the greatest advantage against the variegated setting of bark or rock. A Nighthawk on the ground is all but invisible—and knows it.

While not at any time strictly gregarious, favorable conditions are likely to attract considerable numbers of Nighthawks to a given spot. I have seen dozens of birds at a time winging noiselessly to and fro over the tranquil waters of an inland lake, and on several occasions companies of from one to two hundred executing some grand march, or aerial parade, over a well-watered pasture. These convocations are not necessarily preliminary to the autumnal movement, for I once saw such an assemblage at Goose Lake, in Modoc County, on the 23rd of June (1912). It had snowed the day before, so possibly these birds had been driven in from the hills to a place of assured sustenance, much as swallows are driven to the ponds in early spring. During migration, too, scores of these birds may sometimes be seen moving aloft in loose array, and customarily, at this season, silent.

The eggs of the Nighthawk are heavily mottled with slaty and other tints, which render them practically invisible to the searching eye, even though they rest upon the bare ground or, as oftener, upon an exposed and lichen-covered rock ledge. Except during the very warmest hours (when the sun's rays might addle them) and the coolest (when they might become chilled), the sitting bird is likely to rest beside her eggs instead of on them. The young birds when hatched place great reliance upon their protective coloration, and even permit the fondling of the hand rather than confess the defect of their fancied security. The old bird, meanwhile, has fluttered away over the ground with uncertain wing and drooping tail to drop at last on the very point of death. Or failing in this ruse, she is charging about in midair with plaintive cries. Look upon the babies for the last time, for they will be spirited away before your return—borne off, it is said, between the thighs of the parent bird.

TEXAS NIGHTHAWK
Chordeiles acutipennis texensis

THE NATURE-LOVING PILGRIM camping for a night in some desert wash will have occasion to wonder at a strange burring croak which wells up out of the ground, apparently from nowhere in particular. It is a weird sound, low, monotonous, and impersonal—drowsy, too, if one can ignore the challenge of its mystery. It is the voice of a giant frog grown weary in a waterless land. Or it is the voice of the desert itself murmuring its gratitude before the cooling touch of nightfall. Pan wakes at this hour in yonder mountain glade and summons all his satyrs to revel, but here in the desert silence reigns, silence and the sole mystery of sound. The traveler sleeps, and rousing midway of his dreams, he seems to hear two voices, two deserts answering from nowhere. But each utters the self-same silence, bidding him resign again to slumber.

The most gifted imagination would scarcely ascribe this geophonic serenade to a pair of birds. But the Texas Nighthawks are responsible, as anyone may learn who has the fortune to stumble upon their eggs at nightfall. The hour is important, for were the brooding bird to be disturbed in broad daylight she would merely lift over the sage-brush, flit a few yards, plump down again, and that would be the last of it. But at dusk there is more activity. The bird retires, indeed, but she summons her mate and they set up, at near ranges, always from the ground, that quaint batrachian wail, which is intended, no doubt, rather to charm than to frighten.

Texas Nighthawks bear a close superficial resemblance to the more widely known *Chordeiles minor*, and their appearance a-wing is not particularly different. They are, however, less active and, above all, less venturesome on the wing. They do not favor high levels of air nor attempt the aerial stunts of *minor*, but they flit about modestly over the sage tops, or else leap up off the ground at their winged prey. Texas Nighthawks are also quite sociable, especially toward the close of the breeding season, and hundreds may sometimes be seen in favored valleys, or over such bodies of water as abound in insects. While nesting may be conducted at any remove from water, it is probable that the birds make daily visits to water-holes, and drink "hen-fashion," or else dip on the wing from some of the larger surfaces. Though they endure the extreme heat of the desert, they cannot be quite insensible to it, for they retire to Transition levels with the advancing season. The highest altitude of recorded occurrence is perhaps that of Sugarloaf in the San Bernardinos, where Grinnell found them on August 20th, at 7,500 feet.

It is doubtless improper to speak of the "nesting" of the Texas Nighthawk. Nest she has none, but her two eggs are laid upon the bare ground, and this almost of necessity is of some complexion of sand. The parched spaces between creosote bushes, where the particles of soil, although fine, are still so hot that they hate each other, are one type of bottom. The coarse granitic sand poured out of Tujunga Canyon by the winter freshets is another. The gravel beds of the desert ranges whose component pebbles are sered by volcanic acids are a third. If the eggs have any cover at all, it is the accidental shade of some scraggly bush, and when uncovered they are the very color of the ground.

NORTHERN BLACK SWIFT

Nephoecetes niger borealis

IT MAY BE CONFESSED THAT THE palmy days of bird-nesting *as a sport* are over. Those who still have at heart the interest of oology as a science are not loth to make this admission. Sport in the older sense of the term has ever meant destruction, while science stands or should stand for conservation. A kindlier spirit toward the things of nature is manifesting itself on every hand—a determination to foster and to protect, instead of to destroy. The life of a bird is undoubtedly more important to humanity than its caloric content, and the psychology of a living bird is more fascinating than either its plumage or its egg.

That the turn of the tide came when the task of Science, in this country at least, was nearly ended, is no doubt more than a coincidence. The game has flagged because there are so few new fields to conquer. The quest of the unknown in American birds' eggs is nearly over; for with the exception of certain forms casual or rare along our southern border, and one of the Rosy Finches, there are no more full-fledged species of American birds, believed to breed within the limits of the United States, whose nests and eggs have not been discovered.

What this means for science and for romance the layman may never fully understand. But it means at least that the quest has been very keen of late, and that a bona fide discovery of some long-sought species has marked the discoverer a prince among oologists. When, therefore, an unknown collector, A. G. Vrooman, of Santa Cruz, announced in 1901, through the columns of *The Auk*, that he had found the egg of the Black Cloud Swift (*Nephoecetes niger borealis*), the oological world came to instant attention.

The Black Swift had for decades teased the oological imagination. The bird itself was none of the commonest; but when we did see it, we saw it in roving companies numbering scores or even hundreds. Every movement of these great, black, silent "sky-scrapers" bespoke mystery, no less than ease and power. A lucky day had found them gyrating about the solemn bastions of some basaltic range in eastern Oregon or Washington. Another had seen them madly crossing and recrossing the face of a giant bulwark of the high Sierras, or else hurtling like scimitars through the defiles of a frozen mountain pass. Again, it pleased their whim to descend upon the plains, a thousand strong, and there they hawked at insects, like swallows, albeit with a dash skill unknown to the swallows. At a time, again, they would deploy over the surface of one of the larger lakes, Chelan, Tahoe, or Washington; and the boatman caught the gleam of a beady eye, or else cringed in involuntary terror, as the bird swept over him with the impersonal disregard of a thunderbolt. Sultry days, we used to fancy, drove them low, but even as we gazed and speculated, seeking what manner of meat they fed on, they were gone again, vanished in a trice behind the clouds. There seemed to be no law about their comings and goings, even in the summer season, when all proper fowls are found in the vicinity of their nests. These birds could not nest on lakes or plains. Indeed, I still believe that Black Swifts hunt in flocks at all seasons, and that they enjoy a daily range of hundreds of miles in quest of food.

Comes now Vrooman of Santa Cruz, naturalist, aged forty, and sixteen years steeped in the lore of local collecting haunts. On June 16th, 1901, he is making his annual rounds of those beetling limestone cliffs, which with their indentations front the sea for thirty miles to west and north of the famed resort on Monterey Bay. The country is a rather desolate one, for the unceasing winds have driven even the reluctant redwoods to take shelter in such canyons as occasionally intersect the narrow, sharp-edged table-land. No one but the lookout of a life-saving crew, or a bird-nester, would care to follow this perilous cliff-edge, with only the wind and the snarling surf for company. Shags' eggs are the special quest of the naturalist on this occasion, hence he is equipped with rope-ladder, maul, and pin, as well as with landing-net and tin collecting box. He has just taken two or three sets of cormorants' eggs from the face of a cliff a hundred feet in height, when, as he leans over to land another one, a Black Swift flushes from under his net-pole not four feet away, dives down toward the ocean, and whisks out of sight around the cliff. It all happens in a trice. He thinks he cannot be mistaken, for he has often seen the birds in midair. He has even seen them flash across the face of a cliff in frantic pursuit of some insect too small or too quickly gone for human ken. This must be a Black Swift. The bird is gone, but there, as mute evidence of occupation, lying on an earthen cornice wet with seepage, and partially screened by growing grasses, is an enormous white egg.

In the season of 1914 it was the privilege of the writer to accompany Mr. Vrooman when the annual take was made. After a long motor drive up the coast in the teeth of a fresh gale, we turned in at a point where the cliffs were only sixty-five or seventy feet high. Here the surf, crashing against the abrupt sea-wall, kept the vegetation moist; and here, at a point some thirty feet over the crest of the cliff, the location was made. The Swift, when apprised of our presence by the rattling of Vrooman's "devil box," darted down toward the water, and passing with strong wing-stroke close to the surface of the water, stood straight to sea until lost from sight. A Black Swift I knew it to be at first glance, but this was amazing behavior for a land bird. A Kaeding Petrel or a Cassin Auklet, haled from its burrow and tossed into the air, would have acted just so; but why should this gleaner of heavenly gnats, this inspector of glacier-carpeted fastnesses and habitant of clouds, seek the sympathy or the seclusion of the open sea? *Quién sabe?* Although we knew about where the bird had got up, we did not know the precise spot quitted. The minute search, therefore, required several resettings of the stout steel stake which supported the swinging ladder, and it was nearly an hour before Vrooman appeared aloft bearing that studied, matter-of-fact expression which is the precursor of important news. He had found the egg on a mud cornice some thirty feet down, half hidden in the growing grasses. He had barely returned, however, when a shout from another member of our party, posted on a commanding cliff-edge hard by, apprised us of the return of the bird. She had swept in once, feinted and retreated, but she threatened to return again. Hastily drawing up the ladder, we flung ourselves face down upon a neighboring point, and had the satisfaction of seeing her sweep grandly upward to her nesting ledge. The grass concealed her from inquisitive gaze, even of binoculars, but there she undoubtedly was, brooding on her solitary, titled egg.

It was too good to be true. This mistress of the clouds, this storied, quested, eccentric sky-wanderer, sitting there with wings meekly folded, behind a tussock of grass! We felt like the farmer at the circus, who, having gazed long at the giraffe, declared, "By gum, there ain't no such creature."

CALLIOPE HUMMINGBIRD
Stellula calliope

THIS, THE TINIEST OF OUR SEXTET of California hummers, is also the highest-ranging, at least in the nesting season. It is essentially a mountain-loving species, and is, so far as we have been able to prove, the only breeding hummer of the higher Sierran slopes. There is a 3,000-foot record, by Stephens, of a nest in the San Bernardinos; but 4,000 is the usual minimum, and 8,000 a better average. In the Canadian zone, therefore, the bird knows no restrictions, save that it does not favor the densely timbered sections. In the Sierras it nests nearly up to timber line, 10,000 to 11,500 feet, and follows the advancing season to the limit of flowers. Without doubt the mind remembers longest those birds which visit the mountain heather beds, gorgeous with flowers, and varied beyond description. A bit of heather on a northern peak, where we camped at an elevation of 8,000 feet, yielded thirty-two species of plants in conspicuous bloom within a stone's throw of the breakfast table. The hummers appear to be attracted to the flower-beds by color and position rather than by scent; and as surely as we neglected to rise with the sun, a troop of puzzled honey-hunters hovered by turns over our parti-colored blankets. Once a hummer minutely inspected a red bandana handkerchief which graced the bird-man's neck; and once, I regret to say it, fluttered for some moments before his nose (sunburned!).

But goodness gracious! What an awful temper His Niblets, the Maharajah of Bullypore, really has! Once, in Modoc County, when a Pygmy Nuthatch had, much to my satisfaction, alighted upon the tip of a half-dead juniper, and served notice that he was about to show me his domicile, one of these dashing Star hummers set upon him so viciously that the astonished bird fell off his perch and hugged the tree trunk instead. Even here the nuthatch was not safe, for the hummer darted and buzzed like a giant bumble bee, adding, I believe, a vocal tone to the noise of its wings, until the terrified nuthatch dropped ten feet further and then fled outright. Very valiant, to be sure, the Maharajah looked as he resumed his station on the topmost twig of the juniper, and let the wind toy with his streaming cravat. Then he caught sight of the bird-man and dived down to utter some offensive threats, grinding them out horribly, as between clenched teeth. I should have heeded, too, if the gallant had been, say, a hundred times bigger.

In common with most of our hummers, the Calliope conducts an ardent courtship by means of headlong dashes from the sky. It is a sight well worth seeing when one of these elfin gallants, flashing like a jewel and bristling with self-consciousness, mounts slowly upward on vibrating wings to a height of a hundred feet, then darts back with the speed of lightning to make an affectionate pass at the placid lady on a twig below. Or, occasionally, the tactics are reversed, and the amoret settles slowly through the air as though smitten by Cupid's dart, and invokes the lady's pity on his hapless plight. Pitiful it should be, but the rascal recovers suddenly, bounds aloft and makes again the courting swoop. As he does so, he brings out at the climax a tiny, rasping note—in fact the word "rasp" with a rolled *r*, thus, *rrraspp*, just about expresses it.

An exquisite honeymoon ensues for the happy pair; but when Nature's purposes have been served, the stern madam banishes her ardent spouse, and leaves him henceforth to vent his irascible humors on luckless woodpeckers and wandering chipmunks. The female Calliope is an inconspicuous object, colorwise, but she has a will of her own, and a way which even the collector learns to recognize.

ALLEN'S HUMMINGBIRD

Selasphorus alleni

IT IS, PERHAPS, AS MUCH AS ONE'S REPUTATION is worth in these parlous times of pity to undertake to defend the practice of bird-nesting. But as a hardened offender I shall confess that I have found the keenest delight in the pursuit of hummingbirds' nests. The quarry, albeit abundant, is so elusive, so tiny, and wrought in so fine a harmony with its surroundings, that the collector is put upon his highest mettle. The quest enlists all the faculties of mind, and requires the most alert attention. A flash, a wing-buzz, a suspected bit of moss—these are the things that must be heeded, if success is to come. The trophies themselves are among the most dainty specimens of architecture the world affords, even if one be so well fortified as to resist the appeal of the two tiny, pinkish, elongated pearls which they contain. Moreover, the quest, ardently pursued, leads most certainly, through its exercise of fine discriminations, to an accuracy and intimacy of knowledge of bird life which can come in no other way. Theoretically, the earnest student should be moved to search, irrespective of the trophy; but practically, he never does. Hence, it comes about that the ultra-sentimentalist gets to know as little of the practical psychology and inner workings of bird life as does the skin-man, whose motto is "Shoot first and inquire afterward." Without asserting the full recompense of his own bold claim, the writer may say that a certain cabinet in the Museum of Comparative Oology holds more of fairy treasure, of fragrant memory, and of crystallized experience than may be put into a hundred books, or paintings either.

Enter with me one of those narrow canyons in the Santa Ynez Mountains. We will call it an early May day, although that is between seasons for Allens, and a little early for Costas. A tiny mountain stream babbles over boulders, or gathers darkling in pools under the shade of sycamores, bays, live oaks, and alders. The sides of the canyon, now steep, or briefly precipitous, now sloping and climbable, are occupied by live oaks and ceanothus, with a score of flowering shrubs and a host of bright-hued mints, with sages. Under all, there is the tangle and pluck of wild blackberry vines, and these festoon the lesser cliffs, or face you with impenetrable jungles in the open glades. Here hummers of four species breed. The Black-chins, lately come, are pitching their yellow tents (upside down) in the sycamores and live oaks, without much regard to the water. The Anna Hummers nest anywhere, at any height, save on the ground, or in the vines, but they care less for shade and retirement than do the other species, and their ranks will lessen as we ascend the canyon. Costa Hummers in such circumstances hug close to the water, weaving their little baskets on a descending branch of a willow or a bay tree whose tips nearly drag the water. As for the Allen Hummer, the blackberry tangles are her home, and all such other situations as assure a measure of protection from above. Thus, drooping vines falling over boulders offer ideal sites; for *alleni* is also fond of a swing.

The behavior of the female is quite the most interesting part of hummingbird nesting. Usually the only apprisal one has of the presence of a nest is a little momentary electric buzz summoning you—*somewhere*. Oh! that is the point where the search begins in earnest, for the wing-buzz of the departing bird is a sound ventriloquial in its indefiniteness. Or if the bird returns to squeak her disapproval, that may only add fuel to the fire of your anxiety, without being at all illuminating. Once a female Allen, startled from a nest of unknown location, squeaked lustily from the top of a live oak, until she was sure she had our attention, then she set out on a *Himmelfahrt*, a heavenly flight, winging rapidly upward at an angle of 70 degrees until the eye strained to watch her. Nearer and nearer she drifted to the sun until she suddenly lost herself to view in that orb, and we nearly lost our eyesight. It was, I submit, a clever ruse, quite as effectual as the staple trick of the fleeing highwayman who, to baffle his pursuers, wades the bed of a running stream.

Nests with fresh eggs are, curiously enough, more easily found by observation of the bird than those in which incubation is advanced. At first, the bird, with the nest-making instinct still strong upon her, cannot resist the temptation of a floating bit of down, and she sallies forth noisily to capture it, and add it to her nest-lining. Similarly, she uncovers the eggs at frequent intervals to snap at insects or to sip a beaker of honey, before she has learned to forswear these pleasures for her more exacting duties. And no hummer of refined tastes can be expected to resist the attractions of a cunning bit of moss or a brocaded lichen, but it must be lugged home and added to the collection.

Rufous Hummingbird
Selasphorus rufus

Rufus! What mighty Norsemen have borne that name! None more worthily than the iron-blooded midget of tropic mould who, among six hundred kinsmen, holds the record of "farthest North." Often have I pitied him as on a March day in the Puget Sound country, with the rain pelting and the mercury at 40 degrees, I have come upon him sheltering in the depths of a somber fir tree. Or more pitiful still is the sight of shivering babies in mid-April, the air oozing moisture and the mother gone to search for food. But *rufus* would laugh at our solicitude; and as for hardship, he would say, Lead me to it! Hence it is, he ranges along the Cascade crests and ventures among the glaciers of the mighty Saint Elias Mountain. At Mount Wrangell he is 61° north of the Equator, and his only peer in hardihood is the Chilean Fire-crown (*Eustephanus galeritus*), who attains 55° south in Tierra del Fuego.

Perhaps it is the abounding conceit of the bird which carries it into such perilous places; but if so, the little spitfire makes good all along the way. I thought I had seen hummers before, some tens of thousands of them, but a vision seen on the flowery hills of Shandon (San Luis Obispo County), April 8, 1912, still stands apart in experience. The bird had been moving from flower to flower in the open sage, and came momentarily to rest on a sprig of greasewood. As I saw him quartering from the sun, the center of his gorget glanced molten gold, and his shoulders shot a living flame. As he turned about, his throat-piece darkened suddenly, but whenever it did shine, it was nothing less than cadmium or Saturn red. His back, also, was the very quintessence of rufous, almost flame, and I thought there could be nothing handsomer—until another, his equal, flashed up and displaced him on the same twig.

Rufous Hummers are very fond of the blossoms of the eucalyptus tree, and this towering exotic is not only responsible for the presence of a hundred hummers at once, but in a measure also for the withdrawal of the birds from their humbler and more wonted ranges of observation. It is a pretty sight to see hummers as thick as bees, but it is a bit provoking, as well, to think that there may be as many as six species aloft which are no better than one to you. In the north they are more fortunate who can see these hummers swarming about a lowly bush of flowering currant. At such a time there may be a dozen birds about at once. The bush seems fairly aquiver with their vibrating wings. The birds are exceedingly quarrelsome, and the intrusion of a newcomer may be the signal for a general pursuit and much clashing of tongues.

The rattling noise made by the Rufous Hummer is apparently a vocal sound accompanying flight, rather than a by-product of the wing-beat. One morning in Tacoma, we saw a young dandy in a fine fury. His exhibition of temper was undoubtedly on our account, although there seemed to be no precisely defined objective. The bird first *towered* slowly with bill held straight up, as though in infinite disdain. When at a height of seventy-five feet he darted to one side and then swept down in a passion, giving vent, at the lowest point of the curve, to an explosive rattle of unquestionable ferocity. Then he would face about sputtering and murmuring to note the effect made upon us. Finding us unmoved, rooted to the spot, indeed, with admiration, the little bully repeated the process again and again, pausing only to vary his tactics by a slow and menacing advance with distended gorget flaming in the morning sun. We were cowed, to be sure, and we crept away with the consoling thought that nobody would tell on us if we fled. Or—now, do you suppose there could have been a mischievous coquette applauding softly from behind that screen of dogwood blossoms?

Anna's Hummingbird
Calypte anna

Shrewdest of immortalities, a name! One Anna, sometime Duchess of Rivoli, is held aloft to immortal remembrance in California more surely than as if her statue in imperishable bronze were adorning a space in Golden Gate Park. Lesson, the Frenchman, monographer of hummingbirds, spying a new jewel in a recent importation from Mexico, presented it, *Calypte anna*, with a graceful flourish, to his lady friend; and we, forsooth, were pledged to pay vocal tribute to this unknown lady forever. Was she pretty? Was she witty? Was she worthy and wise? We hope so, for her namesake is all of these; and Anna is his name for better or for worse.

The Anna Hummer, Hyperion of the Golden West, is the California hummer *par excellence*. And while we may not endure to match his beauties against the flaming splendors of certain tropical species, we are well content that such a treasure should be in our portion. Look first upon a singing male as he seats himself on a December day upon the topmost wire of a garden trellis. We must look before we listen. Not only the gorget, but the forehead, crown, and sides of neck as well, are seen to be clad in a resplendent panoply of glancing crimson. At a turn of the head the entire foreparts assume one cast of rose-purple; at another, the gorget will go to velvet of some dark nameless tint in relief, while the side of the head will glance with fires of green and copper. And at another tilt of the head the fires will be wholly quenched in a uniform velvety blackness.

The established article of hummer courtship is, as everybody knows, the tower and dive, and this performance serves as well to intimidate enemies as to win favor with the ladies, though why it should accomplish such diverse ends I cannot for the life of me discern. Perhaps there is a subtle difference in quality which escapes our dull perceptions. Anyhow, the male Anna in courting time is very irascible, and is as likely to try conclusions with a man as with a mouse. Upon sighting a fancied enemy, the little spitfire mounts to a considerable height in midair, and then darts down with great velocity, producing at the climax of its parabola a sudden explosive squeak or squawk—actually a little trying to the nerves of the most hardened offender. This focal squawk (whether vocal or exophonic we do not know) is very brief and is much lower in pitch than the courting squeak of the Costa Hummer. It sounds, in fact, like the whistling cry of the ground squirrel (*Citellus*) or of a cony (*Ochotona*).

The courting flight, with the lady seated on an exposed twig, or modestly hiding in the depths of a bough, is performed with more circumstance. The *squayuck* squeak, or screech, or squawk, is uttered, indeed, at the climax of one downward flight; but the curve of flight on this portion is slight and the speed terrific. It is the grandstand play for an audience of one. After each dash the speed king manages a quick recovery and returns to hover for some moments over his enamorata, as if for applause. The chances are the lady isn't handing out any bouquets today. Nothing daunted, the impetuous suitor ascends, almost vertically, with fiercely vibrant wings, swings over to a proper distance and repeats his dash. Birds do not perspire, but our hero evidently earns his bread by labors more strenuous than sweat of the brow. The coy minx in the grandstand, she knows how to appear quite indifferent, to be sure, but if she does not look out she will overplay the part. Bowles narrates an instance where a swinking swain, outraged at last by the coldness of his lady love, paused before her, and gliding slowly up seized her rudely by the beak and dragged her highness headlong from the perch.

It is thus undoubtedly that hearts are won, for I have witnessed the nuptials—tented all in a bower of oak-leaves. The nuptial kiss occurs as well in midair as upon an oaken bed, but always close to cover and always to a fierce accompaniment of squeaks in which both sexes participate. Indeed, so ingenuous are these happy children of Nature that it is best not to be too inquisitive when one hears a fairy bedlam in the garden.

Kingfishers and Woodpeckers

Western Belted Kingfisher
Megaceryle alcyon caurina

WHEN WE WERE SMALL BOYS and had successfully teased our fathers or big brothers to let us go fishing with them, we were repeatedly admonished not to "holler" for fear of scaring the fish. This gratuitous and frequently emphatic advice would have been discredited if the example of the Kingfisher had been followed. Either because noise doesn't matter to fish, or because he is moved by the same generous impulse which prompts the mountain lion to give fair and frightful warning of his presence at the beginning of an intended foray, the bird makes a dreadful racket as he moves upstream and settles upon his favorite perch, a bare branch overlooking a quiet pool. Here, although he waits long and patiently, he not infrequently varies the monotony of incessant scrutiny by breaking out with his weird rattle—like a watchman's call, some have said; but there is nothing metallic about it, only wooden. Again, when game is sighted, he rattles with excitement before he makes a plunge; and when he bursts out of the water with a wriggling minnow in his beak, he clatters in high glee. If, as rarely happens, the bird misses the stroke, the sputtering notes which follow speak plainly of disgust, and we are glad for the moment that Kingfisher talk is not exactly translatable.

When a fish is taken, the bird first thrashes it against its perch to make sure it is dead, and then swallows it head foremost. If the fish is a large one its captor often finds it necessary to go through the most ridiculous contortions, gaspings, writhings, chokings, regurgitations, and renewed attempts, in order to encompass its safe delivery within.

Kingfishers have the reputation of being very unsocial birds. Apart from their family life, which is idyllic, this reputation is well sustained. Good fishing is so scarce that the birds deem it best to portion off the territory with others of their own kind, and they are very punctilious about the observance of boundaries and allotments. For the rest, why should they hunt up avian companions, whose tastes are not educated to an appreciation of exposed, water-soaked stubs, and a commanding view of river scenery? However, I did once see a Kingfisher affably hobnobbing with a Kingbird, on a barren branch which overlooked a crystal stream in Idaho. I wonder if they recognized a mutual kingliness, this humble fisherman and the petulant hawk-driver?

Kingfisher courtship is a very noisy and spirited affair. One does not know just how many miles up and down stream it is considered proper for the gallant to pursue his enamorata before she yields a coy acceptance; and it is difficult to perceive how the tender passion can survive the din of the actual proposal, where both vociferate in wooden concert to a distracted world. But la! love is mighty and doth mightily prevail.

The parents are very busy birds after the young have broken shell, and it takes many a quintal of fish to prepare six, or maybe seven, lusty fisher princes for the battle of life. At this season the birds hunt and wait upon their young principally at night, in order not to attract hostile attention to them by daylight visits. Only one brood is raised in a season, and since fishing is unquestionably a fine art, the youngsters require constant supervision and instruction for several months. A troop of six or eight birds seen in July or August does not mean that Kingfisher is indulging in midsummer gaieties with his fellows, but only that the family group of the season has not yet been broken up.

NORTHERN RED-BREASTED SAPSUCKER

Sphyrapicus ruber ruber

IT IS ALL VERY WELL FOR THE ECONOMIC ORNITHOLOGIST to tell us
that sapsuckers are somewhat injurious to orchard trees, but the sight
of one of these splendid creatures, dropping with a low cry to the base
of a tree and hitching coquettishly up its length, is enough to disarm
all resentment. From what spilled chalice of old Burgundy has the bird
been sipping? Or from what baptism of blood has he lately escaped that
he should be dyed red for half his length? Recrudescent mythology, ill
at ease in these commercial times, nevertheless casts furtive glances at
him, and longs to account in its inimitable way for the tell-tale color.

For myself, if young fruit trees will lure such beauty from the
woods, I will turn orchardist. Nor will I begrudge the early sap from
my choicest pippins. I am fond of cider myself, but there are worthier.
Drink, pretty creature, drink!

CALIFORNIA WOODPECKER

Balanosphyra formicivorus bairdi

THE CALIFORNIA WOODPECKER IS PREEMINENTLY a sociable bird—
sociable and clannish. Other woodpeckers tend to become solitary, the
larvae-hunting species especially so, because of the comparative scarcity
of their prey. But the California Woodpecker is chiefly dependent upon
mast, and this, if not unfailing, is at least abundant when it is to be
had at all. Now, abundance of food begets gregariousness, of which the
mast-eating pigeon, the extinct Passenger Pigeon of the East, was the
extreme example. Abundance with variability has produced gregarious
but sporadic, or roving, species, as in the case of our own Band-tailed
Pigeon (*Columba fasciata*) and the crossbills (*Loxia curvirostra* and *leucoptera*).
The California Woodpecker is not only gregarious but social, having, by
cooperation in hoarding, solved the question of a variable food supply.

But before we go into that, let us note how well the birds get along among themselves. Bickering and minor differences of opinion there may be, for *Balanosphyra* is an active, noisy bird; but it is astonishing how well they do agree together upon the whole, insomuch that half a dozen woodpeckers may be found working silently upon the same tree. In defense of the common preserves, also, they show a great unanimity of action, combining to drive off marauding Jays and Magpies. This cooperative larder-keeping has in time reacted upon this woodpecker's character, making the species self-contained and self-sufficient to an unusual degree. They are neither wary nor friendly, and, except where persecuted, will go on about their business in total disregard of human comings and goings. Thus, an acorn-ridden oak spans the entrance driveway of a fashionable hotel near Santa Barbara. Automobiles and carriages come and go at all hours, yet at any moment in the year from one to a dozen Woodpeckers may be seen on that tree.

Much time is spent on lookout on the bare tips of elevated stubs or on telephone poles. Frequent sallies are made in midair, chiefly insectivorous, but partly, one suspects, from sheer exuberance of spirits. A most characteristic flight-movement is an exaggerated fluttering wherein progress is at a minimum and exercise at a maximum. In this way, also, they ascend at acute angles, sometimes almost vertically. With this movement alternates much sailing with outspread wings, and certain tragic pauses wherein the wings are quite folded. It is in such a movement of the folded-wing position, apparently, that the Woodpecker may make critical inspection of anything before him, for at other times his downward vision is obscured by the motion of his own wings.

Now, having conscientiously dispatched all other matters, we pause to remark what is perfectly well known to every Californian, that the California Woodpecker is the original artist in inlaid bindings. From time immemorial this bird has riddled the bark of certain forest trees and stuffed the holes with acorns. Speculation is still rife as to the cause or occasion or necessity or purpose of this strange practice, but the fact is indisputable and the evidence of it widely diffused. *Balanosphyra formicivorus bairdi* has taken it for his life work to enshrine all the acorns, one by one, in appropriate wooden niches, so long as life shall last. This is his bounden duty, his meat and drink, his religion, and his destiny.

Why does the bird do it? Ostensibly, of course, for food. Acorns form more than fifty percent of this Woodpecker's diet and by this provident arrangement the bird is able to regale itself on mast throughout the year. These treasure-houses are not "worm cultures" as was formerly supposed. Many of the acorns do become infected, but these represent, apparently, a dead loss to the bird. Care is taken, in selection, to provide sound acorns, and one authority asserts, with what justice I do not know, that the birds are shrewd enough to select sweet ones out of the host of bitter acorns. Acorns so preserved keep sweet and usable much longer than they would upon the ground, and are probably good for more than one season. But the fact remains that the provision made is out of all proportion to any possible use. Chipmunks, California Jays, and other woodpeckers, especially the Lewis, levy upon this horde as often as they dare; but the Californias are very zealous in defense, and do not hesitate to employ platoon tactics when threatened. The feud is especially sharp between the Californias and the Lewises, and one observer tells how a wounded Lewis Woodpecker, escaping from the gunner, sought refuge in a California tree. The Californias set upon him promptly, and one of their number paid forfeit with his life, for, when the huntsman arrived he found the Lewis Woodpecker dead with two of his talons sunk into the California's eyes and two in his pierced skull.

But again, why does the bird hoard treasure on this lavish, irrational scale? For exercise? Perhaps. To be doing something—for the same reason that a high school girl chews gum or a callow youth sucks cigarettes, a matron does embroidery or a middle-aged gentleman of increasing girth trots after a twinkling white ball—to kill time. Possibly, also, from force of habit. Following the blind urge of a provident instinct, the bird over-shoots the mark. Having no accurate criterion of judgment, or inhibitive power, it just goes on forever, *working*.

Red-shafted Flicker
Colaptes cafer collaris

It is perhaps as a musician that the Flicker is best known. The word musician is used in an accommodated sense, for the bird is no professional singer, or instrumental maestro; but so long as the great orchestra of Nature is rendering the oratorio of life, there will be place for the drummer, the screamer, and the utterer of strange sounds, as well as for the human obbligato. The Flicker is first, like all other woodpeckers, a drummer. The long rolling tattoo of early springtime is elicited from some dry limb or board where the greatest resonance may be secured, and it is intended both as a musical performance and as a call of inquiry. Once, as a student, the writer roomed in a large building, whose unused chimneys were covered with sheet-iron. A Flicker had learned the acoustic value of these elevated drums, and the sound of this bird's reveille at four a.m. was a regular feature of life at "Council Hall."

In the early days of April, courtship is in progress, and the lovemaking of the Flicker is both the most curious and the most conspicuous of anything in that order. An infatuated Flicker is a very soft and foolish-looking bird, but it must be admitted that he thoroughly understands the feminine heart, and succeeds in love beyond the luck of most. A bevy of suitors will lay siege to the affections of a fair lady, say in the top of a sycamore tree. Although the rivalry is fierce, one gallant at a time will be allowed to display his charms. This he does by advancing toward the female along a horizontal limb, bowing, scraping, pirouetting, and swaying his head from side to side with a rhythmical motion. Now and then the swain pretends to lose his balance, being quite blinded, you see, by the luster of milady's eyes, but in reality he does it that he may have an excuse to throw up his wings and display the dazzling flame which lines them. The lady is disposed to be critical at first, and backs away in apparent indifference, or flies off to another limb in the same tree. This is only a fair test of gallantry and provokes pursuit, as was expected. Hour after hour, and it may be day after day, the suit is pressed by one and another until the maiden indicates her preference, and begins to respond in kind by nodding and bowing and swaying before the object of her choice, and to pour out an answering flood of softly whispered adulation. The best of it is, however, that these affectionate demonstrations are kept up during the nesting season, so that even when one bird relieves its mate upon the eggs it must needs pause for a while outside the nest to bow and sway and swap compliments.

Nature has not always dealt justly with the western Flicker in the matter of providing an abundance of dead timber for nesting sites. What more natural, then, than that the stinted bird should joyfully fall upon the first "frame" houses and riddle them with holes? The front door of a certain country parsonage testifies to at least one pastoral vacation, by the presence of three large Flicker holes in its panels. The church, hard by, is dotted with tin patches which conceal this bird's handiwork; and the mind recalls with glee how the irreverent Flicker on a summer Sunday replied to the parson's fifthly by a mighty *rat-at-at-at-at* on the weather siding. The district schoolhouse of a neighboring township is worst served of all, for forty-one Flicker holes punctuate its weather-beaten sides—reason enough, surely, for teaching the young idea of that district how to shoot. Indeed, the school directors became so incensed at the conduct of these naughty fowls that they offered a bounty of ten cents a head for their destruction. But it is to laugh to see the fierce energy with which these birds of the plains, long deprived of legitimate exercise, fall to and perforate such neglected outposts of learning. The bird becomes obsessed by the idea of filling a particular wall full of holes, and no ingenuity of man can deter him. If work during union hours is discouraged, the bird returns stealthily to his task at four a.m., and chisels out a masterpiece before breakfast. If the gun speaks, and one bird falls a martyr to the sacred cause, another comes forward promptly to take his place, and there is always some patriotic Flicker to uphold the rights of academic research.

The young are fed entirely by regurgitation, not an attractive process, but one admirably suited to the necessities of long foraging expeditions and varying fare. When able to leave the nest, the fledglings usually clamber about the parental roof-tree for a day or two before taking flight. Their first efforts at obtaining food for themselves are usually made upon the ground, where ants are abundant. These, with grasshoppers and other ground-haunting insects, make up a large percentage of food, both of the young and adults. When feeding upon ants, the Flicker protrudes its tongue, and lets it lie along the ground for a moment until the little victims swarm over its surface and are engaged by its viscid coating. A sudden withdrawal assures a feast and the number of ants which the bird can bag in this fashion is amazing. Five thousand of a small species (*Crematogaster* sp.) were found by Beal in a single stomach—these and a portion of sand incidentally acquired.

MEARNS'S GILDED FLICKER

Colaptes chrysoides mearnsi

IT IS—IT IS—THE GILDED FLICKER! He takes flight from a palo verde, and we get a flash of authentic gold as he lights against the side of a giant cactus (as though it were not at all beset with spines, that should be fearful). He shouts, *Culloo' cullitoo'*, with jovial pretense of fear, and bows emphatically with disarming waggishness. It is our old friend, the Flicker, surely none other, known from seaboard to seaboard, and from New Orleans to—one had almost said "the Pole." Yes; but his voice is a little thinner; and the shafts of his quills, with the accompanying illumination of the webs, are *golden*, instead of grenadine (red). For the rest it is our Flicker, and, save as influenced in habit by special conditions, the self-same bird which blessed our childhood.

The distribution of the Gilded Flicker is almost exactly coincident with that of the sahuaro, or "giant cactus." There is only one conspicuous stand of this plant left in California, that occurring just above the Laguna Dam on the Colorado River. But wherever the presence of the sahuaro affords an excuse for the bird, the latter is apt to occupy neighboring timber as well, whether mesquite, cottonwood, or willow. It is for this reason that the present Flicker population of the Colorado River "bottoms" somewhat exceeds the accommodations provided by the modest remnant of "desert candelabra."

The hospitality of the giant cactus on its native desert is almost unbounded. Its fleshy columns, flanked by fluted arms no less hospitable, shelter not only woodpeckers and owls, but wrens, martins, flycatchers, hawks, doves, and ravens. The gracefully upturned branches, though themselves a dead weight upon the parent stem, will support a man's weight beside, and there is always room for a hawk's nest at their clustering bases. The succulent flesh of the sahuaro is guarded externally by a series of bristling spines, and it is supported internally by a concentric row of woody ribs, which gather strength as the plant rears itself to an impressive height, twenty-five, thirty, or even forty feet. An isolated plant of good size is sure to contain several nesting holes, and a veteran is riddled with them, each the scene of some domestic venture present or past, and most of them cherishing a lively expectation of repeated occupancy. The sahuaro, moreover, furnishes not only lodging, but a very substantial "board," in the shape of luscious fruits borne in profusion upon the growing crown, or upon the ends of the branches. Its body, however, is not largely subject to decay, and the proportion of moribund giants is a small one. When one of them does finally disintegrate, it is a pathetic sight to see in its last stages the weathered outlines of the ancient nesting hollows, each like a quaint gourd, persisting after the supporting tissues have perished. It was the Flicker, no doubt, who discovered, or perfected, this curative hardening process which attends upon any exposure of the sahuaro tissue, as upon the excavation of a nest.

For the Gilded Flicker is at once janitor and high priest of the sahuaro. It is he who prepares, with Cousin Gila (*Centurus uropygialis*), most of the lodgings, and he does this with rare and conscious foresight. Scorning for himself a second-hand dwelling, even his own, the industrious Flicker delves out the nesting hollow *a year ahead*. And whenever this attractive hollow happens to please a braver or less considerate bird, a Purple Martin or an Elf Owl, the poor Flicker has to delve again. And because this has happened many, many times, the patient bird just keeps on digging, so that there will surely be enough for all.

Tyrant Flycatchers

SAY'S PHOEBE

Sayornis sayus

A GENTLE MELANCHOLY POSSESSES the soul of all pewees, and *Sayornis sayus* is the most desponding of the lot. It is impossible to guess what ancestral hardship could have stamped itself so indelibly upon any creature with wings. Perhaps the bird is haunted by the memory of that northern Eden once obliterated by the ice-sheet. Perhaps alkaline waters are bad for little livers. I do not know. Your guess is as good as mine. *Choooory kuteéw*. This "choory" note, heard on a gray day in December, puts one in the same mental attitude as that induced by the modest mewing of a cat. I want to stop and stroke its head, and say in sympathetic falsetto, "Poor little kittens!"

In keeping with its ascetic nature the pewee haunts open, solitary places, drear pastures tenanted by mullein stalks, bleak hillsides swept by wintry gales, dull dobe cliffs with their solemn, silent flutings. Or, since misery loves company, she ventures upon some half-deserted town-site, and voices in unexpectant cadences the universal yearning for green things and cessation of wind. Or, better still, she attaches herself for the season to some farmhouse, culls wintry flies, and roosts disconsolate in the shelter of a cornice—*choooory—choooory—kuteéw*.

Say's Pewee, for all its depressed spirits, is an active bird. Taking station on a fence-post or weed-stalk, it waits for passing insects, and sallies out after them with good form and despatch. If local trade is dull, the bird makes fluttering excursions over the field, snapping right and left at humble quarry, and returning to jet the tail and render mournful thanks. Insects constitute the bird's exclusive diet, save in winter, when, under the spell of adverse weather, dried berries and seeds are sometimes taken.

WESTERN FLYCATCHER
Empidonax difficilis difficilis

THE WESTERN FLYCATCHER INHABITS the deeper woods of lower and moderate levels, chiefly west of the Sierras, though it has its acknowledged centers of abundance in the San Diegan district, and in the humid coast province up to and including the San Francisco Bay region. It is rather partial, also, to watercourses, and especially such as flow through shady retreats or past mossy grottoes. Abundant water and shade lure it to the heart of the Sierras, but only along the valleys of the major streams at altitudes of five or six thousand feet. On the other hand, it is interesting to note an increasing fondness on the bird's part for civilized shade. Given shade, the little fellow will invade the most pretentious estates, or push his way into the confines of cities. The crannies of porches offer him welcome shelter, and he is nowise intolerant of humans, if only they will leave him to his own devices.

Difficilis is typically the gleaner of the middle forest. Though moving about in the shade, he selects a perch devoid of foliage, where he can have a local fair-way. Quiet, for the most part, when settled, he nevertheless shifts position every twenty seconds or so—goes the rounds in search of the lesser hymenoptera and the flies, which together make up two-thirds of his living. Of course these are secured by tiny sallies through the air, and each successful foray is likely to be marked by a self-satisfied shake of the wings when the bird has regained his perch. Birdikins never seems to tire of this sportive gastronomic quest, and we suppose that the flavor of *Hippodamia convergens* (that's a beetle) must be quite equal to pompano or sand-dabs; while the satisfaction of landing *Diabrotica soror* is like bringing a tuna to gaff. Wasps, too, are no mean antagonists, but so relentless is the warfare *difficilis* wages against them, that his older children are fattened up on an almost exclusive diet of wasp meat.

OLIVE-SIDED FLYCATCHER
Nuttallornis borealis

FLYCATCHERS BELONG TO THE SUB-ORDER Clamatores, that is to say, Shouters. Some few of our American flycatchers lisp and sigh rather than cry aloud, but of those which shout, the Olive-sided Flycatcher is easily dean. And it is as an elocutionist only that most of us know this bird, even though our opportunities may have stretched along for decades. On a morning in early May, as surely as the season comes around, one hears a strong insistent voice shouting, *"See here!"* There is not much to see, save a dun-colored bird seated at an impossible height on the summit of a tall fir tree. Its posture is that easy half-slouch which, with the flycatchers, betokens instant readiness for action. While we are ogling, the bird launches from his post, seizes an insect some thirty feet distant, and is back again before we have recovered from surprise. *"See here!"* the bird repeats, but its accent is unchanged and there is really nothing more to see.

Borealis is a bird of the treetops, and nearer you cannot come, save in nesting time, when caution is thrown to the winds, and studies in morbid psychology are all too easy. The birds place a rustic saucer of interwoven twigs and mosses, lined with rootlets, upon the upper side of a horizontal branch, whether of yellow pine, tamarack pine, or fir tree; and as often as otherwise at moderate heights. The small bird usually maintains a prudent aloofness in the early days; but as incubation advances, his solicitude breaks bounds. Then both birds betray uneasiness at the approach of strangers and begin to flit about, with restless, tittering cries, *tew-tew, tew-tew,* or *tew-tew-tew,* sounds which strangely excite the blood of the oologist. Once the nesting tree is made out and the ascent begun, the birds are beside themselves with rage, and dash at the intruder with angry shouts which really stimulate endeavor where they are intended to discourage it.

How fatal is the beauty of an egg-shell! There be those of us who have drunk so oft of this subtle potion that the hand goes out instinctively to grasp the proffered cup. Besides, the product of an Olive-side's skill is of a very special kind—a rich cream-colored oval, warmed by a hint of living flesh, shadowed by lavenders and splotched with saucy chestnut. It is irresistible! But, boys, don't do it! We are old topers ourselves; public sentiment is against us, and our days are numbered. It is right that it should be so. Besides that, and speaking in all seriousness now, while it is desirable and necessary that a few representative collections of natural history should be built up *for the public use,* it does not follow that the public good is secured by the accumulation of endless private hoards of birds' eggs—whose logical end, in ninety-nine cases out of a hundred, is the scrap-heap. You are probably one of the ninety-nine. Think twice before you "start a collection," and then—don't!

Western Wood Pewee
Myiochanes richardsoni richardsoni

THE PREY OF GENTLE MELANCHOLY and the heir to gloom is this pewee of the West. The day, indeed, is garish. The leaves of the fragrant cottonwoods glance and shimmer under an ardent sun; while the wavelets of the lake, tired of their morning romp, are sighing sleepily in the root-laced chambers of the overhanging shore. The vision of the distant hills is blurred by heat pulsations; the song of birds has ceased and the very caddis-flies are taking refuge from the glare. The sun is dominant, and all Nature yields drowsy allegiance to his sway. All but Pewee. He avoids the sun, indeed, but from a sheltered perch he lifts a voice of protest, "*Dear Me!*"

It seems uncalled for. The bird does not appear to be unhappy. Fly-catching is good, and the Pewee cocks his head quite cheerfully as he returns to his perch after a successful foray. But, true to some hidden impulse, as you gaze upon him, he swells with approaching effort, his mandibles part, and he utters that doleful, appointed sound, *dear me*. His utterance has all the precision and finality of an assigned part in an orchestra. It is as if we were watching a single player in a symphony of Nature whose other strains were too subtle for our ears. The player seems inattentive to the music, he eyes the ceiling languidly, he notes a flashing diamond in the second box, he picks a flawed string absently, but at a moment he seizes the bow, gives the cello a vicious double scrape, *dear me*, and his task is done for that time.

But if our musician is faithful to the score of daylight, he makes himself responsible for its comings and its goings. Over how many millions of acres of western woodland is not the dear, doleful precentor the first to break the brooding silence of the night! Or ever the owl and the nighthawk have gone to bed, his voice booms out in the darkness and serves notice of impending day. And he it is who tolls the knell of day departing. Only the Mockingbird, lovesick and comfortless, disputes him—he and the Nuttall's Sparrow, rousing tipsily at goodness knows what hour to shout defiant babblings.

Vireos and Shrikes

WESTERN WARBLING VIREO
Vireosylva gilva swainsoni

IS THERE A MOMENT IN SPRINGTIME more delicious than that in which
the greeting of the returning vireo falls upon the ear? Fresh as apples
and as sweet as apple blossoms comes that dear, homely song from the
willows. How the heart feeds upon it! We tell another bead on life's
jewelled rosary; and, somehow, I think that bead is emerald. The old-
fashioned name "Greenlet," as applied to the vireos, was a misnomer,
if a description of plumage was intended; but if it was intended to
memorialize the bird's fondness for greenery, nothing could have been
more apt. The Warbling Vireo's surroundings must be not only green, but
freshly green, for it frequents only deciduous trees in groves and riverside
copses. It is not an abundant bird, therefore, in California, although
equally distributed, whether in the willows and cottonweeds which gather
about some lonesome spring in the cattle country, or among the crowded
alders and maples of the turbid McCloud. Moreover, the bird is not so
frequently found about parks and shade trees as in the East, although it
looks with strong favor upon the advent of orchards. And the orchardist
may welcome him with open arms, for there is not among all his tenants
a more indefatigable gleaner of bugs and worms.

Because he is clad in Quaker gray there is little need for the Warbling Vireo to show himself as he sings, and he remains for the most part concealed in the dense foliage, a vocal embodiment of the living green. Unlike the disconnected fragments which the Cassin's Vireo furnishes, the song of this bird is gushing and continuous, a rapid excursion over pleasant hills and valleys. Continuous, that is, unless the bright-eyed singer happens to spy a worm *in medias res*, in which event the song is instantly suspended, to be resumed a moment later when the wriggling tid-bit has been dispatched. The notes are flute-like, tender, and melodious, having, as Chapman says, "a singular alto undertone." All hours of the day are recognized as appropriate to melody, and the song period lasts from the time of the bird's arrival, early in May, until its departure in September, with only a brief hiatus in July.

The Warbling Vireo's cradle is swung midway from the fork of some nearly horizontal branch in the depths of a shady tree. In height it may vary from fifteen to twenty-five feet above the ground; but I once found one in a peach tree without a shadow of protection, and within reach from the ground. The structure is a dainty basket of interwoven grasses, mosses, flower-stems, and the like. It is not, however, so durable as that of some other vireos, since much of its thickness is due to an ornamental thatching of grass, bark-strips, green *usnea* moss, and cottonwood down, which dissolves before winter is over. The female is a close sitter, sticking to her post even though nearly paralyzed with fear. The male is usually in close attendance, and knows no way of discouraging the inquisitive bird-man save by singing with redoubled energy. He takes his turn at the eggs when his wife needs a bit of an airing, and even, it is said, carries his song with him to the nest.

Cassin's Vireo

Lanivireo solitarius cassini

NOTHING SO ENDEARS A BIRD to a human admirer as a frank exhibition of confidence. Overtures of friendship on the bird's part may traverse all rules of caution and previous procedure, but henceforth there is a new relation established between them, bird and man, and the man, at least, is bound to live up to it. At the oncoming of a smart shower the bird-man once put into a fir-covered nook for shelter, and had not been there two minutes before a pair of Cassin's Vireos entered for the same reason. They were not in the least disturbed by the man's presence, but cheerfully accepted him as part of Things as They Are. Therefore, they proceeded to preen their dampened feathers at distances of four or five feet, while the bird-man sat with bated breath and glowing eyes. The birds roamed freely about the nook and once, I think *he* made a grimace behind the bird-man's back; for when they came around in front again, I judged she was saying, "Aren't you the wag!" while he tittered in droll recollection.

These vireos roam the half-open woods at all levels, like happy school-children; and their childish curiosity is as little to be resented. If one hears a bird singing in the distance, he need only sit down and wait. Curiosity will get the better of the bird, and under pretense of chasing bugs it will edge over, singing carelessly now and then, by way of covering the inquisitive intent. At close range the song is stifled, and you feel for the ensuing moments as you do when you have overtaken and passed a bevy of ladies on a lonesome street, *all* hands and feet with a most atrocious swagger. Inspection done, the bird suddenly resumes the discarded melody, and you no longer have to "look pleasant."

Like most Vireos, Cassin's sings as he works; and, as he works a good deal of the time, albeit in leisurely fashion, he sings in tiny phrases, separated by unembarrassed intervals of silence, a sort of soliloquizing commentary on life, very pleasant to the ear—*Weé ee-tsiweéoo-tsoo psooipetewer-ptir-sewstrs-piti-wee-sueeé-pisoor*. But our schoolboy does not fully express himself in music so staid and delicate. He has at command a rasping, nerve-grating war-cry, possibly intended by Nature as a defense against cats, but also used, on occasion, when the bird is in particularly fine spirits. The note in question, which I call the nutmeg-grater note, may perhaps be more fitly likened to the violent shaking of a pepper box—a rattling, rubbing, shaking note, of three or more vibrations, ending in a little vocal flourish.

CALIFORNIA SHRIKE
Lanius ludovicianus gambeli

OPEN OR HALF-OPEN COUNTRY is the basic requirement of this audacious and familiar little Butcher-bird. Bird of prey he is for all economic purposes, but he is no prowler, nor yet is he a hoverer, wearing out his wings with incessant flight. He is, rather, the fearless watcher, and he must have for his purpose some practical, elevated station where he may mount his marvelous field glasses; for his eyes are scarcely less in their keenness than in their length of focal range. Telephone poles suit him to a T, and so devoted is the bird to this marshalled soldiery of civilization, that one wonders how he ever fared before the advent of telephone poles. It is on their account, doubtless, that the traveller gets such a strong impression of the Shrike's abundance; for telephone poles and roads are ever close friends.

From a commanding station, if it be no better than a weed-top, this Shrike searches the ground with his eye until he detects a suspicious movement of insect, mouse, or bird. The bird can spot a cricket at sixty feet, Tyler says, and I think that is well within the mark. Then he darts toward his quarry, settles, and strikes with his beak, or else skirmishes nimbly in mid-air if the creature seeks to elude him. From a successful foray the Shrike returns to devour at leisure; but if the victim is large or ungainly, he must have help from a sharp crotch, or a splinter, or the barb of a fence-wire even, to hold it; for here again he is no hawk, and does not know how to clutch with his feet.

In flight, the Shrike moves either by successive plunges and noisy ascensions, or else pitches down from his perch and wings rapidly over the surface of the vegetation. He does not exhibit much local attachment, but rather roves restlessly from post to post, so as not to wear out his welcome with the crickets. All the Shrike's operations are direct and businesslike; and if he pauses a moment to look over his shoulder as you whirl by in your automobile, you get an impression of a very alert bird-person—no loafer, but a Twentieth Century brother in feathers.

The nervous energy which characterizes the California Shrike has got him into trouble with the ladies. He has to be doing something, so when his appetite is satisfied, he just goes right on killing—for the fun of it. He doesn't waste the game, exactly—at least he doesn't mean to—for having killed a mouse or a grasshopper, he hunts up a splinter or a thorn, and neatly impales his victim upon it. He might be hungry some time, you know. That the bird does occasionally return to feast upon this stored-up provender is pretty clearly known; but at the best his killings are far in excess of his needs.

Ravens, Crows, Magpies, and Jays

RAVEN

Corvus corax sinuatus

IN THE RAVEN WE BEHOLD not alone the ranking member of the order Passeres, but the most highly developed of birds. Quick-witted, cunning, and audacious, this fowl of sinister aspect has been invested by peoples in all ages with a mysterious and semi-sacred character. His ominous croakings were thought to have prophetic import, while his preternatural shrewdness has made him, with many, a symbol of divine knowledge.

Although confined now to the wilderness and the waste places, where his persistent misconduct has exiled him, the Raven is still in a sense the dominant bird of the Northern Hemisphere. No other bird, unless it be the regal falcon, successfully disputes his sway; and wherever he deigns to dwell he becomes the *bête noire*, the sable satanic ruler, of the bird-world. In man alone has the Raven met his match; and the story of the eternal conflict between man, the supreme of the mammalian line, and *Carava*, the dusky apex of the avian succession, if it could be told, would afford some of the most thrilling chapters in the history of animal psychology.

In appearance the Raven presents several points of difference from

the Western Crow, with which it is popularly confused. The Raven is
not only larger, but its tail is relatively much longer, and the end of it
is fully rounded. The head, too, is fuller, and the bill proportionately
stouter, with a more rounded culmen. The feathers of the neck are
more loosely arranged, resulting in an impressive shagginess; and
there is a sort of primitive uncouthness about the entire appearance
of these ancient birds, quite in contrast with the unctuous sleekness of
the dapper crows.

As is well known, the Raven remains mated for life. The
companionship of his mate is quite sufficient for him, and the Raven
usually shuns the society of his fellows. But in early springtime it
is different. The social instinct overcomes both sexes alike. Besides
that, vows must be redeclared, even though acceptance be assured.
And how could the dutiful wife know that her hubby was keeping up
with the procession unless he proved himself out in the lists annually,
doing stunts with the other fellows? Anyhow, the court of Venus is
set up every year in the neighborhood of some beetling sea-cliff, or
before some huge monument of sandstone in the cattle country.
One who has been privileged to see a Raven circus in session feels as
though he had caught the Olympians at a back-yard frolic. Dignity
is thrown to the winds, and sable seigneurs don cap and bells, while
prim ladies do aerial skirt dances amid the debris of metaphorical
champagne bottles.

Of the nesting of the Raven a separate volume might be written, a
romance of the wilderness. For, as the Raven's croak is the authentic
voice of the wilderness, so is his nest its rightful citadel. To be sure,
the pressure of civilization has brought the proud bird to some sorry
passes. An observer in Utah tells of a pair of Ravens which nested on
a railroad bridge; and I once found a nest in a deserted barn. But
cliffs are the Raven's proper home, and the further removed these are
from the madding crowd, the better she likes it.

Western Crow
Corvus brachyrhynchos hesperis

Since coming to California I cannot rid myself of the impression that there is something childish about the Crow—scarcely "child-like and bland" either, for he is astute enough, and wary to a degree. It cannot be merely because he is noisy, or that he loves crowds, that he gives the impression of frivolity, or irresponsibility. Doubtless it is rather because of constant comparison with his somber kinsman, the Raven, self-contained black angel and villain of Nature's plot. We have oftener heard in our wanderings the doomful croak of the larger *Corvus*, so when we come plump upon a roistering company of Crows, the lighter quality of their voices strikes us oddly, and we imagine ourselves with a company of school-children at recess time.

These dusky birds are notorious mischief-makers, no doubt of that. But they are not so black, perhaps, as they have been painted. More than any other bird, save the Raven, the Crow has successfully matched his wits against those of man, and his frequent easy victories and consequent boastings are responsible in large measure for the unsavory reputation in which he is held. It is a familiar adage in ebony circles that the proper study of Crow-kind is man; and so well has he pursued this study that he may fairly be said to hold his own in spite of fierce and ingenious persecution. He rejoices in the name of outlaw, and ages of ill-treatment have only served to sharpen his wits and intensify his cunning.

The psychology of the Crow is worthy of a separate treatise. All birds have a certain faculty of direct perception, which we are pleased to call instinct; but the Crow, at least, comes delightfully near to reasoning. It is on account of his phenomenal brightness that a Crow is among the most interesting of pets. If taken from the nest and well treated, a young Crow can be given such a large measure of freedom as fully to justify the experiment from a humanitarian standpoint. Of course the sure end of such a pet is death by an ignorant neighbor's gun, but the dear departed is embalmed in memory to such a degree that all Crows are thereafter regarded upon a higher plane.

Space fails in which to describe the elaborate structure of Crow society; to tell of the military and pedagogical systems which they enforce; of the courts of justice and penal institutions which they maintain; of the vigilantes who visit vengeance upon evil-minded owls and other offenders; or even of the games which they play—tag, hide-and-seek, blindman's buff and pull-away. These things are sufficiently attested by competent observers: we may only spare a word for that most serious business of life, nesting.

A typical Crow's nest is a very substantial affair. Upon a basis of coarse sticks, a mat of dried leaves, grasses, bark strips, and dirt, or mud, is impressed. The deep rounded bowl thus formed is carefully lined with the inner bark of the willow, or with twine, horsehair, cow-hair, rabbit-fur, wool, or any other soft substance available. When completed, the nesting hollow is seven or eight inches across and three or four deep. The expression "Crow's nest," as used to indicate disarray, really arises from the consideration of old nests. Since the birds resort to the same locality year after year, but never use an old nest, the neighboring structures of successive years come to represent every stage of dilapidation.

AMERICAN MAGPIE
Pica pica hudsonia

HERE IS ANOTHER OF THOSE RASCALS in feathers who keep one alternately grumbling and admiring. As an abstract proposition one would not stake a *sou marquee* on the virtue of a Magpie; but taken in the concrete, with a sly wink and a saucy tilt of the tail, one will rise to his feet, excitedly shouting, "Go it, Jackity," and place all his earnings on this pie-bald steed in the race for avian honors. The Magpie is indisputably a wretch, a miscreant, a cunning thief, a heartless marauder, a brigand bold—Oh, call him what you will! But, withal, he is such a picturesque villain, that as often as you are stirred with righteous indignation and impelled to punitive slaughter, you fall to wondering if your commission as avenger is properly countersigned, and—shirk the task outright.

It is indisputably true that Magpies are professional nest robbers. At times they will organize systematic searching parties, and advance through the sage-brush, poking, prying, spying, and devouring, with the ruthlessness and precision of a pestilence. Not only eggs but young birds are appropriated. I once saw a Magpie seize a half-grown Meadowlark from its nest, carry it to its own domicile, and parcel it out among its clamoring brood. Then, in spite of the best defense the agonized parents could institute, it calmly returned and selected another. Sticks and stones shied by the bird-man merely deterred the doom of the remaining larks. The Magpie was not likely to forget the whereabouts of such easy meat.

To say that Magpies are garrulous would be as trite as to say hens cackle, and the adjective could not be better defined than "talking like a Magpie." The Magpie is the symbol of loquacity. The very type in which this is printed is small *pica*, that is, small *Magpie*. Much of this bird's conversation is undoubtedly unfit for print, but it has always the merit of vivacity. A party of Magpies will keep up a running commentary on current events, now facetious, now vehement, as they move about; while a comparative cessation of the racket means, as likely as not, that some favorite raconteur is holding forth, and that there will be an explosion of riotous laughter when his tale is done. The pie, like Nero, aspires to song; but no sycophant will be found to praise him, for he intersperses his more tuneful musings with chacks and barks and harsh interjections which betray a disordered taste. In modulation and quality, however, the notes sometimes verge upon the human; and it is well known that Magpies can be instructed until they acquire a handsome repertoire of speech.

Young Magpies are unsightly when hatched—"worse than naked," and repulsive to a degree equaled only by young Cormorants.

Hideous as they unquestionably are, the devoted parents declare them angels, and are ready to back their opinions with most raucous vociferations. With the possible exception of Herons, who are plebes anyhow, Magpies are the most abusive and profane of birds. When a nest of young birds is threatened, they not only express such reasonable anxiety as any parent might feel, but they denounce, upbraid, anathematize, and vilify the intruder, and decry his lineage from Adam down. They show the ingenuity of Orientals in inventing opprobrious epithets, and when these run dry, they fall to tearing at the leaves, the twigs, the branches, or even light on the ground and rip up the soil with their beaks, in the mad extremity of their rage.

Wherever permitted, the Magpie becomes a faithful pensioner of the slaughterhouse. Stock men take advantage of the birds' weakness for meat, and assail them with shot-gun or poison. The birds learn to be wary of both, but between these attacks and the annual raiding of the nesting grounds, it is perfectly possible to clear the Magpies out of a given range. The first discovery of a "fallen hero" by one of his comrades is the invariable signal for a noisy wake. The clan is summoned by sharp cries, and the members assemble from far and near in quick response. Now one and now another hops up cautiously to view the remains, while all make strident cries which voice their undying indignation at man's cruelty. And, indeed, now that we think of it, what is the use in trying to reduce the varied offspring of Nature to one dead level of mediocrity! If all birds were good little dickey birds, and said *tweet tweet* with pious uniformity, some men, now saintly, would undoubtedly be moved to profane utterance. Here, then, is a toast to the Magpie, cheerful, lovable devil of a bird that he is!

California Jay

Aphelocoma californica

THE CALIFORNIA JAY OCCUPIES A COMMANDING position in the

life of the chaparral and of oak-covered hillsides, throughout California. By "commanding" we do not mean exactly that everything is ordered according to the Blue Jay's will; but it is certain that little takes place without his knowledge. The abundance of the jays and the thoroughness or uniformity of their distribution within any given area will astonish one who has not given close attention to the matter. Try this test: *Kiss* the moistened hand in such diligent fashion as to produce what Coues has so well called a screeping sound. This under a little practice sounds like the distress call of a wounded bird, and a distress note is the rally call of all jays. If you are in jay country at all, first one and then another of the blue-coated rascals will come slipping up through the shrubbery, until you may have a dozen of them poking and peering to discover the source of the commotion.

The time of year or the nature of the season has a good deal to do with the jay's activities, and especially with the publicity thereof. As the time of its own nesting approaches, the jay falls silent, and the adroitness with which this bird will let himself be forgotten is truly amazing. The birds may be nesting in your own front yard; and now that you think of it, you do recall having seen the male bird pottering about on two or three occasions. But as for the California Jay of fame, he is dead. But when the birds have got by with it, when the youngsters, full-fledged, have joined the piratical push, and especially after the mid-summer molting season, then look out for noise! Caution is thrown to the winds, and the world becomes a vast screeching-ground, made only for jays to practice in.

But—but—mischief, thy name is Blue Jay. It falls, now, to the writer's unhappy lot to rehearse the sins of the California Jay, and surely, the recording angel himself has no more laborious task— unless, as we strongly suspect, the office keeps an extra clerk on this job. To see our jay munching an acorn, which is, by most accounts, his proper food, one would extol his exemplary virtue. *Whack, whack, whack* goes the jay's intrepid beak, until Sir Acorn with a groan yields up his substance.

But your jay is no vegetarian. He annexes bugs and slugs as matter of course, indulges a frog or a lizard now and then, and even aspires to mice and shrews. His long suit, however, is the destruction of eggs and young birds. This is his real function and *raison d'etre*. Beginning with the modest fruit of the hen, or the equally humble quail, he works up through successive deglutitive stages until he can boast a discriminating preference for Phainopeplas' eggs, or Hutton Vireo babies. Black-headed Grosbeaks' eggs are a staple in season, while Rufous-crowned Sparrows, Bell Sparrows, California Purple Finches, and Lutescent Warblers pay due toll to the epicurean fancy.

In this role the jay is feared and hated by every other bird, and he is the well-deserving butt of excoriations, vituperations, and personal assaults without number. It is worthy of note in this connection that the jay is not much of a fighter. He "takes punishment," or else flees before the avenging fury of a vireo, a titmouse, or a pewee. All is, he never gives up; so that by hook or by crook he almost always manages to secure the contents of a bird's nest, if accessible, and if its whereabouts is known to him.

In this pursuit the jay not only displays a rare ingenuity, but a satanic fastidiousness as well. He marks the building of a Phainopepla's nest and notes its progress from time to time with an approving eye, but he defers the sacking until the young are of just the right age, say, two days old. Again, he displays a devilish recklessness, for he, too, is an apostle of *Schrecklichkeit*. If the nest is empty, he pulls it to pieces in disgust; or if it is full, he gobbles the contents and then flings out the lining in boisterous contempt. One bird in sardonic mood returned to a Phainopepla's nest, which he had just robbed (within fifty feet of our porch roof), and deposited a half-eaten acorn in lieu of babies.

It goes without saying that Mr. and Mrs. Aphelocoma are models of conjugal fidelity, as well as exemplary parents. It always does stump the righteous to see the wicked observing the rules of the game in these essential matters, but they do. Mr. A. will proffer his spouse a mangled Chipping Sparrow chick, dripping with warm blood, with the same gentle courtesy which you would show in serving a portion of chicken to your lady love. Blue-jay children, I take it, are unusually well behaved, even if their tender nurture has left a woodside mourning. And for these children the jay has caressive and crooning notes which take hold of the very heart of comfort, notes of fond endearment which have come down the ages unmodified, whether by mouth of saint or mug of sinner. A truce to thee, then, old boy blue! Sweet villain! No doubt we'll fight again as we've fought before. And, beyond all peradventure, we'll confiscate those little eggles of yours as fast as found, be they on topmost branch or midmost tangle. But meanwhile, and between whiles, here's to thee, cunning, agile, inconsistent bird! Wag-in-feathers, jack-o'-dreams, rake-hell—Oh, I've a whole thesaurus to hurl at thee yet. Here, take the book! Bang!

Steller's Jay
Cyanocitta stelleri

IT IS A TRUE WORD WHICH SAYS, "It takes a thief to catch a thief." For, to do him justice, it is usually the Steller's Jay who is first to make discovery and outcry if there is any mischief afoot in the woods. Time and again we have had our attention called to the presence of deer or foxes or Horned Owls, which would entirely have escaped our notice had it not been for the zealous proclamations of these birds.

Be sure, also, that the jay is keeping tab on your own movements. If he is feeling hilarious that morning, and he usually is, he will greet the explorer boisterously; but if he "has his doots," he will trail after silently in the treetops, "takin' notes" instead. Upon discovery the Steller's Jay sets up a great outcry and makes off through the thickets shrieking lustily. A favorite method of retreat is to flit up into the lower branches of a fir tree, and, keeping close to the trunk, to ascend the succeeding limbs as by a spiral staircase. The bird, indeed, takes a childish delight in this mad exercise, and no sooner does he quit one treetop than he dashes down to a neighboring tree to run another frenzied gamut.

The diet of these jays is highly varied. They will "try anything once," and so, tiring of bugs and slugs, they are not averse to sampling corn, cabbage leaves, or, best of all, potatoes. While their depredations do not figure much in the larger scheme of things, their attentions to pioneer enterprises and modest "clearings" are a little exasperating. The birds have observed the tedious operations of the gardener in planting, and know precisely where the coveted tubers lie. Bright and early the following morning they slip to the edge of the clearing, post one of their number as lookout, then silently deploy upon their ghoulish task. If they weary of potatoes, sprouting peas or corn will do. Or perhaps there may be something interesting at the base of this young tomato plant. And when the irate farmer appears upon the scene, the marauders retire to the forest shrieking with laughter at the discomfitted swain. Ay! there's the rub! We may endure injury but not insult. Bang! Bang!

As a connoisseur of birds' eggs, too, the Steller's Jay enjoys a bad eminence. The sufferers in this case are chiefly the lesser song birds; but no eggs whatever are exempt from his covetous glance, if left unguarded.

It is well known that the gentleman burglar takes a conscientious pride in the safety and welfare of his own home. Nothing shall molest *his* dear ones. The jay becomes secretive and silent as the time for nest-building approaches. The nest is well concealed in a dense thicket of fir saplings, or else set at various heights in the larger fir trees. If one but looks at it before the complement of eggs is laid, the locality is deserted forthwith. If, however, the enterprise is irretrievably launched, the birds take care not to be seen in the vicinity of their nest, unless they are certain of its discovery, in which case they call heaven and earth to witness that the man is a monster of iniquity, and that he is plotting against the innocent. The youngsters, too, quickly learn to assume the attitude of affronted innocence. At an age when most bird-babies would make a silent get-away under cover of the parental defense, young Steller's jays will turn to and berate the stranger in common with their parents, with all the virtuous zeal of ordained elders.

Swallows

Barn Swallow

Hirundo rustica erythrogaster

ONE HARDLY KNOWS WHAT QUALITY to admire most in this boyhood's and life-long friend, the Barn Swallow. All the dear associations of life at the old farm come thronging up at sight of him. You think of him somehow as a part of the sacred past; yet here he is today as young and as fresh as ever, bubbling over with springtime laughter, ready for a frolic over the bee-haunted meadows, or willing to settle down on the nearest fence-wire and recount to you with sparkling eyes and eloquent gesture the adventures of that glorious trip up from Mexico.

Perhaps it is his childlike enthusiasm which stirs us. He has come many a league this morning, yet he dashes in through the open doors and shouts like a boisterous schoolboy, "Here we are, you dear old barn; aren't we glad to get back again!" Then it's out to see the horse-pond; and down the lane where the cattle go, with a dip under the bridge and a few turns over the orchard—a new purpose, or none, every second—life one full measure of abounding joy!

Or is it the apotheosis of motion which takes the eye? See them as they cast a magic spell over the glowing green of the young alfalfa, winding about in the dizzy patterns of a heavenly ballet, or vaulting at a thought to snatch an insect from the sky. Back again, in again, out again, away, anywhere, everywhere, with two-miles-a-minute speed and effortless grace.

But it is the sweet confidingness of this dainty swallow which wins us. With all the face of Nature before him he yet prefers the vicinage of men, and comes out of his hilly fastnesses as soon as we provide him shelter. We all like to be trusted, whether we deserve it or not. And if we don't deserve it—well, we will, that's all.

The nest of the Barn Swallow is quadrispherical, or bracket-shaped, with an open top; and it usually depends for its position upon the adhesiveness of the mud used in construction. Bringing off the brood is an event which may well arrest the attention of the human household. There is much stir of excitement about the barn. The anxious parents rush to and fro shouting *tisic, tisic,* now in encouragement, now in caution, while baby number one launches for the nearest beam. The pace is set, and babies number two to four follow hotly after, now lighting safely, now landing in the hay-mow, or compromising on a plow-handle. Upon the last-named the agonized parents urge another effort, for Tabby may appear at any moment. He tries, therefore, for old Nellie's back, to the mild astonishment of that placid mare, who presently shakes him off. Number five tumbles outright and requires to be replaced by hand, if you will be so kind. And so the tragicomedy wears on, duplicating human years in half as many days, until at last we see our swallows among their twittering fellows strung like notes of music on the far-flung staff of Western Union.

TREE SWALLOW
Iridoprocne bicolor

THE SWALLOW IS THE SYMBOL OF SUMMER, and by this token we know that we are in the land of perpetual summer, for does not the Tree Swallow "winter" with us? The "Merry Christmas" of the Tree Swallow is, I think, the sweetest greeting the season offers in the Southland. For these birds symbolize purity, liberty, daintiness, and all of gladness that the heart holds dear. In their immaculate garb of dark blue and white, they seem like crystallizations of heaven and its templed clouds, truth and beauty blended, winged fancies, tender tokens of constancy, fragile, yet potent, perennial pledges of the eternal Becoming of Nature.

The Tree Swallow is a lover of water, though doubtless for economic— or shall we say gastronomic?—rather than esthetic reasons. Ponds and lakes are the surest source of supply for insect food, not alone because of the variety and luxuriance of plant life which their borders afford, but because of the comparatively warm atmospheric areas which persist over their surfaces when the weather is turning cold. Swallows are very much attracted, therefore, to favorite watering places; and whatever their wanderings between whiles, they report back every hour or so to headquarters. It is over such places that the migrant species linger longest in the autumn, and it is here that the hardiest of the returning hosts join the Tree Swallows in early spring.

Feather beds will always be in fashion in Swallowdom. As a ribbon to a maid or a bonnet to a dowager, so is a feather to a Tree Swallow. It is one seduction she cannot resist. As a result, the sign of the feather protrudes from the nest, and the youngsters are brought up in a swaddled ease which bodes ill for future usefulness. If the home is disturbed, both parents are very solicitous; and should a feather from the nest be tossed into the air, one of them will catch it and fly about awaiting a chance to replace it. Or if there are other swallows about, some neighbor will snatch it first and make off with it to add to her own collection.

Violet-green Swallow
Tachycineta thalassina lepida

IF WE LAVISHED ANY SUPERLATIVES ON the Tree Swallow—and our memory misgives us that we did—we regret it now. Not but that the Tree

Swallow is strictly deserving—oh, a very deserving bird—but we needed all our superlatives for present use, and one hates to repeat. What shall we do for the Violet-green Swallows? Simply this: we will call them children of heaven.

To appear to the best advantage, this child of heaven should be seen on a typical California day, burning bright, when the livid green of back and crown may reflect the ardent glances of the sun with a delicate golden sheen. The violet of upper tail-coverts and rump comes to view only in changing flashes; but one catches such visions as a beggar flung coins, and adds image to image until he has a full concept of this rainbow hue. At such a time, if one is clambering about the skirting of some rugged precipice in Yosemite, he feels as if the dwellers of Olympus had come down in appropriate guise to inquire his earth-born business. Not, however, that these lovely creatures are either meddlesome or shrewish. Even when the nest is threatened by the strange presence, the birds seem unable to form any conception of harm, and pursue their way in sunny disregard. Especially pleasing to the eye is the pure white of the bird's underparts, rising high on flanks and cheeks, and sharply contrasting with the pattern of violet and green, in such fashion that, if Nature had invited us to "remold it nearer to the heart's desire," we must have declined the task.

The Violet-green Swallows seem to be on excellent terms with those reckless meteors, the White-throated Swifts; and while they will not follow them into some of their Lower Sonoran fastnesses, they are likely to share with them the austere hospitality of the wildest granite walls, Tehipite Dome or El Capitan. In a charmed spot I know near Santa Barbara, an epitome of romance which is yet but a doll's house compared with Sentinel Rock or the desert-frowning bastions of San Jacinto, the following birds rear their young in perfect peace within the space of a stone's cast: Western Red-tailed Hawk, Pacific Horned Owl, Cliff Swallow, White-throated Swift, and Violet-green Swallow.

But throughout the State these children of heaven are exhibiting a most commendable willingness to dwell among the children of men. We are not yet half alive to our privileges, but there are authentic records of Violet-greens nesting in the heart of the city, while such towns as happen to be near their ancient fastnesses are likely to be blessed in triple measure. It is a pretty sight on a sunny April day to see Violet-green Swallows fluttering about a suburban cottage, inspecting knot-holes or recessed gables, or, in default of such conveniences, daintily voicing their disappointment at such neglect on the part of careless humans.

Chickadees, Verdins, and Nuthatches

Oregon Chickadee

Penthestes atricapillus occidentalis

CHICKADEES ARE FRIENDLY LITTLE FOLK, so that wherever they go, except in the busy nesting season, they form the nucleus of a merry band, Western Golden-crowned Kinglets, Sitkan Kinglets, Creepers, Juncoes, Towhees maybe, and a Bewick's Wren or two to guard the terrestrial passage, and to furnish sport for the federated fairies. The chickadees are undisputed leaders, though their name be legion. While they remain aloft, we may mistake their dainty squeakings and minikin ways for those of kinglets, but if we can only determine what direction the flock is pursuing, we may count on the vanguard's being composed of these sprightly, saucy little Black-caps.

Chickadee refuses to look down for long upon the world; or, indeed, to look at any one thing from any one direction for more than two consecutive twelfths of a second. "Any old side up without care" is the label he bears; and so with anything he meets, be it a pine-cone, an alder catkin, or a bug-bearing branchlet, top-side, bottomside, inside, outside, all is right side to the nimble chickadee. Faith! their little brains must have special guy-ropes and stays, else they would have been spilled long ago, the way their owners frisk about. Blindman's buff, hide-and-seek, and tag are merry games enough when played out on one plane, but when staged in three dimensions, with a labyrinth of interlacing branches for hazard, only the blithe bird whose praises we sing could possibly master their intricacies.

Verdin

Auriparus flaviceps flaviceps

AYE, IT IS A CRUEL PLACE, THE DESERT! Cruel, that is, to the body. It denies food to the hungry stomach, and withholds water from the parched lips. The hot sands burn the toiling feet, and there is no living thing which the hand may touch without being pricked or stung or lacerated or enmeshed. If one would shout there is no man to hear, and if one would run there is no whither. A cruel, cruel place is the desert, the abode of all discomfort. But who wants to be comfortable? Not the noble soul; for to be comfortable is to be oblivious, to be unaware of livingness, to be in so far forth unalive.

And so we love (only the noble have read thus far)—we love the bristling cholla cactus, which in its eagerness to impart its delicious pain seems to fairly leap at the passerby. We love the thorny mesquite, and the zizyphus, "all thorns," which hides the hardy thrasher in its depths. Oh, we love them all, but most of all we love the tiny fearless Gnatcatcher and the tiny golden Verdins, the Verdins who cruise about in this parched sea of terrors with never a luffing sail. Surely here is intrepid nobility, or else magic, outright, that a golden-visaged atom should brave these myriad frowns of Nature and pronounce them good, should move happily from thorn to thorn and stop ever and anon to proclaim his boundless satisfaction. It was in the desert that Samson found honey in a lion's carcass, and it is in such another desert that Samson's little brother passes a honeyed existence.

The Verdin is without doubt the least restricted in its local ranging of all the desert birds. It is at home alike in the depths of the mesquite forest or in the monotonous mazes of atriplex which border the shores of the Salton sea, alike in the unending leagues of creosote, or in the varied flora of the "washes," such as sweep down from the Chocolate Mountains; and so the very first sound one listens for upon revisiting the desert is always the pensive *shthilp* of a passing, or it may be an approaching, Verdin.

Truth to tell, there is something a little plaintive and melancholy about the authentic voice of the desert. The birds seem happy enough, and they must be so, else they would not tarry; but their notes confess something of the pathos of unending sands. Verdins are not gregarious, like bush-tits; but also they are never solitary, for they roam the desert in pairs, or in small family groups, or in loose association. It is here that the remarkable penetrative, or carrying power, of the *silp* note serves the Verdin in good stead, for it allows mated birds to hunt, say, a hundred yards apart, without actually losing each other.

SLENDER-BILLED NUTHATCH
Sitta carolinensis aculeate

QUOOK-QUOOK-QUO-EW-EW-EW-EW goes the California Screech Owl in broad daylight. There is an instant hush on the oak-clad hillside—a hush followed by an excited murmur of inquiry among the scattered members of a winter bird-troop. If *you* happen to be the Screech Owl, seated motionless at the base of some large tree and half obscured in its shadows, perhaps the first intimation you will have that the search party is on your trail will be the click, click, click of tiny claws on the tree-bole above your head, followed by a *quank* of interrogation, almost comical for its mixture of baffled anxiety and dawning suspicion of the truth. He is an inquisitive fellow, this Nuthatch, for, you see, prying is his business; but he is brave, as well. The chances are that he will venture down within a foot or two of your face before he flutters off with a loud outcry of alarm. When excited, as when regarding a suspicious object, he has an odd fashion of rapidly right-and-left facing on a horizontal bough—swapping ends, as Jones puts it—as though to try both eyes on you and lose no time between.

Nuthatch is the acknowledged acrobat of the woods—not that he acts for display; it is all business with him. A tree is a complete gymnasium in itself, and the bird is master of it all. In all positions, any side up, this bird is there, fearless, confident; in fact, he rather prefers traveling head downward, especially on the main trunk route. He pries under bark-scales and lichens, peers into crevices, and explores cavities in his search for tiny insects, larvae, and insects' eggs, especially the last-named.

In selecting a nesting site the Slender-billed Nuthatch oftenest chooses an opening prepared by other species—a rotting knot-hole, a weather crack, or a woodpecker's food prospect, giving access to some capacious interior. The hollow may be laboriously remodelled; and this Nuthatch does, on occasion, excavate a nest *de novo*; but the very general avoidance of unnecessary labor on the part of the western bird has probably given rise to its special character, viz., a relatively slenderer and weaker bill. Both sexes share the labor of excavation, and when the cavity is somewhat deepened, one bird removes the chips while the other delves. Like all the hole-nesting species of this family, but unlike the woodpeckers, the nuthatches provide for their home an abundant lining of moss, fur, feathers, and the like. This precaution would not be necessary so far as warmth is concerned, in the lower portions of its range, even though it appears to nest in March; but elsewhere the bird crowds the season, and in the mountains is quite indifferent to lingering snows.

Wrens

Suisun Marsh Wren

Telmatodytes palustris aestuarinus

To THE COOTS AND RAILS BELONG the ooze-infesting morsels of the swamp; but all the little crawling things which venture into the upper story of the waving cat-tail forest belong to the Marsh Wren. Somewhat less cautious than the waterfowl, he is the presiding genius of flowing acres, which often have no other interest for the ornithologist. There are only two occasions when the Marsh Wren voluntarily leaves the shelter of the cat-tails or of the closely related marshables. One of these is when he is driven south by the migrating instinct. Then he may be seen skulking about the borders of the streams, sheltering in the weeds or clambering about the drift. The other time is in the spring, when the male shoots up into the air a few feet above the reeds, like a ball from a Roman candle, and sputters all the way, only to drop back, extinguished, into the reeds again. This is a part of the tactics of his courting season, when, if ever, a body may be allowed a little liberty. For the rest, he clings sidewise to the cat-tail stems or sprawls in midair, reaching, rather than flying from one stem to another. His tail is cocked up and his head thrown back, so that, on those few occasions when he is seen, he does not get credit for being as large as he really is.

Since his sphere of activity is so limited, we may proceed at once to the main interest, that of nest-building. And this is precisely as the Marsh Wren would have it, else why does he spend the livelong day making extra nests, which are of no possible use to anyone, save as examples of Telmatodytine architecture? It is possible that the female is coquettish, and requires these many mansions as evidence that the ardent swain will be able to support her becomingly after marriage. Or, it may be that the suitor delights to afford his lady love a wide range of choice in the matter of homes, and seeks thus to drive her to the inevitable conclusion that there is only one home-maker for her. However this may be, it is certain that one sometimes finds a considerable group of nest-balls, each of apparent suitability, before any are occupied.

Cactus Wren

Heleodytes brunneicapillus couesi

FULLY CONSCIOUS OF HIS LARGER SIZE and of the envy which it may incite, our giant wren is the most wary and secretive of the Troglodytine race. We are welcome to study his architecture, since there is no help for it, but his person is sacred from all eyes.

We have no choice, then, but to begin our studies with an investigation of those great globular, or foot-ball-shaped, masses of grass and fine weeds which we shall find imbedded in almost any cactus patch, or upborne by some taller stem of cholla, in fine scorn of concealment. The mistress will inevitably have slipped away—the conspicuous position of the nest guarantees that; but if incubation is well along, or young are in the basket, an anxious head will presently be thrust up from a concealed vantage point in a neighboring thicket. A glance, and down again. Or if the bird is descried on top of a cholla in the distance, it is in a strained, alert attitude. The male parent voices his anxiety by song, the very same with which he charmed his mate, for he has never felt the urge of harsher passions. Soft and low it comes, a rich yodeling alto of uniform tone—uniform, that is, save for the light crescendo with which the series opens, and the fading murmur of its closing note.

The remaining wonder is how these birds, be they never so agile, can make their way about the cruel cactus spines with impunity. They do not achieve immunity by instinct, for I have seen young birds lacerate themselves cruelly in first attempts. Yet they took their punishment uncomplainingly, or exhibited but the mildest surprise that their world should be so beset. Theirs is a hard life, inexplicable, save as we cast the blame upon the "lure of the desert," which claims many victims, and those most willing, among human kind.

BEWICK'S WREN
Thryomanes bewicki

A CAREFUL LIST OF THE DOZEN MOST prominent birds of California must make early mention of the Bewick's Wren. "Prominent" is not exactly the word to use, either, if it suggests large size or brilliant plumage or bold behavior. The Bewick's Wren has none of these marks—but he is one of the dozen most abundant, best distributed, most versatile, most adaptable, and most characteristic birds of the West. *Dominant* is, perhaps, a better epithet, though "prominent" is recognized as suitable by one who has mastered the intricacies and varieties of the Thryomanian song.

The Bewick's Wren freely invades the haunts of men; it even disputes much territory claimed by the House Wren *(Troglodytes aëdon parkmani)* but timber slashings, rocky hillsides, sunny arroyos, and the chaparral are more to its taste. Thus, the Canyon Wren, the Rock Wren, the House Wren, the Winter Wren, and the Wren-tit are brought into active competition with it; and while each in turn goes to places where the Bewick's Wren will not follow, it is the Bewick's

Wren which dominates the general situation. Whether in chaparral or log-heap or cactus bed, therefore, the Bewick's Wren knows his ground. And he lets you see exactly as much of himself as he intends and no more. If there is any unusual appearance or noise which gives promise of mischief afoot, then the Bewick's Wren is the first to respond. Flitting, gliding, tittering, the bird comes up and moves about the center of commotion, taking observations from all possible angles and making a running commentary thereon. His attitude is alert and his movements vivacious, but the chief interest attaches to the bird's mobile tail. With this expressive member the bird is able to converse in a vigorous sign language. It is cocked up in impudence, wagged in defiance, set aslant in coquetry, or depressed in whimsical token of humility. Indeed, it is hardly too much to say that the bird makes faces with its tail.

For all that the bird is so common, nests of the Bewick's Wren type are comparatively rare in collections. This is due, perhaps, as much to the lawless variety of sites used, as to the caution of the bird. A cranny of suitable size is the *sine qua non*, and this may be in a rock-pile, in a canyon-wall, in an old woodpecker-hole, in the mouth of an old tunnel of a Rough-winged Swallow, under a root, behind a sprung bark-scale, in an old shoe or a tin can, or the pocket of a disused coat.

If the Bewick's Wren is sly and secretive during the nesting season, a more generous spirit fills its breast when the young are well astir. Nothing could be more charming than the sight of a family group of *bewickis* taking a Sunday stroll. Bugs are the ostensible object of pursuit, but bug-hunting languishes when the stranger seats himself on a mossy log, and a gentle ripple of veiled inquiry assures him that he is of more interest than many bugs. One by one the questing babies hop out into the open, select a comfortable perch and survey the big brother with friendly curiosity. Many childish comments are passed, and the mischief of the party may even start a snicker, but it is all in good part, and the bird-man feels the flattery of a dozen admiring eyes. Even the mother, a little reluctant, is lured into the open by the confident declarations of her children; and under pretense of righting a rumpled feather, accepts compliments upon the fine appearance of her gentle brood. Admiring eyes have signed a truce, and the ancient misunderstanding is forgotten.

Canyon Wren
Catherpes mexicanus

Save in the brimful Sierras and along the dank coasts of the north, the cataracts of California go dry in the summer season. The torrential water-courses which carry off the surplusage of March are silent by April, and in May a worm might crawl unrebuked across the face of a rock worn smooth by the flood waters of winter. How the moment is redeemed, then, when a bird comes tumbling down a precipice of song, hurling himself recklessly from rock to rock till he seems to lay the vocal tribute at your very feet. The descent is through nearly two octaves; and the notes, whose crest, heard in the distance, seem purest whistle-tones, are seen at near quarters to be double and vibrant in character.

Heard across the wastes of chaparral, or in the cool depths of some rugged ravine, this song of the Canyon Wren is at once the most stirring and imaginative, and the most delightful which the wilderness of California has to offer. Heard a dozen times, perhaps, or ever its author is seen, one has formed in advance a picture of a very engaging bird-person. And for all save dignity (no wren can be dignified) the Canyon Wren meets the expectation. Whether the bird plays at hide-and-seek through trailing vines, or posts quietly on a rock-knob, or comes clinking over the face of a rocky exposure, it is easily seen to be the handsomest of North American wrens. The white of the throat, where alone the plumage is immaculate, shades on the breast into the rich warm brown or auburn of the hinderparts; and everywhere else there is speckling of black-and-white or a barring of black. The bird, however attentive, cannot resist a peeping spider or an insulting midge, and whatever the danger, he manages to divide his time impartially between observation and insect-catching.

There is no place forbidden to a Canyon Wren, no rock wall which frights him, no tunnel's mouth, nor intricacy of talus bed. He has no special predilection for the picturesque, however, as his name might seem to imply. A brush pile or a heap of old tin cans will do as well as a miner's cabin or an old Mission. What a merry soul it is, and his life how full of adventure! There is a wondrous variety in the world which he explores—log-heaps, stone-piles, crannied walls, labyrinths of roots undermined by a stream, stemmy jungles, tangled vines, rain-fretted gullies, and all the infinite disarray of Nature. And the plucky bird charges into some cavern, dark with nameless terrors, as though it were a nesting-box, and he exorcises all its dank ghosts with a merry *clink clink*, which is sunshine itself. Now and then he does make amazing discoveries, which he reports in a sudden explosion of *clinks*. After such a passage, it is moments on end before he gets calmed down enough to clink coherently. In and out, down, around, across and under—who would not envy the happy diversity of this midget's daily round!

Dippers, Kinglets, and Thrushes

AMERICAN DIPPER OR WATER OUZEL

Cinclus mexicanus unicolor

Advancing and prancing and glancing and dancing,
And dashing and flashing and splashing and clashing;
And so never ending, but always descending,
Sounds and motions forever and ever are blending,
All at once and all o'er, with a mighty uproar;
And this way the Water comes down at Lodore.
—Roubert Southey, "The Cataract of Lodore"

BUT THE SCENE OF AQUEOUS CONFUSION was incomplete unless a leaden shape emerged from the spray, took station on a jutting rock, and proceeded to rub out certain gruff notes of greeting, *jigic, jigic, jigic*. These notes manage somehow to dominate or to pierce the roar of the cataract, and they symbolize henceforth the turbulence of all the mountain torrents of the West.

The Water Ouzel bobs most absurdly as he repeats his inquiry after your health. But you would far rather know of his, for he has just come out of the icy bath, and as he sidles down the rock, tittering expectantly, you judge he is contemplating another one. Yes; without more ado the bird wades into the stream, where the current is so swift you are sure it would sweep a man off his feet. He disappears beneath its surface and you shudder at the possibilities; but after a half minute of suspense, he bursts out of the seething waters a dozen feet below, and flits back to his rock, chuckling cheerily. This time, it may be he will rest, and you have opportunity to note the slightly retroussé aspect of the beak in its attachment to the head. The bird has stopped springing now, and stands as stolid as an Indian, save as ever and again he delivers a slow wink, upside down, with the white nictitating membrane.

The Water Ouzel feeds largely upon the larvae of the caddis, or "May" fly, known locally as periwinkles. These are found clinging to the under surface of stones lining the stream, and their discovery requires quite a little prying and poking on the bird's part. Great numbers of the adults of this and other forms of Ephemeridae fall upon the surface of the water and are snapped up before the greedy trout can get them.

The Ouzel is non-migratory, but the summer haunts of the birds in the mountains are largely closed to them in winter, so that they find it necessary at that season to retreat to the lower levels. This is done, as it were, reluctantly, and nothing short of the actual blanketing of snow or ice will drive them to forsake the higher waters. The bird is essentially solitary at this season, as in summer, and when it repairs to a lower station, along late in November, there is no little strife engendered by the discussion of metes and bounds.

The Ouzel places its nest beside some brawling stream, or near or behind some small cascade. In doing so, the chief solicitude seems to be that the living mosses, of which the bulky globe is composed, shall be kept moist by the flying spray, and so retain their greenness. Indeed, one observer reports that in default of ready-made conveniences, the bird itself turns sprinkler, not only alighting upon the dome of its house after returning from a dip, but visiting the water repeatedly for the sole purpose of shaking its wet plumage over the mossy nest.

Ruby-crowned Kinglet
Corthylio calendula calendula

The sight of a Ruby-crowned Kinglet, no matter where, begets in one a feeling akin to reverence. It is too beautiful, too sudden for mere flesh and blood, and we know that we are getting a winged message from the Creative Infinite.

It seems only yesterday I saw him—Easter Day in old Ohio. The significant dawn was struggling with heaped-up clouds—the incredulities and fears of the world's night; but now and again the invincible sun found some tiny rift and poured a flood of tender gold upon a favored spot where stood some solitary tree or expectant sylvan company. Along the river bank all was still. There were no signs of spring, save for the modest springing violet and the pious buckeye, shaking its late-prisoned fronds to the morning air, and tardily setting in order its manifold array of Easter candles. The oak trees were gray and hushed, and the swamp elms held their peace until the fortunes of the morning should be decided. Suddenly from down the river path there came a tiny burst of angel music, the peerless song of the Ruby-crown. Pure, ethereal, without hint of earthly dross or sadness came those limpid welling notes, the sweetest and the gladdest ever sung—at least by those who have not suffered. It was not, indeed, the greeting of the earth to the risen Lord, but rather the annunciation of the glorious fact by heaven's own appointed herald.

The Ruby-crowned Kinglet has something of the nervousness and vivacity of the typical wren. It moves restlessly from twig to twig, flirting its wings with a motion too quick for the eyes to follow, and frequently uttering a titter of alarm, *chit-tit* or *chit-it-it*. On occasions of unusual excitement, as at the presence of an owl or a cat, the bird delivers what I call electric spark notes. *Chit it chit it chit it chit it chit it*, and so on *ad infinitum* in a sustained, vibrant series. If two birds become concerned over the same discovery, the Lilliputian bedlam which follows sounds like a six-unit wireless transmitting station. During migrations the birds swarm through the treetops like warblers, but are often found singly or in small companies in thickets or open clusters of saplings. In such situations they exhibit more or less curiosity; and if one keeps reasonably still, he is almost sure to be inspected from a distance not to exceed four or five feet.

A Sabbath spent on Shasta! apotheosis of rest! ultimate of soul's desire!—save Heaven. Best of all, the Ruby-crowned Kinglet sings! It is the Ruby-crown who captivates the imagination. Tireless he shouts from the treetops, and though charmed to the full with the rapture of the bird's shouting, one still wonders why he sings. For many moon cycles he has been a bachelor, a mere unit in the winter throng, careless of aught but himself and his gnawing belly. Spring roused him to thought of mating. The urge of hot blood led him to notice, to pursue and capture, to mate and then to celebrate in an ever-recurring note of ecstasy. But now? Now his mate sits demurely upon the nest. Love's favors are past, and there remains for him, what? Remains loyalty! Devotion! That swerveless passion of love which is above the heat of the blood and the expectation of favors. The singer—surely he knows not why—still shouts his joy from treetop to treetop, and all that his mate may be comforted in her long vigil. The bird rises above himself, and is, for a season, of that altruistic fellowship of which God is the founder, and we humans but unworthy members. For a season! Alas! There is the strange blighting pity of it. Summer ends, the necessity is over. Nature's subtle purposes have been accomplished, and the birds forget—are to each other henceforth as though they had never been.

Almost our singer in his ecstasy has seemed to grasp the reality of soul-life and to demand entrance into the fellowship of the immortals. And then, even while we are moved to call him "brother," the bird forgets—becomes again a mere animated atom, a craving bundle of selfishness, the very symbol of inconstancy.

Wherefore, O Bird, I take your protestations *cum grano salis*. You are not you, *ipse cognitus*, you are only a prophecy, an expression of a Greater, who is for a time moved to express a high purpose through a bit of clay, and will presently withdraw himself again. Him I hear, and rejoice. But you? Shall I respect you in very sooth, Birdikins? Nay, not with my soul.

My ear, indeed, is charmed. My eye has ceased not to mark with delight your very dainty motions. Imagination has been purified and aspiration stimulated. But—but—not with my soul. You—you have no soul. You are not yourself. You have—you are no self. For a Self were by very definition immortal. And I love only the *immortals*. Farewell! poor—dear—*bird*.

WHITE MOUNTAINS HERMIT THRUSH
Hylocichla guttata polionota

HE WHO HAS NOT IN HIS HEART a separate place for the Hermit Thrush is no bird lover. He who has never heard the evening requiem of the Hermit has missed the choicest thing which Nature in California has to offer. He who, having listened to that song, does not feel a responsive glow and a quickening of the spirit, has need of more than Nature's ministries. He needs most to find his God and to have his sins forgiven.

It is not alone for the lofty associations of Alpine meadow and Sierran grove that we prize the bird, though such choice of setting were gratifying evidence of a poetic nature. It is not for any marked vivacity, or personal charm of the singer that we praise his song; the bird is gentle, shy, and unassuming, and it is only rarely that one may even see him. It is not that he excels in technique such conscious artists as the Catbird, the Thrasher, and the otherwise matchless Mockingbird; the mere comparison is odious. The song of the Hermit Thrush is a thing apart. It is sacred music, not secular. Having nothing of the dash and abandon of Wren or Ouzel, least of all the sportive mockery of the Western Chat, it is the pure offering of a shriven soul, holding acceptable converse with high heaven. No voice of solemn-pealing organ or cathedral choir at vespers ever hymns the parting day more fittingly than this appointed chorister of the eternal hills. Mounted on the chancel of some low-crowned fir tree, the bird looks calmly at the setting sun, and slowly phrases his worship in such dulcet tones, exalted, pure, serene, as must haunt the corridors of memory forever after.

The associations of timberline, otherwise delectable, are unalterably hallowed by the recollection of that shy, modest presence and that voice "all breathing human passion far above." And although I have dwelt among the Sierra Hermit Thrushes for happy weeks, I never could get up any enthusiasm for making the bird a subject of scientific inquiry. I have found nests, of course, and left them. Also we may suppose that the birds eat something or other. Mischa Elman is said to have a weakness for pretzels, and Galli-Curci spends a certain number of hours out of the twenty-four in bed—snores, perchance; but it is not by these things that Art is remembered or the divinity of Song made glorious. I refuse to spy upon the Hermit Thrush, or to prattle of cosmetics and preferences in cheese.

Northwest Robin

Planesticus migratorius caurinus

"EVERYBODY KNOWS ROBIN. He is part and parcel of springtime, chief herald, chief poet, and lord high reveler of that joyful season. It is a merry day when the first flock of Robins turns itself loose on the home landscape. There is great bustle and stir of activity. Some scurry about to note the changes wrought by winter, some wrestle with the early and unsophisticated worm, while others voice their gladness from the fencepost, the gable, the treetop, anywhere. Everywhere are heard interjections of delight, squeechings and pipings of ardent souls, and no end of congratulations over the home-coming.

"Robin has cast in his lot with ours, for better or for worse. Our lawns are his lawns, our shade trees were set on purpose to hold his homely mud-cup, and he has undertaken with hearty good will the musical instruction of our children. He serves without pay—oh, a cherry now and then, but what of that? The fruit-grower never had a more useful hired man; and it is written: 'Thou shalt not muzzle the ox that treadeth out the corn.' I wonder if we realize how much of life's good cheer and fond enspiriting we owe to this familiar bird." [William Leon Dawson and John Hooper Bowles, *The Birds of Washington*]

All of which foregoing is only partially true of California. For save in favored sections of the Sierran uplands, the northeastern plateau region, and the humid coast belt south to, and lately including, San Francisco, the Robin is not the familiar of childhood nor the poet of common day. For the most part the bird nests in our cooler mountain climate in "Transition" or "Canadian" faunal zones, even up to the limit of trees, so that it is only as an irregular winter visitant—shy, silent, fugitive, but often excessively numerous—that urban California knows the Robin. Only the stout-hearted Sierran, the prospector, or the semi-professional camper-out knows the Western Robin as he deserves to be known.

The Robin's song in its common form is too well known to most of us to require particular description, and too truly music to lend itself well to syllabic imitation. There is something homey and substantial about it which makes us give thanks for common things, and accept without analysis—as we do salt and sunshine and breath of orange blossoms.

When the Robin is much given to half-whispered notes and strains unusually tender, one may suspect the near presence of his fiancée. If you are willing to waive the proprieties for a few moments you will hear low murmurs of affection and soft blandishments, which it would tax the art of a Crockett to reproduce. And again, nothing can exceed the sadness of a Robin's lament over a lost mate. All the virtues of the deceased are set forth in a coronach of surpassing woe, and the widower declares himself forever comfortless. It is not well, of course, to inquire too particularly as to the duration of this bereaved state—we are all human.

The Robin is an ardent lover, no doubt of that; and by the same token he is willing to back up his claims against all comers. Before Robins have become common about the streets and yards of a mountain village, partners have usually been selected; but there still remains for many of the cocks hard-contested battles before peaceful possession is assured. These are not sham fights either; a Robin will fight a hated rival beak and claw, till he is either thoroughly winded or killed outright.

And he is no less brave as the head of a family or as an upright neighbor. No other protestations, as of invaded nesting rights, have quite the moral earnestness of Robin's. (I should hate to gather Robins' eggs for a living!)

VARIED THRUSH
Ixoreus naevius naevius

TO HAVE EARNED THE RIGHT TO SPEAK appraisingly of the Varied Thrush as a bird of California, one must have lingered in some deep ravine of Humboldt County, where spruce trees and alders and crowding ferns contend for a footing, and where a dank mist drenches the whole with a fructifying moisture. Here and here only, in California, is the Varied Thrush at home, but his domain extends northward to the limit of trees in northwestern Alaska. For the Varied Thrush loves rain as a fish loves water; while as for the eternal drizzle, it is his native element and vital air. Sunshine he bears in stoical silence or else escapes to the depths of the forest glade. But let the sun once veil his splendors, let the clouds shed their gentle tears of self-pity, let the benison of the raindrops filter through the forest, and let the leafage begin to utter that myriad soft sigh which is dearer than silence, and our poet thrush wakes up. He mounts the chancel of some fir tree and utters at intervals a single long-drawn note of brooding melancholy and exalted beauty—a voice stranger than the sound of any instrument, a waif echo stranding on the shores of time.

There is no sound of the northwestern woods more subtle, more mysterious, more thrilling withal, than this passion song of the Varied Thrush. Somber depths, dripping foliage, and the distant gurgling of dark brown waters are its fitting accompaniments; but it serves, somehow, to call up before the mind's eye the unscaled heights and the untried deeps of experience. It is suggestive, elusive, and whimsically baffling. Never colorless, it is also never personal, and its weird extra-mundane quality reminds one of antique china reds, or recalls the subdued luridness of certain ancient frescoes. Moreover, this bird can fling his voice at you as well from the treetop as from the ground, now right, now left, the while he sits motionless upon a branch not fifteen feet above you.

The Varied Thrush is known by a variety of names, none more persistent or fitting than that of "Winter Robin." It is a Robin in size, prevailing color, and general make-up; and it appears in the lowlands in large numbers only in the wintertime, when the deep snows have driven it out of the hills. The Thrush is much more shy than the Robin, and although it moves about in straggling companies, and does not shun city parks, it keeps more to cover. It also feeds largely upon the ground, and when startled by a passerby it flutters up sharply into the trees with a wing-sound whose quality may soon be recognized as distinctive. At such times the bird makes off through the branches with a low chuck, or *tsook*, or else tries the air by low notes which are like the song, only very much more subdued. This is manifestly an attempt to keep in touch with companions, while at the same time attracting as little hostile attention as possible. This note is, therefore, barely audible, and has very little musical quality, *aarue*, or *üür*.

The Varied Thrush is chiefly a ground-feeder and nothing edible that is likely to strew the ground comes amiss. It is on this account that the birds venture out from hedges and coppices to take sly nips at the festive angleworms. Never shall I forget how, while seated by the window in one of the most luxurious homes of Montecito, I saw a Varied Thrush not twenty feet away, hopping across the perfect lawn in search of a vulgar worm. The audacity! And, like the Robin, the Varied Thrush gratefully accepts the largess of fallen olives. Indeed, it is to be suspected that the wily Thrush gets about two olives to Robin's one, for, mind you, he is "devilish cute." Or, where olives fail to tempt, or birds resist, the Christmas berry yields its yuletide cheer, and the unfailing pepper berry *(Schinus molle)* gives a palatable consolation.

WESTERN BLUEBIRD

Sialia mexicana occidentalis

MIU-MIU-MIU—MUTE YOU ARE, or next thing to it, you naughty little beauties! Why don't you sing, as do your cousins across the Rockies? You bring spring with you, but you do not come shifting your "light load of song from post to post along the cheerless fence." Is your beauty, then, so burdensome that you find it task enough to shift that?

It is always interesting and sometimes amusing to trace the early struggles of truth. Preconceptions die hard. The Eastern Bluebird warbles delightfully; therefore, the Western Bluebird *ought* to—but it doesn't! In an experience of some thirty-nine years, the author has never heard from the Western Bluebird's beak an utterance which deserves the name of song, or anything more musical than the threefold *miu*.

From this it is clear that the Western Bluebird is no musician, but he *is* a beauty; and he does have the same gentle courtesy of bearing which has endeared the bluebird wherever known. It is impossible to treat of Bluebird's domestic life without recourse to humanizing terms. Bluebird is a gentleman, chivalrous and brave, as he is tender and loving. Mrs. Bluebird is a lady, gentle, confiding, and most appreciative. And as for the little Bluebirdses, they are as well-behaved a lot of children as ever crowned an earthly affection.

Both parents are unsparing in their devotion to the rising generation, and so thoroughly is this unselfish spirit reflected in the conduct of the children that it is the subject of frequent remark. Mr. Finley tells of an instance in which a first brood, just out of pinafores, turned to and helped their parents provide food for another batch of babies, and this not once, nor twice, nor casually, but regularly, until the second brood were well matured. Instinct! Instinct! say you? But, wherefor? Is it not rather a foregleam of ethical life, an out-cropping of that altruistic tendency which hints a deeper kinship with the birds than we have yet confessed?

And real gallantry between the sexes may not be less ethical. On a day in Ohio, I located a bluebird's nest in the knot-hole of an apple tree, and planted the camera in a commanding and somewhat threatening position. The cavity held callow young, but after the parents had visited their charges once and were somewhat relieved in anxiety, I saw a very pretty passage which took place between them. In a neighboring apple tree the male secured an elegant fat grub and was most devoutly thrashing it when the female appeared upon the scene. With a coaxing twitter she approached her mate; but he backed off, as much as to say, "Wait, wait, dear, he isn't dead yet!" But she was hungry and pressed her suit, until he in good-natured impatience flitted across to another limb. Here he whacked the worm vigorously, striking him first against one side of the limb and then the other by a swinging motion of the head. The female followed her lord and cooed: "Oh, I know that will taste good. Um! I haven't tasted one of those white grubs for a week. So good of you, dearest! Really, don't you think he is done now?" The valiant husband gave the luckless grub just one more whack; and then, with every appearance of satisfaction, he hopped over toward his better half and placed the morsel in her waiting beak, while she received the favor with quivering wings and a soft flood of tender thanks. Altogether I think I never saw a prettier exhibition of conjugal affection, gallantry, and genuine altruism than the sight afforded. It was not only like the behavior of humans; it was like the best in human life, a pattern rather than a copy, an inspiration to nobility and gentleness of the very highest type.

Mountain Bluebird
Sialia currucoides

GENTLE AND DEMURE, AS WELL AS brave and high-spirited, is this sky-born thoroughbred of the Sierras, this bit of heaven's own blue incarnate. We shall think only of the milder qualities when we come upon a company of Mountain Bluebirds deployed over some south-sloping hillside on a sunny winter's day. Pasture weeds or fence-posts serve for lookout stations, whence the mountaineer may spy the crawling beetle, and seize daintily with flutterings of purest azure. Some pensive notes, *chee'ry* or *dear'ie*, like those of the Eastern Bluebird (*S. sialis*), but not so clear-cut, will be heard; or, if we press too closely, certain thrush-like *tsooks* of dainty alarm. Other song the birds have none, save an emphatic *whew* (never *miu*), uttered under stress of emotion. For here, again, the entire song tradition, including the "delightful warble" attributed to the bird by Townsend, appears to be quite without foundation, as in the case of *S. m. occidentalis*.

The Mountain Bluebird is a frequent and most endearing sight of the timberline association in the Sierras. Here, amidst retreating snowfields and bursting greenery, where everything is fresh and clear-cut and radiant, our azure incarnation seems exactly at home. The jagged peaks are cutting the horizon into blue tatters, anyhow, and it is no matter for surprise when detached shreds of the cerulean wreckage flutter over the heather, or lose themselves by the margin of some turquoise pool. And here, where gnarled pine trees have felt the tooth of the frost and have yielded sheltering hollows, the Mountain Bluebirds make their nests. Or, perchance, some hardy woodpecker has paved the way and left a princely excavation, which the bluebirds have only to line with soft dead grasses and call their own.

From five to seven dainty eggs, the palest possible blue, furnish occasion for pride and solicitude, and a little later for gallantries of ministration and defense, the sweetest and the bravest which this gallant old world knows. And if I had not seen a score of male bluebirds whose sole concern was to protect their home with its precious contents, I should not tell this tale of another not so gallant. There were seven babies, and the very least excuse for cowardice in this case, but I had marked this bird as a timorous fowl, who would not even venture up to have his picture taken. So when, one day, a great outcry arose with reference to a Clark's Crow, I hurried over. Some determined avenger was after the miscreant, and he doubled and twisted hither and yon (but always yonner if possible), uttering wild cries of rage and execration, while many lesser fowls joined the hue and cry in a less determined way. While this commotion was going on, our bluebird *père*, who happened to be seated on a stump a hundred feet from the nest, was a study. Instead of joining the pursuit he simply crouched and shuddered, as he turned an apprehensive eye aloft. He was paralyzed with fear. And lo and behold, when all the excitement was over, it was his mate, *mère* bluebird if you please, who emerged from the fray panting and triumphant! Now what do you think of that? Certainly the ladies of California are coming to their own! It is only fair to add that while the heroine was recovering her breath the male bird went dutifully after a worm.

Thrashers and Mockingbirds

CALIFORNIA THRASHER
Toxostoma redivivum

HOMELY APOLLO, HISTORIAN OF THE CHAPARRAL, poet of the common weed, apostle of dewy morn, mediator of sun and shadow, woodland recluse, and shy intimate of back-yard tryst, minstrel alike of blue-gray-green spring and dun summer, brown wraith of California, thou dost work alike havoc in our gardens, harmony in our ears, and a heavenly hubbub in our hearts. Would, oh, would that there were more of thee, and more beautiful and more constant.

The California Thrasher is preeminently a chaparral bird, and as such enjoys a fairly uniform distribution up to about six thousand feet. It seeks its food chiefly upon the ground, where it rustles among the leaves and fallen wastage for beetles, ants, and scattered seeds. After a fresh rain it loves to delve in the earth itself—for grubs and cut-worms, however, rather than buried seeds; and the "havoc" wrought occasionally in an outlying garden is really beneficial plowing. Berries and wild fruit are eaten freely in season; and *Rhus* seeds, both harmless and poisonous, are a staple article of diet. The bird is strong on its feet, but rather weak a-wing, and oftener escapes by hopping through the shrubbery or running along the ground than by exercise of the grand manner.

Screeping in the brush is always generously responded to, for *redivivum* has a lively bump of curiosity. He is, moreover, a duly constituted patrolman of the under chaparral; and because he is always dressed in service khaki, instead of the loudly advertised blue of Sergeant Aphelocoma, he is able to come to closer grips with the lesser malefactors of the leafy half-world.

It is the impulse of song alone which brings the Thrasher to plain view. Song requires the topmost bough of ceanothus or scrub oak, and the earnest gesticulations of the sickle-shaped mandibles are a commonplace to the observer who carries glasses. The song of the California Thrasher is most nearly comparable to that of the Mockingbird. It is, however, more broken, more impetuous, and a partisan might say of a fresher quality—at any rate, less conventional and civilized. Now and then a singing Thrasher borrows from his neighbors, and we have unquestionable imitations, of Wren-tit, Flicker, or Jay, interspersed with his own improvisations. The effect is rarely as convincing as in the case of our true Mockingbird, breathless, hurried, and disguised rather; but here, as always, it is individual ability which counts.

These common powers bring Thrasher and Mocker into frequent comparison, and some of us have been privileged to hear the two species comparing notes on their own account, with no little suspicion of jealousy in the premises; but we shall decline a decision. It is the age-old question of country-mouse and town-mouse, and such are settled by prejudices, not judgments.

Western Mockingbird
Mimus polyglottos leucopterus

TRILLETS OF HUMOR—shrewdest whistle-wit—
Contralto cadences of grave desire
...midnights of tone entire—

Tissues of moonlight shot with songs of fire;—
Bright drops of tune, from oceans infinite
Of melody, sipped off the thin-edged wave
And trickling down the beak,—discourses brave
Of serious matter that no man may guess—
Good-fellow greetings, cries of light distress.

'Twas Sidney Lanier [in "To Our Mockingbird"] who with such unerring finger pointed out the cadence, the content, and the very spirit of the Mockingbird's song. No admirer has done the bird more equal justice and none is likely to. And it is no disparagement of other songsters to admit that the Mockingbird is the best known and the best famed of all American song birds. In the mouths of the world's best critics, only the Nightingales of Europe and the Bulbuls of the Orient are brought into comparison with the American Mockingbird. As virtuosos these others may possibly excel, but the Mockingbird gains a favorable decision, however biased, because he frankly commits his cause to human keeping. By establishing his mate in our climbing rose bush, and himself mounting guard above upon the cottage chimney, he has made us partners in interest. His cause is ours, and woe betide him who dares impugn the musical virtues of the American Mockingbird. He has touched our honor.

The Nightingale sings only in a northern springtime—or so they tell us. With the Mockingbird it is eternal spring. If bird-song expresses, as we hold, joy in life, rather than merely a passing desire to capture a mate, then is the Mockingbird the most joyful of birds. He is always at it, winter and summer. Or if in the springtime his songs are a little more earnest, a little more passionate, he is not more partial than the rest of us. Spring is the joy-time par excellence, and if one sings in the autumn, is it not because spring has been entrapped and carried over in the heart? Or if in winter, this is doubtless, also, because spring is coming.

Song is the Mocker's *raison d'etre*. It is his own true love, his passion, his obsession, no less than his trade. Not content with his own inspirations, masterly, varied, and abundant as these are, the singer lays under tribute everything else that sings, or yodels, or squawks withal. The plaintive notes of a Say's Phoebe and the regal scream of the Western Redtail interest him alike. No other bird-song is too foreign, too intricate, or too delicate for his own rendition. Of the passing migrants he takes toll, no less than of his familiar neighbors. Two Mockers that I heard in Arizona, and these a hundred miles apart, had each preserved the recollection of the exquisite gushing song of the Lincoln Sparrow (*Melospiza lincolni*). These mimics, too, had been unusually favored, for I myself never heard the Lincoln Sparrow sing, save in his breeding haunts high in the mountains, where, of course, the Mocker does not penetrate.

But the Mockingbird is, after all, very "human." We shall not leave him in heaven, even for the space of this page; nor shall we hasten to deify him without having first examined the feet of clay. Even in the utterance of song he is something of a wag, not to mention a buffoon; while the elsewhere noble instinct of solicitude for young has in the Mockingbird degenerated into an exaggeration of petulance, which would be repulsive, were it not so entertaining and harmless.

To speak of the buffoonery first: it is well known how the Mocker plays the fool whenever his lady love appears. Though he flutters up to her with drooping wings, his flattery is mingled with intentional bombast, and she cries *yăă yăă* in the same mocking tone with which a girl in pigtails greets an awkward brother: "*Yăă*, Mr. Smarty, why don't you stand up and fall over?" It is fair enough, of course, that music should enter a bird's feet, as it does a man's; but when the Mocker attempts to dance, he invites ridicule rather than respect. His heart interferes with his heels, until one cries in derision, "Softy, softy!"

When the young birds are hatched out, the Mockingbirds become the most jealous and aggressive of guardians. Not content with persecuting all other birds and driving cats out of bounds, they quarrel with their most intimate human friends, no matter of how long standing. The ordinary note of appraisal, *choop* or *tsook*, comes out like the crack of a whip, beyond imitation, the most intense and upbraiding sound of which a California bird is capable. If the danger is very real, the birds fall back on an ancestral thrasher cry, *choory*—sometimes piteously prolonged, *choooory*—and this is moving enough, but they spoil it all with floods of those mocking *yăăă* cries, which arouse only resentment.

SAGE THRASHER
Oreoscoptes montanus

IN A LAND SO BLESSED WITH arid and semi-arid vegetation, we are apt to overlook the virtues of that homely plant, the "sage" (*Artemisia tridentata*). To be sure, its area of maximum distribution lies to northward and eastward, but we have here and there wholesome touches of it; while upon our eastern and especially our northeastern borders lie great areas which entitle California to recognition among the Also Blest. It is a wonderful weed, not alone for its pungent odor—the sweetest of life's bitters—but for its hospitality, its sturdy heroism, and, above all, for its fidelity—unflinching in its task of covering the hills, be they never so unending. I love the sage! So does our hero, miscalled, "Oreoscoptes," "Mountain Viewer." Call him rather Agapatos Artemidos, Beloved of Artemis, from whom his favorite flower is named. Born of the sage, he has no outlook beyond it, and needs none. Listen!

The hour is sunrise. As we face the east, heavy shadows still huddle about us and blend with the ill-defined realities. The stretching sage-tops tremble with oblation before the expectant sun. The pale dews are taking counsel for flight, but the opalescent haze, pregnant with sunfire, yet tender with cool greens and subtle azures, hovers over the altar, waiting the concomitance of the morning hymn before ascent. Suddenly, from a distant sage-bush bursts a geyser of song, a torrent of tuneful waters, gushing, as it would seem, from the bowels of the wilderness in an ecstasy of greeting and gratitude and praise.

It is from the throat of the Sage Thrasher, poet of the bitter weed, that the tumult comes. Himself but a gray shadow, scarce visible in the early light, he pours out his soul and the soul of the sage in a rhapsody of holy joy. Impetuous, impassioned, compelling, rises this matchless music of the desert. To the silence of the gray-green canvas, beautiful but incomplete, has come the throb and thrill of life—life brimful, delirious, exultant. The freshness and the gladness of it touch the soul as with a magic. The heart of the listener glows, his veins tingle, his face beams. He cannot wait to analyze. He must dance and shout for joy. The wine of the wilderness is henceforth in his veins, and drunk with ecstasy, he reels across the enchanted scene forever more.

And all this inspiration the bird draws from common sage and the rising of the common sun. How does he do it? I do not know. Ask Homer, Milton, Keats.

The Sage Thrasher appears to live life in its ultimate simplicity, for there is no other bird bred amidst more uniform surroundings; and yet if we could know, I suppose life would seem to be made up of pleasant variety enough—a thousand sorts of bugs to choose for food, a thousand fair ladies from whom to win a mate, and twice ten thousand times ten thousand sage-bushes, any one of which is fit to support that modest cradle which shall house his children. What d'ye lack, my masters?

Pipits, Waxwings, and Phainopeplas

AMERICAN PIPIT

Anthus spinoletta rubescens

THE AMERICAN PIPIT DOES NOT SUSTAIN the habitual dignity of the boreal breed. He is no clown, indeed, like our Western Chat, nor does he quite belong to the awkward squad, with young blackbirds; a trim form and a natty suit often save him from merited derision, but all close observers will agree that there is a screw loose in his make-up somewhere. The whole Pipit race seems to be struggling under a strange inhibitory spell, cast upon some ancestor, perhaps, by one knows not what art of nodding heather bells or potency of subtly distilled Arctic moonshine. As the flock comes straggling down from Oregon they utter unceasing *yips* of mild astonishment and self-reproach at their apparent inability to decide what to do next.

In social flight the Pipits straggle out far apart, so as to allow plenty of room for their chronic St. Vitus's dance to jerk them hither or thither or up or down, without clashing with their fellows. Only a small percentage of those which annually traverse the State fly low enough to be readily seen; but when they do they are jolting along over the landscape and complaining at every other step. The note is best rendered *tlip-yip*, less accurately *pip-it* (whence of course the name); and a shower of these petulant sounds comes spattering down out of the sky when the birds themselves are nearly or quite invisible.

The Pipit is probably the best distributed and most characteristic bird of our southern beaches in winter. At this season the flocks are more or less dispersed and individuals pay little attention, or none, to possible comrades. In these circumstances a Pipit is the special despair of all properly constituted bird photographers. The bird appears to get up from under your feet the first time, when of course you weren't looking for him; but thereafter let one so much as focus a thought upon him and the bird begins to fidget forthwith, to step stealthily, to forget his proper business of fly-catching, and to mutter about a forgotten engagement. At sixty feet—the bird being at that distance about as large on a photographic plate as the small end of a dull pin— he scuttles to the top of a stranded kelp root and declares his intention of leaving instanter if you do not abate your rudeness. He stands his ground, however, till you are about to swing at an unsatisfactory range of forty feet, when he springs into the air with an exultant bound and shouts derisively, "*pipit thlipit.*" Pip it! and also drat it!

CEDAR WAXWING
Bombycilla cedrorum

OUT OF THE PEPPER-TREE COMES a chorus of excited squeaks. The passerby pauses to see what the commotion may be, and finds the tree alive with birds—birds of a ravishing beauty, albeit engaged in a scramble for food as unseemly as that of an American pie-eating contest. You would suppose that a bird so beautiful would behave with becoming decorum, or at least pause for admiration. But no, it is gobble, gobble, gobble, and the red berries disappear almost faster than one can count. At a squeak, a little louder than the rest, perhaps, though we cannot tell it, the whole company bursts out of the sheltering greenery, effects an instant and graceful squadron formation, and either retires, squeaking, to a conspicuous outpost, such as a leafless sycamore tree, or else plumps unquenched into some other green fountain of peppery consolation.

Thus the normal Bombycilline day divides itself into frequent periods of disgraceful gluttony, alternating with periods of dignified retirement. Needless to say, the latter period is concerned chiefly with digestion; but when we know how little these greedy beauties really get out of their food, we may pardon their apparent voracity. As Dr. Grinnell has pointed out, it is only the viscid coating of the kernel of a pepper berry which has an agreeable flavor and furnishes nourishment, so that the papery hulls and the peppery centers require to be disgorged. This operation appears to involve momentary distress, and is accomplished by two or three coughs and a sidewise jerk of the head, which disposes of several kernels at once. Aside from these exspuitive interruptions, the sight of a snug company of Cedarbirds lined up on a telegraph wire, or bunched in a treetop, is pleasing in the extreme. The soft body-plumage of melting browns and saffrons and Quaker drabs, set off by the abrupt black "trimmings" of the head, the military crest, and the erect soldierly pose of the figure, give one a somewhat awed impression.

And that squeak! The Cedarbird, being so singularly endowed with the gift of beauty, is denied the gift of song. He is, in fact, the most nearly voiceless of any of the American Oscines, his sole note being a high-pitched, sibilant squeak. Indeed, so high-pitched is this extraordinary note, that many people, and they trained bird-men, cannot hear it at all, even when the Waxwings are squeaking all about them. Cedarbirds are especially noisy when scrambling for food but the self-same squeaks issue from a motionless company in the treetop; and the bird seems to have settled upon this note because it requires least effort. Discussion is liveliest just before flight, and the squeaking continues while the birds are a-wing.

PHAINOPEPLA
Phainopepla nitens

CERTAIN BAFFLING CONTRADICTIONS, and many elusive qualities besides, mark this wayward son of the desert. Handsome he is, indeed, and they have given him a high-sounding Grecian title in appreciation of his magnificence. Yet is he ever the soul of modesty, and the sudden consciousness of a spying eye will scatter all his show of finery, and send him dashing into the bush with *peps* of disgust. Shy he is to a fault, insomuch that the other side of a bush has always the preference both in approach and in escape. The waste places are his proper home; yet he will conduct his small affairs in a crowded suburb, and he will set his nest in a spreading oak tree which overshadows a human habitation. Curiosity will tempt him to answer a cat-call from the depths of a mesquite—a cat-call, mayhap, with a gun behind it—while caution will drive him forth at a hundred yards and keep him a skulking wraith in the offing while the home-trees are being searched. Gallantry struggles in his breast with spiteful tyranny, daintiness with gourmandizing greed, dignity with buffoonery, courage with cowardice, and last but not least, diligence and devotion alternate in his purpose with the most shocking caprice.

To speak soberly, therefore, of the Phainopepla, one's first impression is of a shining black beauty, graceful and active, enlivened by a mobile crest, a fiery red eye, a snowy mantle (in interrupted pattern, shown only in flight), and a bird possessed, withal, of a voice which promises all sorts of good things. But this favorable first impression pales with familiarity, and one admits after long acquaintance that the Phainopepla is, without doubt, a little queer, his voice a little disappointing, his psychology not quite understandable, and his manners hopelessly alien.

Having said so much, we have perhaps said too much. Any prisoner at the bar is entitled to the services of an attorney, and any bird sitting at the bar of our poor human judgment is entitled to sympathetic consideration. He is entitled, moreover, to be judged by a jury of his peers; and if we would deal exact justice, or even approximate justice, to the Phainopepla, we must doubtless become birds ourselves for the nonce. Here is a motion, then, for a new trial.

Pep pep—it is a musical, half-plaintive, haunting note which first apprises us of the arrival of the "shining flycatchers" from their winter home in the desert. The males arrive first, but are followed in four or five days by the modest gray females, who, likewise, call *pep pep*, or *perp perp*, in solicitude, or resentment of human attention. The male is discreet, but a well-screened observer may sometimes catch one in a transport of ecstasy. He leaps into the air, turns a somersault, returns to the perch with quivering wings, swaps ends violently, displays the crest to the utmost, and produces all the while a flood of jumbled, weak notes intended for song. Besides the song and call notes, one hears a *scrat* or *kuteerp*, which betoken apprehension, or distress, or at least disagreement of opinion at home.

The flight of the Phainopepla, though oftenest *direct*, is both languid and ostentatious, so that one catches distinct views of the white blotch on the wing of the male, or the corresponding pale area on that of the female. In going any considerable distance, the birds rise to several times the height of the tallest vegetation, so as to obtain an unobstructed view; and upon reaching the intended destination, they dive abruptly down, with much display of putting on brakes by means of the ample tail. Now and then some smart Aleck will play drunk, and go reeling about hither and thither in the air in the most eccentric fashion.

In building a nest the male Phainopepla takes the initiative and does at least nine-tenths of the work. Indeed, he seems to be jealous of any attention to this drudgery on the part of the female, and will even drive her away if she meddles over much. Visits of inspection are, however, permitted, and the virtuous architect is not insusceptible to words of praise. "Architect" is, perhaps, an over-pretentious word; for a Pep's nest is a mere aggregation of soft substances, such as, by reason of a general stickiness, will under pressure assume some sort of coherence. Twigs there may be, but these are used for filler rather than as structural support. Sage-leaves, string, catkins, dried flowers, lichens, bits of wool, cobwebs, soft shredded bark—anything which will lend itself to a soft gray or greenish gray ensemble—is acceptable. The nest is settled into branching twigs or forks, whether upright, horizontal, or declining; or occasionally it may be balanced upon the shaft of a bare branch.

Wood Warblers

Yellow Warbler

Dendroica stiva

TAKE A WILLOW CATKIN BURSTING with powdered gold and nestling against a cluster of its own vivid leaves, and you will have the model after which the Yellow Warbler was painted. The bird was made for the tree—perhaps in a sense he was made *by* it—and this associational bond is a very strong one. Roughly speaking, the Summer Warbler breeds wherever willows are found, and this means that his summer home in California is nearly confined to the Upper Sonoran faunal zone and to the vicinity of water, whether running or stagnant. Transition tongues of alder and cottonwoods, mingled with willow, sometimes tempt the birds into the upper reaches of some mountain valley, but here more than ever he is dependent upon water.

The Yellow Warbler, while frequenting wooded streams, is, nevertheless, a bird of sunshine. It does not keep to the depths of the larger trees, but hunts over the thickets and saplings, with occasional bold excursions to outlying rose briars or even to the sage. As it moves about, to thread some willow clump with sunshine—that we speak not of such prosaic matters as bug-catching—it pauses momentarily for song.

The song is sunny, too, and while not elaborate, makes substantial contribution to the good cheer of spring. Heard in the boskage it sounds absurdly as if some wag were shaking an Attic salt-cellar on a great green salad. The notes are almost piercing, and sound better, perhaps, from across the river than they do in the same tree.

The male Yellow is very domestic in his tastes, insomuch that, quite unlike other warblers, he will often venture to sing from the very bush in which his mate is sitting. Unless well accustomed to the presence of humans, the female will not sit patiently under the threat of close approach. She slips off quickly, and her vigorous complaints serve to summon her husband, when both flit about close to the intruder, and scold roundly in fierce, accusing notes, which yet have a baby lisp about them.

Audubon's Warbler
Dendroica auduboni auduboni

Audubon's Warbler is *par excellence* the warbler of the West. Cheerful, aggressive, capable, the bird symbolizes, as we would fain believe, the best in western tradition. For your true Westerner needs no artificial aids. Pride of family, education, circumstance, these are flung aside in that fundamental democracy which faces Nature unafraid and wrests from her the prizes which she is obliged to bestow upon the resolute. And how splendid an example the bird sets! Without tools or furnishings, without connections or backing, without so much as a hand-bag in which to keep a few cherished belongings, this brave young argonaut faces the world. This world is full of winged assassins, feline prowlers, serpents, storms, glaciers, fogs, droughts, and a thousand nameless terrors. "Ho ho! Who cares!" says Sir Audubon. "The world is mine. Not a tree, but I shall explore it; not a canyon, but I shall quaff water from its depths; not a mountain, but I shall mock at its glaciers; not a tempest, but I shall know how to escape its fury. Ho ho!" And so this tiny warbler, penniless and homeless, threads mazes which no surveyor has ever chained, scales heights which no aneroid has ever measured, sleeps in a hundred and forty different beds, from the lowly weed to the fir tree's loftiest pinnacle, lunches at ten thousand counters, and comes back to us winter by winter, artless, unspoiled, cheerful, and courageous. Oh, who would not be such a bird!

One is tempted to declare that the Audubon's Warbler is the commonest bird in California, in mid-winter. Doubtless this would be an exaggeration, for there are Gambel Sparrows, not to mention House Finches, to consider; but it is certain that these warblers are more in evidence on a winter day in the interior valley and south of the Tehachapi than are the presumably more abundant birds skulking in the chaparral. It is nothing, for example, to see two hundred Audubons in the course of a morning's tramp. When they are as thick as this, they string out along the telephone wires, or deploy over the ground of open fields. Their movements are always desultory and individually independent, so that they remind one at times of irresolute Pipits. Best of all, we see them in numbers on the sand dunes and over the beaches. Having known Sir Audubon as a dweller at timberline, I am not even yet reconciled to seeing him perched on a stranded kelp root and snapping at flies. For the rest, every wayside hedge claims him; and as for the eucalyptus trees, they are surely made on purpose to house Audubons.

Audubon's Warbler as a songster deserves some notice. His song, to be sure, is brief and its theme nearly invariable, as is the case with most warblers; but there is about it a joyous, racy quality, which flicks the admiration and calls time on spring. The singer posts in a high fir tree, that all may hear, and the notes pour out rapidly, crowding close upon each other, till the whole company is lost in a cloud of spray at the end of the ditty.

Few warblers express such a frank concern for the welfare of their domicile as do these lordly Audubons. When the young are grown, the parents throw discretion to the winds and advance within a foot or so of the intruder, prostrating themselves along the branches, or spreading their tails and wings in frantic efforts to arouse a distracting cupidity. The young are gentle, well-behaved little creatures, whom no one could possibly wish to harm. When the nest is quitted, they follow their parents dutifully through the treetops; or if the season is early, the male takes charge of his brood while his mate prepares another nest. When the season is ended, the family party works slowly over the mountainside above timberline. Such parties I met in July at ten thousand feet on Shasta, where the only other birds one might expect were Thurber Juncoes, or, perhaps, the heavenly Rosy Finch.

YELLOWTHROAT
Geothlypis trichas

"CAT-TAIL YELLOWTHROAT" WOULD BE A more appropriate name, if only we had the courage to apply it, because for every pond or swamp in the Southland which can boast the presence of the giant bulrushes (*Scirpus lacustris occidentalis* and *S. californicus*) which alone are properly called tules, there are a dozen where only cat-tails (*Typha latifolia* or *T. angustifolia*) dwell. And for every cat-tail patch there is a pair of Yellowthroats—more, if there is room.

Given a cat-tail or tule patch as an assured base of operations, *Geothlypis* will roam about adventurously enough. Rank grass, coarse herbage, stunted bushes—these and the promise of insects will lure him away several hundred yards, but always he sings, "My heart's in the cat-tails." Yellowthroat is a restless, active, little body, and he is among the first to come forward when you enter the swamp. His method is hide-and-seek and the game would all be his, if he did not reveal his presence from time to time by a harsh accusing note, a sort of Polish, consonantal explosion, *wzschthub*—a sound not unlike that made by a guitar string when struck above the stop. If you attempt to follow the bird, the game ends in disappointment. But if the observer pauses, curiosity gets the better of the bird, and he is soon seen peering out from a neighboring bush, roguery only half hidden by his highwayman's mask.

The female, having no mask, keeps to the background, but she is not less interested than her mate in the progress of events. When the scout returns to report, there is often a curious outbreak of discussion, in which the husband, as like as not, finds it necessary to defend his opinion with a perfect torrent of *wzschthubs*.

Nests of the Yellowthroats are the commonplace of all swampy localities—commonplace, yet never without interest, because of their varied architecture and their diverse setting. A nest may be sunk firmly into a damp tussock of grass barely clear of the ground or water, or it may be lashed firmly to the stalks of an investing clump of cat-tails, or it may be deftly hidden under a canopy of weed-tops a hundred yards from water. The nest may be composed chiefly of brittle weathered leaves of grass or sedge, so incoherent as to be scarcely removable, or else it may be settled into a veritable fortress of coiled cat-tail leaves, sturdy and dependable. The lining, too, may be of coiled grasses almost as light in color as the speckled white eggs which they support, or it may be of black horsehair, throwing the jewels into prized relief.

WESTERN CHAT

Icteria virens longicauda

STRUCTURALLY ALLIED TO THE WOOD WARBLERS, the Chat has yet such a temperamental affinity with the Catbird that it is difficult, for me at least, to dissociate the two birds in thought. Both love the thickets; both excel in song; both plague their neighbors by mimicry; and both alike are dearly provoking bundles of contradictions. The Chat is, perhaps, the greater buffoon, as he is certainly the more handsomely dressed of the two. Beyond this we must consider him on his own merits.

Ten to one you know him, if at all, only as a voice, a tricksy bushwhacker of song, an elusive mystery of the thicket; or you have unconsciously ascribed his productions to half a dozen mythical birds at once. But look more closely. It is well worth the quest to be able to resolve this genius of roguery. Be assured he knows you well enough, by sight, for he does not poke and pry and spy for nothing, in the intervals of song. He has still the proverbial curiosity of woman. Seat yourself in the thicket, and when you hear the mellow, saucy *Kook*, with its whistled vowel, bounded by consonants barely thought of, imitate it. You will have the bird up in arms at once. *Kwook*, returns the bird, starting toward you. Repeat it, and you have won. The bird scents a rival and he will leave no stem unclasped but he finds him. As the bird alternately squints and stares from the brush, note the rich warbler olive of his upperparts, the gorgeous yellow of the throat and breast, the white brow-stripe and the malar dash, offset by black and darker olive. It is a warbler in color-pattern, a Yellowthroat done larger, but waggish, furtive, impudent, and resourceful beyond any other of his kind.

The full song of the Chat is usually delivered from some elevation, a solitary tree rearing itself above dense cover. The music almost defies analysis, for it is full of surprises, vocal somersaults, and whimsy turns. Its cadence is ragtime, and its richest phrases are punctuated by flippant jests and droll parentheses. Even in the treetop the singer clings closely to the protecting greenery, whence he pitches headlong into the thicket at the slightest intimation of approach.

The love song of the Chat, the so-called "dropping song," is one of the choicest of avian comedies, for it is acted as well as sung. The performer flings himself into mid-air, flutters upward for an instant with head upraised and legs abjectly dangling, then slowly sinks on hovering wing, with tail swinging up and down like a mad pump-handle—Punch, as Cupid, smitten with the mortal sickness. And all this while the zany pours out a flood of tumultuous and heart-rending song. He manages to recover as he nears the brush, and his fiancée evidently approves this sort of buffoonery.

The Chat is a skilled mimic. I have traced the notes of such diverse species as Bullock's Oriole, Slender-billed Nuthatch, and Magpie to his door. Once, down on the Rio Grande, we rapped on a vine-covered cottonwood stump to dislodge a Flicker that had been shrieking *Klyak* at us for some minutes past, and we flushed a snickering Chat instead.

It is perhaps as a singer of the night that one finds the versatile Chat most impressive. The bird has no compunction about awakening a tired ornithologist; and the prudent camper will, therefore, measure his hours so as to allow for several nocturnal interruptions. It is that incurable malady of the heart again! Chaucer might have said of our hero as he did of the knight:

So hote he loved that by the nightertale
He slep na more than doth the nightingale.

Be that as it may, the Western Chat will assail the midnight with guttural reproaches, explosive cackles, cat-calls and shrieks until the would-be sleeper is fairly frenzied. Then the bird will pour on a sudden ointment of sound in tones of richest ravishment. The mollified sleeper sinks to rest again amidst a silence palpable.

Skilled minstrel though he is, the Western Chat, like the eastern bird, has small taste for architecture. A careless mass of dead leaves and coarse grasses is assembled in a bush at a height of three or four feet; and a lining of finer grasses, when present at all, is so distinct as to permit of removal without injury to the bulk of the structure. From three to five eggs are laid, and so jealously guarded that the birds are said to destroy the eggs once visited by man. So cautious are the Chats that even after the young have hatched out, they take care not to be seen in the vicinity of their nest, but a low, anxious *chuck* sometimes escapes from the harassed mother in a neighboring thicket.

Tanagers, Grosbeaks, Sparrows, Juncoes, and Towhees

WESTERN TANAGER

Piranga ludoviciana

RED, YELLOW, AND BLACK—can anyone imagine a more dashing color combination? And the colors are all guaranteed pure—prime, or "spectrum" yellow for the collar, rump, epaulets, and underparts; spectrum red for the forehead, crown, and as much of the remainder of the head as the age of the wearer entitles him to; black, also of the purest, albeit not glossy, and picked off appropriately on wings and tail with white, and on the back with yellowish edgings. It is a costume for a king!

Seen in the hand, this vivid costume would seem to assure a very conspicuous bird, but afield it is not so. Seen against the changing green of willows, pines, or fir trees, these brilliant colors are lost to any but the most attentive eye. A resplendent male does not hesitate to stand quietly upon the end of a branch and survey you until his curiosity is fully satisfied. This quiet attitude of genteel curiosity seems to be characteristic of all tanagers. Apart from its psychological bearings, sedateness would seem to play an effective part in modifying the attractions of bright plumage.

While chiefly silent during the migrations, the arrival of the birds upon their chosen summer sites is betokened by the frequent utterance of a pettish *pit'ic* or *pit'itic*. The full-voiced song grows with the season, but at its best it is little more than an étude in R. "It is remotely comparable to that of the Robin, but it is more stereotyped in form, briefer, and uttered at intervals rather than continuously sustained. The notes are sharp-edged, and rich in *r*'s, while the movement of the whole, though deliberate, is varied, and the tone cheerful." I can detect no constant difference between the song of the Western Tanager and that of the Scarlet Tanager (*P. erythromelas*), save that that of the former is oftener prefaced with the call note, thus: *Piteric whew, we soor a-ary e-erie witooer*. This song, however, is less frequently heard than that of the Scarlet Tanager, East. Its perfect rendition, moreover, argues the near presence of a demure little lady in olive, a person who looks like nobody in particular to our undiscriminating gaze, but who exerts a strange fascination over our brilliant squire. Young males of the second summer sing hopefully, but they are less often successful in love than their ruddier rivals.

It behooves the tanager maiden to be exacting in her choice, for all the help she will get out of him at best will be sympathy and song. When it comes to real work, like nest building, she must do it. *He* will graciously advise as to the situation, some horizontal branch of fir or pine, from six to fifty feet high, and from three to twenty feet out. He will even accompany her on her laborious trips after nesting material, cooing amiable nothings, and oozing approval at every joint—but help her?—*nevaire*!

BLACK-HEADED GROSBEAK
Hedymeles melanocephalus melanocephalus

BIX, AND AGAIN, *BIX*. It is our own bird that speaks from the shrubbery on an August day, and by this alone we know that the minstrel of springtime is with us still. How he gladdened those fresh hours! And how he sang on, cheerful, melodious, content, until June had silenced other singers of the lower levels. The Black-headed Grosbeak is a bird beloved of Californians. Gentle, modest, unassuming, he moves about with quiet dignity which proclaims his worth; and when he does consent to be interviewed, the reporter is sure to wax enthusiastic over his somewhat bizarre beauty. For my part, I never hear those first mellow flutings of springtime without being seized with a wild desire to see the singer, and to quench the thirst of long abstinence by a satisfying vision of black and white and ochraceous tawny.

The glory of the Black-headed Grosbeak is his song—not often a brilliant or wonderful song, but always a jovial, rolling, or eumoirous song. Sometimes it is a little argumentative, as though the singer, having taken a brief for optimism, had encountered a skeptic. Sometimes the singer's heart is so full that he carries his song about with him while he works. Bug-catching is a very necessary occupation, so he follows it dutifully, but song breaks out after every third or fourth bug, and it follows him about as he threads the mazes of willow and alder or mountain birch. At such times, too, his progress is further punctuated by *bixes*, all harmless, apparently, but delivered with such energy that a camper caught at close quarters starts to his feet.

The happiness which fills the Grosbeak's breast carries into the nesting season. He is so proud to have Mrs. G. honor him with her company that he is willing to help build the nest, or at least to pretend to—singing is always more important on such occasions—and he is willing, more than willing, to take his turn at sitting upon those precious eggs. This means that he is a model husband and father. The glory of paternity fills his being. The wonder of life amazes him. The graciousness of Mrs. G. is extraordinary. The eggs which she has deposited in the family basket are nothing less than superb. So this doting, marveling, and altogether amiable idealist sings as he works, sings as he contemplates his offspring-to-be, the imprisoned mysteries within those walls of freckled blue; and as he feels the warm, round wonders pressing against his breast, he breaks ever and again into joyous song.

A Grosbeak family makes a pretty group at, or just before, nest-leaving time. Few birds show more clearly the essential values and sexual differences of parenthood. The mother is timid as well as tender, indefatigable, indeed, in household ministrations, but a little pensive withal, a clinging vine. The father is a hustler as well as an idealist. He manages to bring in great loads of food every ten or fifteen minutes, and the youngsters thrive amazingly. Nor does this model parent allow increasing cares to weigh down his spirits. Even with his "market basket" laden to the brim, he shouts a cheerful snatch of song to herald his approach; and the children greet his return with clamorous applause. Lucky children of "Big Bill"! he has a big heart, as well as a big beak.

WESTERN LARK SPARROW

Chondestes grammacus strigatus

THERE IS A SPOT NEAR SHANDON so endeared by reason of its verdure and its unspoiled simplicities, that one hesitates to draw invidious attention to it. If you will promise not to plot "improvements," you shall join us on an afternoon in early April. It has been raining off and on for a week, but the sky is clear now, and the lush grasses welcome our feet with the abandonment of fullness. A lazy country road skirts this scene of beauty; and, upon either side, its intermittent strand of fence-wire, sagging indolently, supports a gallant crowd of the merriest, sweetest sparrows to be found in the whole glad realm. No, they are not a crowd, either, for although the Western Lark Sparrows foregather here annually to pass the season of courtship, and although one may count a hundred of them in the length of a dozen panels, they are not animated to any considerable extent by flock impulses, nor does one think of them *en masse.*

Whether it be running nimbly along the ground, or leaping into the air to catch a risen grasshopper, one feels instinctively that here is a dainty breed. The bird endears itself, moreover, because of its fondness for wayside fellowship. If you are on horseback, the Lark

Sparrow, like the Horned Lark, loves to trip ahead coquettishly along the dusty road, only to yield place at last to your insistent steed with an air of gentle reproach. As it flits away, you catch a glimpse of the rounded tail held half open, with its terminal rim of white; and you know that you have met the aristocrat of the sage.

Or it may be you have caught the bird singing from a fencepost, and rather than lose his run (for poesy also has its mechanics), he will pause momentarily instead of seeking safety in flight. Then that marvelous head comes into full view. What a striped beauty he is! A finger-ring slipped over the Quail-head's head will pass *twenty-three* patches of pure color—black, white, chestnut and buffy, before it encounters a streaky admixture of flaxen, black, and rufous-tawny on the hindhead. The rest of the bird is "sparrow-color," above, relieved only by the flashing white tips of the fanshaped tail. If you are very lucky or very well-behaved, the song will resume. And the song of the Lark Sparrow is one of Nature's sacraments.

Nor is it alone the emotions of springtime which provoke this minstrel to utterance. In fall or winter, when they are flocking, a special dispensation of sunshine will set them all to singing. No less than a score of them are huddled together in a treetop, and a merry *eisteddfod* we shall have of it. Little Welshmen! That's what I call them, for they excel in song as they do in gladness of heart. Aye, aye, what a merry mad bird house it is! No two of them singing alike in theme or tempo, but all of them pitching in at once with a royal good will! Isn't it glorious—tinkling, bubbling, gushing, trilling! Who says that a December day in California is not as good as June anywhere else?

RUFOUS-CROWNED SPARROW

Aimophila ruficeps ruficeps

THERE IS NOTHING SINISTER ABOUT the stealthiness of this creeping sparrow. He is neither plotting mischief nor playing at hide-and-seek, and he seems to be so pleasantly absorbed in the interests of his little world of grass and weeds as to be quite oblivious to scrutiny or impending danger. There is something so demure, so winsome, so unaffected in his manner as he steps out into the open a dozen feet away, culls a bug and dissects it appreciatively, or else hums a half-forgotten song, that prejudice is immediately disarmed and thoughts of collector's envy dismissed. If the bird notices you at all it is only to bestow a friendly glance, after which he pursues the even tenor of a way which you are sure embraces all the beatitudes. In fine, the Rufous-crowned Sparrow must impress everyone who observes him at all as an amiable and gifted poet of content, a sort of embodiment of sunshine and solitude and homely cheer.

Few lives are so devoted to the humbler levels. Even the Savanna Sparrow will go rocketing off through the air when disturbed. But the Rufous-crown steps about through the grass-stems or tufted cover of a rocky hillside without ostentation or appearance of effort; and even when hard-pressed seems to regard flight as unprofessional, a pitiful and degrading last resort. Yet as the breeding season approaches, the Rufous-crown does not hesitate to explore the upper reaches of last year's weed-tops, or to sing from prominent stations on rock or bush.

If anyone supposes that because the Rufous-crown is a fairly plentiful bird in southwestern California, the nests are common likewise, then he is entitled to another guess. The discover of one of these obscure cradles, sunk flush with the ground on some weed-strewn hillside, is something of an exploit. Or perhaps it is fairer to say that discovery of a Rufous-crown's nest is a fortunate accident—a bird flushed at close range, or almost stepped on—for deliberate tracing of the bird to a nest is all but impossible, owing to the exceeding wariness of the bird's approach.

SIERRA JUNCO

Junco oreganus thurberi

ONE'S FIRST ENCOUNTER WITH JUNCO in the Southland is likely to take place on some little oak-sprinkled ridge, the coolest of that section. First one bird, then another, will quit the ground, most unexpectedly to you, and take refuge in a live oak tree. It's a game of hide-and-seek henceforth with you for "it," unless you resolutely sit down and efface yourself until such time as the birds are ready to play a game of their own choosing.

There is a jovial restlessness about these birds in flock which is contagious. Their every movement is accompanied by a happy titter, and the pursuit of necessities is never so stern that a saucy dare from one of their number will not send the whole company off pell-mell like a rout of school-boys. Whenever a Junco starts to wing, it flashes a white signal in the lateral tail-feathers; and this convenient "recognition mark" enables the birds to keep track of each other throughout the maddest gambols in brush-lot or treetop.

In the early days of March the Juncoes gather now and again for a grand concert. The males mount the bush-tops and hold forth in rival strains, while the females lurk under cover and take counsel of their hearts. Junco's song is a sweet little tinkling trill, not very pretentious, but tender and winsome. Interspersed with this is a variety of sipping and suckling notes, whose uses are hard to discern. Now and then, also, a forcible kissing sound may be heard, evidently a note of repulsion instead of attraction, for it is employed in the breeding season to frighten enemies. During the progress of the concert some dashing young fellow, unable fully to express his emotion in song, runs amuck, and goes charging about through the woodsy mazes in a fine frenzy without, however, quite spilling his brains. Others catch the excitement and the company breaks up in a mad whirl of amorous pursuit.

But before the songs are altogether sung out, or "life's great decision" made, the companies begin to climb the hillsides. Up, up they will go with the ascending season, so that Junco's year may be appropriately described as mountain climbing. Now and again a pair will pause, marriage can no longer be deferred; or else the coolness of a suitable locality betrays them into a belief that they are high enough for happiness.

The variety and interest of Junco's nesting habits are scarcely exceeded by those of any other bird. In general, the birds appear to be guided by some thought of seclusion or protection in their choice of nesting sites. Steep hillsides or little banks are, therefore, favorite places, for here the bird may excavate a cool grotto in the earth, and allow the drapery of the hillside—mosses and running vines—to festoon and guard the approaches. In the foothills the upper banks of road-cuttings are frequently occupied, while in mountain meadows I have seen haystacks in whose disheveled sides the Juncoes sheltered their young.

WHITE-CROWNED SPARROW
Zonotrichia leucophrys

PURE QUALITY PERTAINS TO the White-crowned Sparrow. He is chieftain of his *gens*, or clan. His central crown-stripe is purest white, and the bordering bands of black are, if possible, a little blacker, certainly a little silkier, than those which adorn the lesser members of his race. Moreover, the black invades the lores, and this mark is accepted, in this instance at least, as conclusive evidence of superiority.

Two special circumstances conspire to raise *leucophrys* to preeminence in our regard. In the first place, we do not see him in winter. Winter is at best a time of letdown, a time of vulgar flocking, a time of sordid scrambling for food. It is, therefore, a time of disillusionment for bird-lovers. Picture a company of our favorite film stars crowded together in a restaurant, a cafeteria perhaps, with only ten minutes in which to bolt a cup of coffee, sandwich, *and* a piece of pie, before the stage starts for Caesar's Camp in Francisquita

Canyon, L.A.! Ah, well for us, no doubt, that the White-crowned Sparrow conducts his winter business in Chihuahua, beyond our troubled ken.

But the thing which endears the chieftain to us most is his choice of the high Sierras for a summer home. Here is an expression of taste which meets our unqualified approval. The birds gather dignity from the mountains, and they grace in turn the wildest fastnesses, the snow-bound meadows, and the crystal brooks of "timberline." When a bird really prefers to wrest a living from reluctant snow-drifts, to pay court to ladies beside roaring cataracts, or to sing lullabies from the vantage of storm-twisted pines, it is a sign that his heart is in the right place, and that all his actions must be viewed indulgently. Only the Rosy Finch deserves a higher place in our regard, and he, alas! does not sing.

Nuttall's Sparrow
Zonotrichia gambeli nuttalli

When you enter a bit of shrubbery at the edge of town in April or May, your intrusion is almost sure to be questioned by a military gentleman in a gray cloak with black-and-white trimmings. Your business may be personal, not public, but somehow you feel as if the authority of the law had been invoked, and that you would better be careful how you conduct yourself in the presence of this military person. Usually retiring, the Nuttall's Sparrow courts exposure where the welfare of his family is in question, and a metallic scolding note, *zink*, or *dzink*, is made to do incessant service on such occasions. A thoroughly aroused pair, worms in beak, and crests uplifted, may voice their suspicions for half an hour from fir-tip and brush-pile, without once disclosing the whereabouts of their young.

Nuttall's Sparrow is the familiar spirit of brush-lots, fence tangles, berry patches, and half-open situations in general. He is among the last to quit the confines of the city before the advancing ranks of apartment houses and sky-scrapers, and he maintains stoutly any vantage ground of vacant lot, disordered hedgerow, or neglected swamplet left to him. Even Golden Gate Park boasts its breeding population of Nuttall's Sparrows; and I have known them to invade Union Square in the heyday of the spring migration. With the local Song Sparrow he shares the honor of being the commonest sparrow in the northwestern coastal strip of California; and in some places, no doubt because of his less slavish attachment to water, *nuttalli* is more abundant than *Melospiza*.

As a songster this sparrow is not a conspicuous success, although he works at his trade with commendable diligence. He chooses a prominent station, such as the topmost sprig of a redwood sapling, and holds forth at regular intervals in a prosy, iterative ditty, from which the slight musical quality vanishes with distance *Hee ho, chee weé, chee weé* and *Hee, wudge, i-wudge i-wudge i-wéééé* are vocalized examples.

Gambel and Nuttall's Sparrows mingle more or less in winter, at least from San Francisco southward; and it is idle to try to separate them. They are jolly fellows in a crowd; and if to the general excitement of early springtime is added the special interest of bedtime, the noise these rascals can make is fairly deafening. There is always hilarious discussion of the merits of upper and lower berths; and when to their jostling notes—*woods woods a woods*—are added sharp *dzinks* from the grouches, the resulting babel compares favorably with *Passer domesticus* in Bedlam.

Song Sparrow
Melospiza melodia

EUPHONIAS AND PYRRHULOXIAS AND VOLATINIAS are very beautiful, no doubt, but there is a little brown-streaked bird of modest mien whose image is conjured up by the word "home," and whose homely, honest song would bring glad tears to the eyes of any American wandering amid tropic delights. Disregarding for the nonce those subtle and fleeting characters of difference which oblige us in California to speak of the Song Sparrows, let us fix our attention upon the bird itself, *the* Song Sparrow. For where is the bird-lover whose face does not unconsciously relax, or whose heart does not turn tender at the mere mention of this magic name, Song Sparrow! He is the poet of common day. He is the familiar of childhood; for knowledge of him comes at a time of life when one can poke about without rebuke in little cool dingles, or, perchance, accompany recreant water-courses in their perilous journeys to the sea.

Water loving, as a species, throughout their American range, the Song Sparrows of California are even more notably attached to water. Only in the extreme Northwest, where conditions of humidity are widespread, do they suffer themselves to range above half a mile or so from some stream or swamp or saline marsh. A plot of their distribution in summer, therefore, would look like a partial blueprint of our hydrographic system. Even in the interior the bird exhibits a strong aquatic tendency. Not only will the bird build its nests in tussocks entirely surrounded by water, but it will itself plash about carelessly in shallow water; and it sometimes seizes and devours small minnows. This hydrophilous tendency has become especially fixed in the saline marshes bordering upon San Francisco Bay. The extreme example is found in the Alameda Song Sparrow (*M. m. pusillula*), which scarcely deserts the salicornia barrens for a single hour, and which rears its young, as it gleans its living, on the brink of the tide channels.

Silver-tongue is also a bird of the ground and contiguous levels. When hiding he does not seek the depths of the foliage in trees, but skulks among the dead leaves on the ground, or threads his way through log heaps. If driven from one covert the bird dashes to another with an odd, jerking flight, working its tail like a pump-handle as though to assist progress. Ordinarily the bird is not fearful, although retiring in disposition. Bug-catching claims a great deal of attention, and the tules, at least, must be very grateful for the incessant purging of insect pests, especially grubs, which is contrived by this indefatigable gardener. The Song Sparrow is not above scratching for a living either.

At this task he kicks with both feet, after the fashion approved by *Pipilo* and others. He makes a business of it, too, for every once in a while a clod flies out behind as though it had been flung from a buzz-saw.

It is as a songster, however, that we know this sparrow best. Silver-tongue's melody is like sunshine, bountiful and free and ever grateful. Mounting some bush or upturned root, he greets his childish listeners with *"Peace, peace, peace be unto you, my children."* And that is his message to all the world, "Peace and goodwill." Once on Puget Sound, we sat stormbound at the mouth of our tent, and, mindful of the unused cameras, grumbled at the eternal drizzle. Whereupon the local poet flitted to a favorite perch on a stump hard by, and, throwing back his head, sang, with sympathetic earnestness, "Cheer up! Cheer up! Count your many mercies *now*." Of course he did say exactly that, and the childish emphasis he put upon the last word set us to laughing, my partner and me, until there was no more thought of complaint.

But no matter how gentle a bird's disposition may be, there is ample use, alack! for the note of warning and distrust. When, therefore, the Song Sparrow's nesting haunts are invaded, the bird emits a *chip* or *chirp*, still musical, indeed, but very anxious. In winter, resident birds deny themselves even this characteristic cry; and, except for the occasional outbursts of full song, they are limited to a high nasal *tss*, which seems to serve the purpose of a flocking, or recognition, call. Song Sparrows are not really gregarious birds; nor are they even seen in close proximity save in mating time, but they like to assure themselves, nevertheless, that a dozen of their fellows are within call against a time of need.

Spotted Towhee
Pipilo maculates

THE SPOTTED TOWHEE BULKS LARGE in the economy of the underworld. He is, in fact, its acknowledged prince; not, of course, in the Mephistophelian sense, but as the undoubted aristocrat among those humble folk who skulk under dark ferns, thread marvelous mazes of interlacing sticks and stalks, sort over the leafy wastage of the careless trees, and understand the foundations of things generally. To really get Master Towhee's point of view, one must be willing to creep on hands and knees among the bristling stems of mountain lilac and chamise of a southern mesa, or else go belly-wise through the rootage and cast-off duffle of a northern forest. It is a wonderful world the serpent sees (albeit a mussy one), a basic, essential world, where all flesh meets you on a common level. If dinner be the quest, here is a table always spread. Help yourself, for "self-service" is the inflexible rule, and "*hors d'oeuvres*" the exception. Under a fragment of a tree's cast-off garment lies a grub in wriggling invitation; and here where weeds of two generations have cast their bones, a spider, not adroit enough by half, has concealed a hamper full of toothsome eggs. Dinner is from six to six (and again from six to six for the night shift), and the full belly is to the industrious. Towhee is thoroughly at home here, and scratching for food is his job. This he pursues not by the methodical clutch and scrape of the old hen, but by a succession of backward kicks, executed with spirit by both feet at once, and assisted by a compensatory flash of the wings. By this method not only lurking insects but fallen seeds of a hundred sorts are brought quickly to light, and these the bird swiftly devours.

But we started to speak of Towhee's preeminence, not of his dining. His chieftainship is due in part, no doubt, to a certain fatherly alertness manifested on behalf of the clan. No sound or movement, whether hostile or friendly, escapes his notice. If the bird-man's entrance into the local bird setting be accomplished with a becoming modesty, he presently hears a mild, questioning voice, *me ay?* or *me ayuh?* But if the man is unduly offensive, he hears instantly an indignant *marié, marié,* which sends the clan scattering. But when the bird-watcher glimpses the chief's costume, the secret of his ascendancy is out. Fine feathers still do make fine birds. Black-and-white and earth red, picked out here and there with white spots, "maculations," make an impressive uniform, and one to which we all yield cheerful respect. But the marvel is how anything so spick and span can emerge from such a chaos; or how beauty can maintain itself in constant association with bugs and slugs and the innumerable horribilia of the Kingdom of Underfoot.

BROWN TOWHEE

Pipilo crissalis

FAMILIAR OBJECTS, WHATEVER THEIR WORTH, come to be dear to us through association. There is, honestly, no particular reason why we should be fond of this prosy creature, save that he is always around. In appearance, the bird is a bit awkward, slovenly, and uncouth; or at least, we are obliged to see him oftenest in every-day duds, and he seems to have no company manners. And for color—never was a more hopeless drab. But surely the bird must have some redeeming qualities. He sings, perhaps? Not at all; his efforts at song are a farce, a standing joke—though he is himself entirely devoid of humor. He is, to be sure, a gleaner of crumbs and odds and ends, but so are the ants; and the bird's presence in a garden is far from being an unmixed blessing. Really, there is no reason why one should espouse the cause of this local ash-man. Yet I suppose there are few Californians who would willingly spare the homely, matter-of-fact presence of this bird under foot. Brown Towhees are just birds—the same way most of us are just folks.

Truth to tell, the sober color of our hero does match very well the universal dryness of the under scrub, during the long rest period which Californian vegetation indulges (and which dutiful Californians pretend to like). When other birds, therefore, have forsaken the mesa and have gone to higher, greener levels, the Towhee feels no need of change. He has come into his own. Trusting to his brown coat, he moves about fearlessly in the open, and is much more active than Thrasher or Wren-tit dares to be, away from cover. Wren-tit is, doubtless, the first bird to respond to the screeping call of the bird-man, but if the Wren-tit is not on hand, the Brown Towhee is sure to be. His name is legion, and some one of him marks the downsitting and the uprising of every human in western or southern California.

The Brown Towhee is the typical Hans when he gets with other birds. When he is consorting with the Crown Sparrows, as he often does, or tries to, he apes all their motions of fright or flight, but he does it so awkwardly and exposes himself in such yokel fashion, according to their standards, that the crowd is jeering at him before he has rejoined it in the shelter of the bush. Save for the afflictions of the noble passion, the Towhees get along well enough with their own kind. There is likely to be amiable twittering—good-natured banter, it would seem—whenever they meet; and nothing could be more suggestive of homely joys than the sight of a wedded pair taking "the kids" out for an airing of a Sunday afternoon. The excursion, perhaps, is conducted through the garden. Bugs and worms are not overlooked. Fallen seeds are seized and bolted outright, or else shelled deftly with that curious nibbling motion which always looks babyish or affected in these large-beaked birds. Fresh herbage is sampled freely, too freely, perhaps, as we shall learn presently. Whatever the parents do the children imitate in grateful obedience; but there are baby hours whiled in the leafy shade, when they are more prone to snatch up what father or mother has uncovered by energetic backward kicks than to rustle (quite literally) for themselves.

Cowbirds, Orioles, Blackbirds, Meadowlarks, and Bobolinks

COWBIRD
Molothrus ater

IT MAY BE URGED WITH SOME SHOW OF JUSTICE that every bird-person deserves a sympathetic biographer. Even criminals on trial for their lives are entitled to legal defense. Well, then, let who will be defender. I will be prosecuting attorney. "*J'accuse.*" The prisoner at the bar is a demirep, a ne'er-do-weel, a slattern, a shirk, a harpy, a traitor, an anarchist. Destitute of all natural affection, she cares neither for the wrongs of others nor for the undermined pillars of her own virtue. She is the unchaste mother of a race gone wrong, an enemy of bird-society, a blight upon the flower of Progress. Despised and hated by her fellow birds, harried and anathematized by her victims, this avian marplot lives only by stealth and by the secret practice of violence. All that may possibly be urged on behalf of this culprit is that she is the victim of an unfortunate heredity. Such a defense is in itself an accusation. The Cowbird stock is indeed polluted: of haphazard and unknown paternity, conceived in an infamy of indifference, she was dumped at birth into a strange cradle, and left to make shift as best she might, an unblessed and pitiless bastard. Nourished by uncomprehending or reluctant strangers, and winning a place in their affections solely at the cost of the lives of their own innocent babes, this foundling first accepts their untiring ministrations, and then escapes, an alien ingrate, to join herself to the beasts of the field. What wonder, then, that at maturity she welcomes the pirate band, joins them in their obscene revels, and perpetuates, in turn, her dissolute race. Out upon her!

But even degeneracy may be picturesque—of interest, that is, when viewed dispassionately as a phenomenon instead of a moral issue. Hear, then, with what tolerance you may, the story of a changeling:

Beginning, say, in mid-August, before the bird has ever seen another of its own kind, we find it closely attached to some group of horses or cows, following them about slavishly, now being nosed out of the way as the animals feed, or evading as by instinct the misplaced hoof. Perhaps it is oftenest the foregathering of the animals which leads the birds themselves together. At any rate, the corral soon boasts a little company of these dun-colored youngsters with light undervests, and, though they early learn to come and go freely, the association with horses and cattle is lifelong.

In winter there is a general retirement into Mexico, although a few of the dwarf variety linger through the season upon the Colorado Desert and along the Colorado River. In February or March, according to altitude, there is a return movement of Cowbirds, oftenest in company with other blackbirds. But if the main flock halts for refreshments and discussion en route, a group of these rowdies will hunt up some disreputable female of their own kind, and make tipsy and insulting advances to her along some horizontal limb or fence rail. Taking a position about a foot away from the coy drab, the male will make two or three accelerating hops toward her, then stop suddenly, allowing the impulse of motion to tilt him violently forward and throw his tail up perpendicularly, while at the same moment he spews out the disgusting notes which voice his passion.

Of the mating, Chapman says: "They build no nest, and the females, lacking every moral instinct, leave their companions only long enough to deposit their eggs in the nests of other and smaller birds."

The egg, thus surreptitiously placed in another bird's nest, hatches in ten or eleven days, usually, therefore, two or three days before those of the foster mother, and the infant Cowbird thus gains an advantage which he is not slow to improve. His loud clamoring for food often drives the old birds to abandon the task of incubation; or if the other eggs are allowed to remain until hatched, the uncouth stranger manages to usurp attention and food supplies, and not infrequently to override or stifle the other occupants of the nest, so that their dead bodies are by-and-by removed to make room for his hogship. It is asserted by some that in the absence of the foster parents the young thug forcibly ejects the rightful heirs from the nest, after the fashion of the Old World Cuckoos. I once found a nest which contained only a lusty Cowbird, while three proper fledglings clung to the shrubbery below, and one lay dead upon the ground.

When the misplaced tenderness of foster parents has done its utmost for the young upstart, he joins himself to some precious crew of his own blood, and the cycle of a changeling is complete.

BULLOCK'S ORIOLE
Icterus bullocki

THANK GOD FOR WONDER! What is it but a pleased interest in the unfolding panorama of life? We consider it the special attribute of childhood, because life is new to the child; but woe to us when we cease to wonder! It is a sign that we have ceased to live. For in the last analysis, Wonder is Worship—a recognition of the presence of God and ecstatic joy thereat.

It is not otherwise with the soul and God. Our Heavenly Father has devised the myriad show of Nature, and has brought us to view it. If we gaze with unseeing eyes, if we turn quickly away, we offend him. He has labored in vain, and the Creator's heart is in so far saddened. But if, on the other hand, we enter with deep appreciation into the storehouse of Nature, if we pass with reverent ecstacy from one marvel to another, or if we gaze with kindling enthusiasm upon a single example of his perfect work, we declare ourselves to be of his sort. We are manifestly pleased, and his pleasure is in the sight of ours. We hold communion with him in wonder no less than in praise. Rightly considered, wonder is worship, and God hath not wrought in vain.

And what marvel in all nature shall exceed that offered in the delicate, fantastic traceries of a Bullock's Oriole's egg! On a background of palest bluish gray, the calligraphist, having dipped his pen in a well of purplish black, proceeds to scrawl and shade, to zigzag and flourish and vibrate— all this while the obedient oval turns round and round. Now as the egg revolves for a dozen turns, the artist bears on with laborious care. Now he lifts the pen; and now, returning, he loiters while the ink runs out upon the page in little pools of indelible blackness. Quaint and fanciful, indeed, are the divagations of the Icterine genius. With all the world before him, why should he not choose to be fantastic? On a specimen before me there are traceries which vary in width from one twentieth of an inch to one ten-thousandth. Some of them stand forth like the lines of an engraved visiting card, while others require a magnifying glass to recall their nebulous course to visibility. On another egg twelve independent lines pass unheeding within a total space of one tenth of an inch, while the smaller end of the same egg is perfectly bare. Here the weird image of a goblin piper braces itself on legs set rakishly awry, and strains away at a splintered flute—all within the space of a barley-corn. There a cable of twisted purple ropes frays suddenly and goes off into gossamer hysterics. Another egg, tottering under its burden of pigment, shows lines curiously shadowed, or "side-wiped." It is all so fascinating, so bewildering, and so mysterious! What is it all for?

RED-WINGED BLACKBIRD
Agelaius phoeniceus

SPRING HERSELF BEING LISTED AS a "winter resident" in California, we are never quite certain when the official season does open. Certainly not, as elsewhere, with the coming of the Redwings. Such as are not already resident in the State, arrive from the North in late autumn, and spend the winter with us. Neither their comings nor their goings are as conspicuous with us as they are in the North; but if in mid-February or early March we come upon a boisterous company of Redwings crowding a treetop, we may be sure that they are mustering for the northern journey. What a world of jubilation there is in their voluble whistlings and chirpings and gurglings, a wild medley of conquest which will strike terror to the faltering heart of that northern winter. A sudden hush falls upon the company as the bird-man draws near the tree in which they are swarming; but a dusky maiden pouts, "Who cares?" and they all fall to again, hammer and tongs, timbrel, pipes, and hautboy. Brewer's Blackbirds and Cowbirds occasionally make common cause with the Redwings in the northern migrations, but it is always the last-named who preponderate, and it is they who are most vivacious, most resplendent, and most nearly musical. The Redwing's mellow *kongqueree* or occasional tipsy *whoop-er-way-up* is the life of the party.

An annual visit to the cat-tail swamp is as necessary as a birthday to the life of any well-regulated bird-lover. The reedy mazes grow ever dearer year by year, and the chorus of expostulating blackbirds, which is their inevitable accompaniment, renews our racial youth as if by magic. We must not forget the date of first nesting, April 15th, for almost before we know it, our friends to the number of a dozen pairs or more have taken up their residence in the old cat-tail swamp—nowhere else, if you please, unless driven to it—and here a dozen baskets of matchless weave are swung, or lodged, midway of growing plants. Our distant approach has been commented upon from the tops of bordering willows by *keyrings* and other notes. Now at close range, the lordly male, he of the brilliant epaulets and the proper military swagger, shakes out his fine clothes and says, *Kongqueree*, in a voice wherein anxiety is quite outweighed by vanity and proffered good-fellowship withal. But if we push roughly through the outlying sedges, anxiety obtains the mastery. There is a hubbub in the marsh. Bustling, frowsy females appear and scold us roundly. The lazy gallants are all fathers now, and they join direful threats to courteous expostulations as they flutter wildly about our intruding heads. To the residual small boy in us the chance of calling out these frantic attentions is irresistible, even though no harm is intended, or done. Perhaps we love to play the part of bogey, that we may rejoice in our own restraint. Perhaps we perceive, if we stop to think at all, that our own anxieties may be as mildly amusing to some benevolent Presence, and as ill-founded.

Of course the Redwings are the self-appointed guardians of the swamp. They are not less jealous of unlicensed avian intruders than of humans. Sometimes they fail to discriminate, and their pugnacity leads either to ridiculous or dangerous lengths. Once, at Los Banos, I saw a company of Bicolored Redwings set upon an unoffending Marsh Hawk, a handsome blue male bird who was attending strictly to his own business. The big fellow stood the abuse for a while, then, quick as a flash, seized a blackbird in his talons and bore it away. A moment later, to our astonishment, he released the little bully, who flew off promptly and, let us hope, gratefully. It was just as though the Marsh Hawk had purposely restrained his power, and had done it all to teach the saucy little fellows a salutary lesson.

Yellow-headed Blackbird
Xanthocephalus xanthocephalus

OH, WELL FOR THE UNTRIED NERVES that the Yellow-headed Blackbird sings by day, when the sun is shining brightly, and there are no supporting signs of a convulsion of Nature! Verily, if love affected us all in similar fashion, the world would be a merry mad-house. The Yellow-head is an extraordinary person—you are prepared for that once you catch sight of his resplendent gold-upon-black livery—but his avowal of the tender passion is a revelation of incongruity. Grasping a reed firmly in both fists, he leans forward, and, after premonitory gulps and gasps, succeeds in pressing out a wail of despairing agony which would do credit to a dying catamount. When you have recovered from the first shock, you strain the eyes in astonishment that a mere bird, and a bird in love at that, should give rise to such a cataclysmic sound. But he can do it again, and his neighbor across the way can do as well—or worse. When your nerves have somewhat recovered, modesty overcomes you, and you retire, not without a chastened sense of privilege that you have lived to hear the Yellow-head pop the question—"and also you lived after."

For all the Yellow-head is so decided in utterance, in disposition he is somewhat phlegmatic, the male bird especially lacking the vivacity which characterizes the agile Brewer's Blackbird. Except when hungry, or impelled by passion, he is quite content to mope for hours at a time in the depths of the reeds; and even in nesting time, when his precincts are invaded, he oftener falls to admiring his own plumage in the flooding sunshine than tries to drive off the intruder. Let the homely and distrait female attend to that.

WESTERN MEADOWLARK
Sturnella neglecta

SUMMER SILENCES THE BIRDS SO GRADUALLY, and we ourselves have become so much absorbed in business during the prosy days of September, that we have almost forgotten the choruses of springtime, and have come to accept our uncheered lot as part of the established order of things. But on a nippy October morning, as we are bending over some dull task, there comes a sound which brings us to our feet. We hasten to the window, throw up the sash and lean out into the cool, fresh air, while a Meadowlark rehearses, all at a sitting, the melodies of the year's youth. It all comes back to us with a rush: the smell of lush grasses, the splendor of apple blossoms, the courage of lengthening days, the ecstacies of courtship—all these are recalled by the lark-song. It is as though this forethoughted soul had caught the music of a May day, just at its prime, in a crystal vase, and was now pouring out the imprisoned sound in a gurgling, golden flood. What cheer! What heartening! Yea; what rejuvenation it brings! Wine of youth! Splashes of color and gay delight!

It is impossible not to rhapsodize over the Meadowlark. He is a rhapsodist himself. Born of the soil and lost in its embraces for such time as it pleases him, he yet quits his lowly station ever and again, mounts some fence-post or treetop, and publishes to the world an unquenchable gladness in things-as-they-are. If at sunrise, then the gleams of the early ray flash resplendent from his golden breastplate—this high-priest of morning; and all Nature echoes his joyous blast: "Thank God for sunshine!" Or if the rain begins to fall, who so quickly grateful for its refreshment as this optimist of the ground, this prophet of good cheer! There is even an added note of exultation in his voice as he shouts: "Thank God for rain!" And who like him can sing farewell to parting day! Piercing sweet from the meadows come the last offerings of day's daysmen, peal and counterpeal from rival friendly throats, unfailing, unfaltering, unsubdued: "It is good to live. It is good to rest. Thank God for the day now done!"

The Meadowlark is an assiduous nester. This not because of any unusual amativeness, but because young Meadowlarks are the *morceaux delicieux* of all the powers that prey—skunks, weasels, minks, raccoons, foxes, coyotes, snakes, jays, magpies, crows, and ravens; and if there be any other power of darkness, be sure it has its hand in here. Hawks and owls otherwise blameless in the bird-world err in respect to the Meadowlark—the game is too easy. Even the noble Peregrine does not disdain this humble, albeit toothsome, quarry; and the Kestrel (*Cerchneis sparverius*) will stoop for a young Meadowlark when all other avian offerings are virtuously passed by.

Fecundity then is the only recourse—this, and concealment. Not relying altogether upon its marvelous protective coloration, the lark exhibits great caution in approaching, and, if possible, in quitting its nest. In either case it sneaks along the ground for a considerable distance, threading the mazes of the grass so artfully that the human eye can follow with difficulty, or not at all. At the approach of danger a sitting bird may either steal from her nest unobserved and rise at a safe distance, or else seek to further her deception by feigning lameness, after the fashion of the shore-birds. Or, again, she may cling to her charge in desperation, hoping against hope till the last possible moment, and taking chances of final mishap. In this way a friend of mine once discovered a brooding Meadowlark imprisoned underneath his boot—fortunately without damage, for she occupied the deep depression of a cow-track.

BOBOLINK
Dolichonyx oryzivorus

ROBERT OF LINCOLN! APOSTLE OF MIRTH! Merriest madcap artist of spring! Symbol of divine unrest and divine—oh, divine Hope! He is here! Turn out, you Native Sons! and muster, you sons of millionaires, to do him honor! You whose fathers struck oil, or whose grandsires struck pay dirt, what will you ever strike one-half so rich as this fountain of song, this well of gladness, pure and unrestrained! Hail! blessed brother bird! And hail! tumultuous minstrel Bobolink!

Next after Bluebird, the coming of Bobolink marks the broadest step in the golden stair of springtime, by which we yearly attain the height of ornithological joy. His coming heralds that tidal wave of migration which begins somewhere during the last week of April, and sweeps over us till the middle of May. Without waiting for their more modest mates, the males press northward, hot-winged, to riot for a while over the dank meadows in bachelor companies, and to perfect that marvel of tumultuous song. Oh, how they sing, those Bacchanals of springtime! From fence-post or treetop, or quivering in midair, they pour forth such an ecstacy of liquid, gurgling notes as must thrill the very clouds. Such exuberance of spirit, such reckless abandon of mirth-compelling joy would cure a sick preacher on blue Monday. As the bird sings, he bows and scrapes and pirouettes till, as Wheaton says, "he resembles a French dancing master in uniform, singing, fiddling, dancing, and calling off at the same time."

But when some fine morning, about a week later, a shy, plainly attired, brown lady drops from the sky with a soft *dink*, then it is that the passionate soul of the singer is fairly consumed by the inner fires of melody and desire. He dashes like mad after his lady love and pursues her at breakneck speed through the thickets of weeds and about fence-rows until he loses her in the grass. Then he hovers, or rather dances, in the air, over the spot where she vanished, or else retires to a fence-post hard by, to make frantic protestations of his devotion. *Oh geezeler, geezeler, gilpity, onkeler, oozeler, oo*, comes from that perfect throat; and somewhere between two blades of grass the lady is watching him—the sly minx—and chuckling softy to herself.

Finches and Old World Sparrows

CALIFORNIA EVENING GROSBEAK
Hesperiphona vespertina californica

THE EVENING GROSBEAK IS NEITHER the most beautiful nor the most tuneful of the Fringillidae, if he is by common consent rated the oddest. His garb is a patchwork; his song a series of shrieks; his motions eccentric; his humor phlegmatic; and his concepts beyond the ken of man. Although at times one of the most approachable of birds, he is, on the whole, an avian freak, a rebus in feathers.

Perhaps we make too much of a mystery of him, just as we rate the owl highest in wisdom for the single discretion of silence, which any dunderhead may attain. But now take this group in the park; just what are they about? They sit there solidly in the rowan tree where all the passersby may take note of them, giving vent ever and anon to explosive yelps, but *doing nothing* by the hour, until an insane impulse seizes one of their number to be off to some other scene no better, be it near or far, and the rest yield shrieking consent by default of alternative idea. It is all so unreasonable, so uncanny, that it irritates us.

If a student runs through the brief published annals of this bird, he will be surprised to see how much of its history has been written in or near the cities. Just why these birds should be especially attracted to the centers of population, it is hard to say. Perhaps they love the stir and uproar of urban life, the din which they help so valiantly to promote. At any rate, it is easy enough to see why they are more noticeable here, for their showy and patchy coloration marks them as distinguished visitors in town, whereas in the forest their colors so melt into and harmonize with their surroundings that it is difficult to follow their movements.

Sierra Nevada Rosy Finch, or Dawson's Leuco
Leucosticte tephrocotis dawsoni

IN ONE SENSE AT LEAST THE American Leucostictes stand at the very apex of evolutionary progress. If life began, as the biologists assert, in the depths of the ocean, then it is the "Leuco" who has carried life's banner highest. Today he flaunts it from the mountain peaks, from Shasta and Whitney no less than from Blanca and Baker and Robson. If lofty association means anything for character, also, the Sierra Nevada Rosy Finch ought to be the very best of birds, for it is his privilege to spend a lifetime wrestling with the eternal snows.

What, now, does our divinity—eat? To all intents and purposes, *snow*. Watch a company of them deploy over a snowfield, hopping sedately from crest to crest of the tiny ridges, or else escalading into the pits which the sun has made. They are pecking industriously at the surface as they go, and accumulating—well, not snow-flakes, nor yet snow-balls, but *frozen insects*, instead. It is marvelous what a varied diet is offered to these patient gleaners of the glaciers. The warm winds wafted up from the great interior valley bear moths and beetles, bugs and winged ants—they know not whither; and these, succumbing to the sudden cold of the Sierran heights, fall in a beneficent shower over the Leuco's table.

As the season advances and the area of the snowfields is reduced, the Leucos resort to the south slopes of the peaks, where yellow-winged locusts and deer-flies and the hardy butterflies, notably *Vanessa californica*, hold forth. These they pursue on the ground, or else seize in midair by dextrous leaps from below. They feed also at the lower levels over the heather beds and in the vicinity of the cirque lakes.

No bird, however, could be more thoroughly at home, or more matter-of-fact in its behavior, about precipices or in ice-bound couloirs. Whether in nest-hunting, mate-hunting, or in the ordinary quest for food, a Leucosticte will flit from crevice to point up the face of a twelve-hundred-foot escarpment as though it were a garden dike. The crannies are explored in leisurely fashion in quest of lurking bugs; and if it is mating time, the bird pauses to sing, or rather, chirp, from some eminence that would make an Alpensteiger dizzy. The *bergschrund*, or chasm where the rock-wall and ice-wall part company, has no terrors for the Leuco. Once I saw a precocious infant (of *L. t. hepburni*) which had tumbled into one of these places some thirty feet in depth; but mama was feeding him, and he was as cheerful as a cricket, expecting, no doubt justly, to win out again after his wings were a little stronger.

If there are nesting activities on, they are conducted *sub rosa*. There is no eagerness to display domestic secrets. These must be ferreted out. But there is lavish display of romantic interest. Males are chirping loudly from vantage points; and as often as one of them discovers a female, presumably unengaged, he darts down into her neighborhood, then sidles over to her, hat in hand, so to speak, and pours forth a strident flood of amorous professions. The antics in which one of these hot-hearted bachelors engages are lush beyond description. If the lady will endure his presence at all, the male fairly perspires adoration. His wings quiver and his whole frame trembles. He turns about, slowly, in order that his enamorata may see how his every feather is engulfed; or if he pauses, he puts up a wing affectedly, as though to shield himself from the lady's overpowering glances. If the lady is cold—cold, but not impossible—in the very extremity of despair the smitten one procures a wisp of straw, seizing it by the middle, and bearing it about like a huge moustachio, the while his eloquent pleas are pouring forth. By this act, of course, he signifies that he speaks of conjugal affection. The lady must be won to a sense of responsibility. The days are long but the snows are melting. "Oh, will you? won't you? say, why don't you cast your lot with mine?"

These advances have various denouements. If the female is indeed smitten, as must in the nature of things sometimes happen, the couple adjourn to some cave among the rocks and carry out the purpose of love in secret. If the lady is only shy, she sidles off, or flits, and there is instant pursuit. The couple charge about like meteors amuck, and if they do not dash their brains out, it is a good sign that love is *not* blind. But if, as oftener happens, the lady is either previously engaged, or minded to try out the young swain's professions, she makes spiteful dabs at her admirer while he falls back in pretended and ecstatic alarm. Oftener still, the swain is addressing a lawfully wedded wife, for it seems to be his principle to try all doors till one of them yields. In that case, the lady tells him quickly to be off about his business, and is obeyed, or else—an avenging bolt falls out of the blue. The lawfully wedded husband, who nine times in ten is on the job, whether near or remote, falls upon that young rascal and either chases him clear out of bounds, or administers an actual drubbing. There seem to be more males than females, and it is proper form for the ladies to be always attended in public by their mates.

WILLOW GOLDFINCH

Astragalinus tristis salicamans

BRIGHT APOSTLE OF MIDSUMMER! Herald and poet of sunlit hours! How the drooping heads of waterless daisies lift up when they catch his cheerful salutation! *Per chic' i chic'—Perchic' opee,* says the rollicking beak as he throws his pendant loops of flight. *Perchic-ichic, perchic*—and lo, the minstrel is suddenly quenched in a riot of thistledown. Or else it is a great fruiting sunflower which has engaged his attention, and he must pause upon the instant and test the ripeness of those luscious seeds. *Dayick? Dayick?* he questions, but the stolid ranks of little striped elves stand silent. They are not quite ready yet. Whereupon the happy minstrel remarks *puchew* or *chu wëë oo*, in a forgiving voice, and flies with an indulgent titter to another prospect.

In the winter season Willow Goldfinches are everywhere very much less in evidence. They do not migrate, apparently, but they take on a duller plumage, and they live more quietly. Just as the impression gets about that they are gone, one stumbles upon a large company stealing about in the tops of the sycamore trees, or else sunning themselves at the edge of a ceanothus patch. If too much disturbed, they will *perchic perchic opee* as of yore; but it is a pale reflection of midsummer glory.

California Linnet, or House Finch
Carpodacus mexicanus frontalis

I SUPPOSE THERE IS NOT ANOTHER BIRD in the West which is responsible for so much amiable discourse, so much friendly camaraderie, so much homely good cheer withal, as this ubiquitous "Linnet." The bird is part and parcel of our California life, as much to be taken for granted as sunshine and dry weather. The Linnet is the bread-and-butter of the bird feast which life daily spreads before us. We may pass it over, for the nonce, in favor of more notable dainties, but it is staple. We will come back to it. For my part, I confess without shame that I am fond of the Linnets. They may litter my porches and they may strip my vines if they like. I will take my pay in music—that incessant, uplifting chorus of commonplace joy. It is reward enough to see the happy creatures breeding and brooding under our very noses, and lavishing upon us that flattery of confidence which they possess in common with our own children. They are not angels; and sometimes we call them dirty little brats—the birds, I mean—but the home that is not surrounded by an investing halo of Linnets, I hold it to be unblest.

The House Finch is without question the most abundant bird in California. It probably outnumbers all other resident species three to one, and in some localities ten to one. It does not to any large extent invade the chaparral nor the deserts, per se, nor does it seek to possess the mountains; and yet within its range it gives an impression of ubiquity which is very nearly supported by the facts. The bird's adaptability is marvelous. It is practically without associational restraints, and although its preference is for cultural surroundings, it makes its home in the most secluded barrancas, or haunts alike the cliffs which front the cattle range, and those which face the sea.

In its nesting habits the California Linnet exhibits the utmost diversity of taste and the utmost degree of accommodation to varied conditions. The bird does nest about houses and outbuildings, multitudinously; but the very name House Finch is so often challenged by experiences afield that one is sooner inclined to call it devil finch or spook finch. Does one penetrate the fastnesses of the cattle country, where the Dalton gang and the James boys used to hold forth, it is to study the mighty eagle, or to trace the "bullet hawk" (*Falco mexicanus*) to its ledge. But lo, the "House" Finch has set its little tepee in a cranny beside the noble falcon; and while the falcon hurls its thunders from the blue, this tedious chit simpers and chirps as though its tiny affairs were Nature's chief concern. Does one visit the cliffs at Pismo to get the salty sting of the gales, or "to hear old Triton blow his wreathed horn," lo! the House Finch has come before. Here upon these storied cliffs, where birds of high and rare degree, Peregrines, Surf-birds, Royal Terns, pause, in passing, to greet the shore, these irreverent commoners gossip and flutter, or gather straws. Not even the occasional presence of the White-throated Swift, the speed demon of the upper air, daunts these hardy sans-culottes. They, too, disport themselves aloft, or wing placidly across some yawning chasm which the sea has cleft, mews. House Finch, indeed! Why, there is no juniper tree where a heedless alike of the buffeting wind and of the fretful sea-man may be alone with his Maker, but this bird hops in its branches and twangs his little lute!

Choice of nesting materials is as catholic as that of nesting sites. Again the catalog comprises anything soft and available: straw, grass, weed-stems, flower-heads, string, wool, cotton, vegetable down, bark strips, moss, horsehair, and, rarely, feathers. There is, however, real artistry among the House Finches, and often the builder makes choice of a single material, so that there is a tasteful simplicity in the finished product. The young birds are little tyrants, yet as "cunning" as they are insatiable. They follow their parents about with importunate cries when we would judge them fully able to care for themselves. But mother doubtless knows best, and it certainly is a pretty sight to see a busy mother stuffing food down the throat of a tremulous hobbledehoy who looks at least half a size larger. And the youngster doesn't forget his manners, either. If he does say "Please" pretty often and pretty emphatic, he also says "Thank you" all over, with quivering wings, which to my notion are most expressive and grateful.

And when the family life of the House Finch is merged in the greater life of the flock, this charm of manner is not all forgotten. Though the songs of springtime are hushed, the keep-in-touch notes are still cheerful and friendly. And when a cloud rises, two or three thousand strong, from a wayside weed-patch to settle on the telephone wires, the heart of the passerby insensibly warms as he hears pleasant greetings and a babel of polite discussion. Surely, these are amiable bird-folk, and we may thank our lucky stars that California has bred gentlemen-commoners instead of gibbering assassins.

English Sparrow

Passer domesticus

WHAT A PIECE OF MISCHIEF IS THE SPARROW! how depraved in instinct! in presence how unwelcome! in habit how unclean! in voice how repulsive! in combat how moblike and despicable! in courtship how wanton and contemptible! in increase how limitless and menacing! the pest of the farmer! the plague of the city! the bane of the bird-world! the despair of the philanthropist! the thrifty and insolent beneficiary of misguided sentiment! the lawless and defiant object of impotent hostility too late aroused! Out upon thee, thou shapeless, senseless, heartless, misbegotten tyrant! thou tedious and infinite alien! thou myriad cuckoo, who dost by thy consuming presence bereave us daily of a million dearer children! Out upon thee, and woe the day!

Without question the most deplorable event in the history of American ornithology was the introduction of the English Sparrow. The extinction of the Great Auk, the passing of the wild pigeon and the turkey—sad as these are, they are trifles compared to the wholesale reduction of our smaller birds, which is due to the invasion of this wretched foreigner. To be sure he was invited to come, but the offense is all the more rank because it was partly human. His introduction was effected in part by people who ought to have known better, and would, doubtless, if the science of ornithology had reached its present status as long ago as the early fifties.

If there are those who still require evidence that the English Sparrow is an undesirable alien, I beg to submit for their consideration the following charges, each confirmed by experience no less than by authority.

1. The English Sparrow destroys fruits, berries, grains, buds, garden-seeds, and tender shoots.

2. The bird destroys as many beneficial insects as it does injurious.

3. It is a frequent destroyer and almost inevitable disseminator of disease, through its use of poultry litter and other trash in nest-building.

4. It harbors and disseminates chicken-lice (*Dermanyssus gallinae* Redi), as well as bird-lice (*D. avium* De Geer).

5. The English Sparrow reduces the number of desirable native birds through destruction of their eggs and young, and through usurpation of their nesting sites.

6. It discourages and drives out desirable native species by continual annoyance and by the employment of mob tactics.

7. It defiles shrubbery, ornamental vines and trees, houses, and public buildings, by its excrement; and it builds bulky, disfiguring nests out of unsightly trash.

8. Its unwelcome presence defiles the more remote woodland sanctuaries and mars the serenity of the everlasting hills, no less surely than it does that of the cities and the rural centers.

It requires no further testimony to show that the presence of this bird is absolutely undesirable. It is a scourge to the agriculturist, a plague to the architect, and the avowed and determined enemy of all other birds. Its nests are not only unsightly but unsanitary, and the maudlin racket of their owners unendurable. The bird is, in short, in the words of the late Dr. Coues, "a nuisance without a redeeming quality." Although we assent to this most heartily, we are obliged to confess on the part of our race to a certain amount of sneaking admiration for the [English] Sparrow. And why, forsooth? Because he fights! We are forced to admire, at times, his bull-dog courage and tenacity of purpose, as we do the cunning of the weasel and the nimbleness of the flea. He *is* vermin and must be treated as such; but, give the Devil his due, of course.

Appendix

CURRENT COMMON AND SCIENTIFIC NAMES

TAXONOMY IS NOT STATIC. Since 1923, the development of ornithological science has led to the reclassification of many species. This appendix lists, in their order of appearance in this book, any species whose common or scientific name has changed since Dawson's time. Dawson's common name is listed first, followed by the current common name (if it has changed) and the current scientific name (if it has changed).

Dawson often employs trinomial nomenclature to refer to a particular subspecies. Unless it is absolutely clear that the same subspecies is recognized today (as in the case of the Northern Black Swift, once *Nephoecetes niger borealis*, now *Cypseloides niger borealis*), this appendix only lists the current species-level, binomial classification. The two main sources for this information were the Official California Bird Records Committee's State Bird List and the Berkeley Natural History Museums' online catalog (http://bnhm.berkeley.edu/browse/vertebrates_all.php).

Loons and Grebes
Horned Grebe, *Podiceps auritus*

Albatrosses, Shearwaters, and Petrels
Short-tailed Albatross, *Phoebastria albatrus*
Dark-bodied Shearwater (Sooty Shearwater)
Beal's Petrel (Leach's Storm Petrel)

Cormorants and Pelicans
Farallon Cormorant (Double-crested Cormorant)
Baird's Cormorant (Pelagic Cormorant)

Herons, Bitterns, and Ibises
Pallid Great Blue Heron (Great Blue Heron)
Wood Ibis (Wood Stork)
White-faced Glossy Ibis, *Plegadis chihi*

Ducks, Geese, and Swans
Mallard, *Anas platyrhynchos*
Cinnamon Teal, *Anas cyanoptera*
Shoveller, *Anas clypeata*
Pintail, *Anas acuta*
Canvasback, *Aythya valisineria*
American Golden-eye (Common Goldeneye), *Bucephala clangula*
Whistling Swan (Tundra Swan), *Cygnus columbianus*

Falcons, Hawks, Eagles, Condors, and Vultures
American Kestrel, *Falco sparverius*
Marsh Hawk (Northern Harrier)
Sharp-shinned Hawk, *Accipiter striatus*
Western Goshawk (Northern Goshawk), *Accipiter gentilis*
Western Red-tailed Hawk, *Buteo jamaicensis*

Quail and Grouse
Catalina Island Quail (California Quail), *Callipepla californica*
Oregon Ruffed Grouse (Ruffed Grouse)

Cranes, Rails, and Coots
Virginia Rail, *Rallus limicola*

Shore-Birds
Northern Phalarope (Red-necked Phalarope), *Phalaropus lobatus*
Long-billed Dowitcher, *Limnodromus scolopaceus*
Least Sandpiper, *Calidris minutilla*
Western Sandpiper, *Calidris mauri*
Black-bellied Plover, *Pluvialis squatarola*

Killdeer, *Charadrius vociferus*
Snowy Plover, *Charadrius alexandrinus*

Gulls and Terns
Glaucous-winged Gull (Glaucous Gull)

Doves
Western Mourning Dove, *Zenaida macroura*

Road-runners and Cuckoos
California Cuckoo (Yellow-billed Cuckoo)

Owls
American Barn Owl (Common Owl), *Tyto alba*
Arizona Elf Owl (Elf Owl), *Micrathene whitneyi*

Goatsuckers, Swifts, and Hummingbirds
Nuttall's Poorwill (Common Poorwill)
Pacific Nighthawk (Common Nighthawk)
Texas Nighthawk (Lesser Nighthawk)
Northern Black Swift, *Cypseloides niger borealis*
Allen's Hummingbird, *Selasphorus sasin*

Kingfishers and Woodpeckers
Western Belted Kingfisher, *Ceryle alcyon*
California Woodpecker (Acorn Woodpecker), *Melanerpes formicivorus*
Red-shafted Flicker (Northern Flicker), *Colaptes auratus*
Mearns's Gilded Flicker (Gilded Flicker)

Tyrant Flycatchers
Western Flycatcher (Pacific-slope Flycatcher)
Olive-sided Flycatcher, *Contopus cooperi*
Western Wood Peewee, *Contopus sordidulus*

Vireos and Shrikes
Western Warbling Vireo, *Vireo gilvus*
Cassin's Vireo, *Vireo cassinii*
California Shrike (Loggerhead Shrike)

Ravens, Crows, Magpies, and Jays
Western Crow (American Crow)
American Magpie (Black-billed Magpie), *Pica pica*
California Jay (Scrub Jay)

Swallows
Tree Swallow, *Tachycineta bicolor*

Chickadees, Verdins, and Nuthatches
Oregon Chickadee (Black-capped Chickadee)
Slender-billed Nuthatch (White-breasted Nuthatch)

Wrens
Suisun Marsh Wren, *Cistothorus palustris aestuarinus*
Cactus Wren, *Campylorhynchus brunneicapillus*
Bewick's Wren, *Thryomanes bewickii*

Dippers, Kinglets, and Thrushes
Ruby-crowned Kinglet, *Regulus calendula*
White Mountains Hermit Thrush (Hermit Thrush), *Catharus guttatus*
Northwest Robin (American Robin), *Turdus migratorius*

Thrashers and Mockingbirds
Western Mockingbird (Northern Mockingbird)

Pipits, Waxwings, and Phainopeplas
American Pipit, *Anthus rubescens*

Wood Warblers
Yellow Warbler, *Dendroica petechia aestiva*
Audubon's Warbler (Yellow-rumped Warbler), *Dendroica coronata*
Black-throated Gray Warbler, *Dendroica nigrescens*
Tolmie's Warbler (MacGillivray's Warbler, Mourning Warbler)
Western Chat (Yellow-breasted Chat)

Tanagers, Grosbeaks, Sparrows, Juncoes, and Towhees
Black-headed Grosbeak, *Pheucticus melanocephalus*
Sierra Junco (Junco)
Brown Towhee (California Towhee)

Cowbirds, Orioles, Blackbirds, Meadowlarks, and Bobolinks
Bullock's Oriole, *Icterus bullockii*

Finches and Old World Sparrows
California Evening Grosbeak (Old World Finch)
Sierra Nevada Rosy Finch (Gray-crowned Rosy Finch)
Willow Goldfinch (American Goldfinch), *Carduelis tristis*
California Linnet (House Finch)
English Sparrow (House Sparrow)

About the Editor

The Western Anna (Anna Marie Cecilia Neher) hails from the Pacific Northwest but has learned to thrive on the urban detritus of the San Francisco East Bay's pubs and coffee shops. To learn something of the Anna's ways, one need merely penetrate the recesses of a used bookstore and wait: singing carelessly to disguise her inquisitive intent, she will soon edge over to peer at you from behind a neighboring bookshelf.

A CALIFORNIA LEGACY BOOK

Santa Clara University and Heyday Books are pleased to publish the California Legacy series, vibrant and relevant writings drawn from California's past and present.

Santa Clara University—founded in 1851 on the site of the eighth of California's original twenty-one missions—is the oldest institution of higher learning in the state. A Jesuit institution, it is particularly aware of its contribution to California's cultural heritage and its responsibility to preserve and celebrate that heritage.

Heyday Books, founded in 1974, specializes in critically acclaimed books on California literature, history, natural history, and ethnic studies.

Books in the California Legacy series appear as anthologies, single author collections, reprints of important books, and original works. Taken together, these volumes bring readers a new perspective on California's cultural life, a perspective that honors diversity and finds great pleasure in the eloquence of human expression.

Series editor: Terry Beers
Publisher: Malcolm Margolin
Advisory committee: Stephen Becker, William Deverell, Charles Faulhaber, David Fine, Steven Gilbar, Ron Hansen, Gerald Haslam, Robert Hass, Jack Hicks, Timothy Hodson, James Houston, Jeanne Wakatsuki Houston, Maxine Hong Kingston, Frank LaPena, Ursula K. Le Guin, Jeff Lustig, Ishmael Reed, Alan Rosenus, Robert Senkewicz, Gary Snyder, Kevin Starr, Richard Walker, Alice Waters, Jennifer Watts, Al Young

Thanks to the English Department at Santa Clara University and to Regis McKenna for their support of the California Legacy series.

CALIFORNIA
LEGACY

OTHER CALIFORNIA LEGACY BOOKS

One Day on Beetle Rock Sally Carrighar

Unfolding Beauty: Celebrating California's Landscapes Edited by Terry Beers

Essential Mary Austin Edited by Kevin Hearle

Essential Muir Edited by Fred D. White

Tales of the Fish Patrol Jack London, introduction by Jerry George

Storm George R. Stewart, foreword by Ernest Callenbach

Eldorado: Adventures in the Path of Empire Bayard Taylor,
  foreword by James D. Houston

The Anza Trail and the Settling of California Vladimir Guerrero

Death Valley in '49 William Lewis Manly, edited by LeRoy and
  Jean Johnson

Mark Twain's San Francisco Edited by Bernard Taper

If you would like to be added to the California Legacy mailing list,
please send your name, address, phone number, and email address to:

California Legacy Project
English Department
Santa Clara University
Santa Clara, CA 95053

For more on California Legacy titles, events, or other information,
please visit www.californialegacy.org.

HEYDAY INSTITUTE

Since its founding in 1974, Heyday Books has occupied a unique niche in the publishing world, specializing in books that foster an understanding of the history, literature, art, environment, social issues, and culture of California and the West. We are a 501(c)(3) nonprofit organization based in Berkeley, California, serving a wide range of people and audiences.

We are grateful for the generous funding we've received for our publications and programs during the past year from foundations and more than three hundred individual donors. Major supporters include:

Anonymous; Anthony Andreas, Jr.; Barnes & Noble bookstores; BayTree Fund; S. D. Bechtel, Jr. Foundation; Fred & Jean Berensmeier; Butler Koshland Fund; California Council for the Humanities; Candelaria Fund; Columbia Foundation; Compton Foundation, Inc.; Federated Indians of Graton Rancheria; Wallace Alexander Gerbode Foundation; Marion E. Greene; Walter & Elise Haas Fund; Hopland Band of Pomo Indians; James Irvine Foundation; George Frederick Jewett Foundation; Guy Lampard & Suzanne Badenhoop; LEF Foundation; Michael McCone; Middletown Rancheria Tribal Council; National Audubon Society; National Endowment for the Arts; National Park Service; Philanthropic Ventures Foundation; Poets & Writers; Rim of the World Interpretive Association; River Rock Casino; Riverside-Corona Resource Conservation; Alan Rosenus; San Francisco Foundation; Santa Ana Watershed Association; William Saroyan Foundation; Sandy Cold Shapero; Service Plus Credit Union; L. J. Skaggs and Mary C. Skaggs Foundation; Swinerton Family Fund; Victorian Alliance; Tom White; and the Harold & Alma White Memorial Fund.

For more information about Heyday Institute, our publications and programs, please visit our website at www.heydaybooks.com.